SYSTEM OF ETHICS

Socratic Method and Critical Philosophy

SYSTEM OF ETHICS

BY

LEONARD NELSON

TRANSLATED BY NORBERT GUTERMAN

FOREWORD BY H. J. PATON

INTRODUCTION BY JULIUS KRAFT

NEW HAVEN

Yale University Press

LONDON · GEOFFREY CUMBERLEGE · OXFORD UNIVERSITY PRESS

1956

As though to test his youthful vigor, divinity thrust man into conflict with Nature, which contests him every step of the way and at the outset largely has the better of him. Every step he must wrest from her alien power. Yet every step he does achieve is to his good, for he himself violently foists on Nature an alien law that issues solely from his own heart.

JAKOB FRIEDRICH FRIES

Moral man, and he alone, is wholly free.

FRIEDRICH VON SCHILLER

Contents

Foreword

NEARLY THIRTY YEARS have passed since Leonard Nelson died at the early age of 45. A man of amazing energy, he had already attracted considerable attention in Germany; but conditions in that country were unpropitious for a balanced and reasonable philosophy—that is to say, they were unpropitious for philosophy as such. Nelson's doctrines seem to have been swept away by a torrent of unreason before they had time to spread.

In commending the present translation of his *System of Ethics* to all who are interested in philosophy, I am at a disadvantage; for my knowledge of his published work is superficial as well as limited—too superficial to justify any attempt at an objective assessment of its permanent value. All I can do is to explain why I have felt attracted and impressed, and indeed excited, by what little I have been able to read. I will try to do this by stating in language perhaps misleadingly objective what I seem to have found in him even on a hurried reading and what I hope others may find also.

Nelson is manifestly a creative philosopher, a seeker after truth who has arrived at his convictions by independent thinking and is confident—possibly too confident—that his methods and doctrines are sound. Although his main interests are ethical and extend to practice as well as theory, he has a wide range, and he endeavors to work out his philosophy as a systematic whole—had he lived, he might well have made further contributions to modern logic and the theory of mathematics. The framework of his thinking is firm and definite, and he writes with an enviable lucidity—not always the outstanding merit of German philosophers. He appears to be sustained by an intellectual excitement which communicates itself to his readers. Although he assigns to a priori thinking a much greater rôle than is commonly allowed in these days of self-assured empiricism, he has a shrewd eye for the facts of experience and of moral action. Even if he may seem to attach too much importance to what he calls his "deduction" of particular duties and ideals, he is essentially humane and never ceases to be animated by the ideals of sanity and common sense.

The main stimulus to his thinking, though by no means the only one, was given by Immanuel Kant, and it might almost be said that he is trying to adjust the Critical Philosophy to modern problems. Curiously enough, he appears to have come to Kant partly from the study of Fries, a writer by whom, perhaps through my own fault, I have failed to be impressed. He is, however, no unquestioning disciple of Fries or even of Kant, but a robust thinker with a philosophy of his own: he attempts to correct Kant's errors as well as to develop and expand his doctrines. Although we may not be prepared to accept all Nelson's strictures or proposed improvements, they challenge us to re-think the Kantian philosophy; and where doctrines already explicit or implicit in Kant are placed in a different setting and expressed in a different language, we may be helped to acquire a new insight into their meaning. Some readers will find Nelson easier to understand than his master, and his views are always suggestive and worthy of examination. He seems to me to have recaptured something of Kant's philosophical attitude and spirit. He has a far better claim to be regarded as carrying on and developing the Critical method than either the German idealists or the Marburg school of commentators, to whom he was so strongly, and in my opinion so wisely, opposed.

Although Nelson's work has a special interest for students of Kant, it is put forward as an independent philosophy which is intelligible in itself and has to be judged on its own merits. The present volume may be described as the application of fundamental ethical principles already examined in the author's *Kritik der praktischen Vernunft;* and it comes before us as, so to speak, an experimental confirmation of these principles. The principles are, however, made sufficiently clear in themselves, and the reader will have no sense of incompleteness, unless he is looking for something more than is commonly expected today. What we are offered is at once a systematic application of principles and a dispassionate review of our moral duties and ideals—such a review as has seldom been attempted in recent years. The distinction between duties and ideals—or between categorical imperatives and categorical optatives—is one of Nelson's interesting innovations. His treatment of them in detail varies considerably in thoroughness, perhaps because he did not live to complete his final revision. Some of his judgments are highly unconventional—for example, about suicide and about our duties to animals—and he may at times be more stimulating than convincing; but his appeal is always to reason and never to authority or to mystical emotion. Particularly valuable are his discussions on the ideals of friendship and on the ideals of public life. On the latter topic he may be perhaps be forgiven if in spite of his dispassionately theoretical approach he is unable to conceal his hatred of tyranny and love of freedom.

Time moves inexorably on, and some may think that a philosophy produced more than thirty years ago can have little bearing on the problems that interest us today. Although Nelson had much of the modern analytic spirit and a great desire for rigor in philosophic thinking, it may be admitted that if he were writing at present, he would sometimes express himself differently, or at least would have to offer more defense for some of the methods and some of the language that he uses as a matter of course: for example, in spite of his careful analysis of ethical concepts he may be thought to use too easily the concept of what he calls "the will." But all philosophies of all ages (including our own) have their unexamined assumptions, and Nelson has at least made a strenuous effort to unearth and defend the presuppositions of his thinking. The errors of parochialism can be avoided only by studying the philosophy of other times and other countries, so that differences in interest and in vocabulary may be a gain as well as a loss. In any case the changes made by the passage of some thirty years ought not to be exaggerated, and Nelson's problems seem to me still very much our own.

The permanent enemies of philosophy are dogmatism and skepticism. Both have their roots in an irrational or semirational distrust of reason and tempt men to take refuge in the wilder forms of romantic and mystical speculation. To all such movements Nelson is deliberately and vigorously opposed. His great merit is that he offers us a defense of reason in action as well as in thought. He holds, if I understand him aright, that the principles of moral action are as rational as those of scientific thinking; that they can be discovered and formulated and justified in a consistent philosophy; and that they can be confirmed by being applied successfully in detail to the whole field of human conduct. This ideal he has attempted with great courage and thoroughness to realize, and his attempt merits the serious consideration of contemporary philosophers. His interest, it may be added, is not merely a theoretical one; for he believes that without clear thinking we can have no defense against violence and anarchy. I could wish that I had made his acquaintance earlier.

H. J. Paton.

Oxford University
June 30, 1956

Introduction

THE NAME of Leonard Nelson (1882–1927) does not figure among the famous philosophers of the 20th century. Trivial though the point is, it is worth remembering that fame and greatness—particularly in philosophy—do not coincide. Public opinion is capricious and therefore anything but a sober judge of philosophical merit.

There has always been a hidden history of philosophy which has had to wait patiently for the acknowledgment of congenial minds: to wit Russell's discovery of Frege and Husserl's recognition of Brentano's and Bolzano's merits. To these should be added Nelson's rediscovery of Fries' outstanding contribution to Critical Philosophy * which had been (and is still) buried under the dead weight of Hegelianism and its consequences.

Since Fries was a disciple of Kant, Nelson is thus in the direct tradition of Kantian philosophy, though not in its "idealistic" distortion by the school of Fichte, Schelling, and Hegel. That falsification is today continued by the existentialist "interpretation" of the *Critique of Pure Reason*—actually the sworn enemy of all dogmatic metaphysics—as an essay in existentialist anthropology. Sober contributions to Critical Philosophy have a difficult time indeed nowadays.

Yet it would be wrong to say that Nelson's work found no echo at all. He is well known to symbolic logicians in connection with the Nelson-Grelling paradox of autological and heterological words. He is known to scholars of Neo-Kantianism through his challenging theory that the "problem of knowledge" is a pseudo problem. He is known and respected by philosophers of law through his equally challenging demonstration that positivistic jurisprudence is a *Rechtswissenschaft ohne Recht*. But Nelson is scarcely known and even less adequately appraised in that field to which he devoted his greatest intellectual efforts: the foundation and reconstruction of ethics.

* A discussion of this rediscovery may be found in my Introduction to Nelson's *Socratic Method and Critical Philosophy*, New Haven, Yale University Press, 1949. Reprinted here as Appendix, pp. 263–75.

Nelson's *Lectures on Ethics* fall into five parts published in three volumes. The first volume, *Critique of Practical Reason*, appeared in 1917.* In this work Nelson not only attempted to validate our basic ethical postulates but logically and axiomatically analyzed all possible methods by which ethics might be established, and all logically possible ethical systems. A small circle has continued to study and discuss this profound work intensively,† but it has remained largely unknown. This is true as well of the volume Nelson published next (even though logically it should come last): *System of the Philosophy of Law and Politics*. Nelson felt that the political upheavals of the first World War and its aftermath made it important for the philosopher to enter the political arena to the limits of his capacity and he therefore hastened publication of this work, which appeared in 1924. He died in 1927 at the age of forty-five; and the second volume, *System of Ethics and Pedagogics* (1932), received final editing at the hands of his co-workers, Grete Hermann and Minna Specht. The first part of this volume is here published in translation.

Nelson's *System of Ethics* does not establish or validate ethical rules; that is the task of a critique of practical reason. In his *Ethics* Nelson demonstrates what a system logically derived from given ethical rules should look like. Hence it is not a collection of aphorisms, nor does it offer long-winded, disconnected preachings, nor overwhelm the reader with historical scholarship. Instead, Nelson's *Ethics* offers a rigorous logical development, derived from a few clearly formulated assumptions, the epistemological analysis and validation of which forms the subject matter of his *Critique of Practical Reason*.

Nelson's *Ethics* proceeds as Spinoza proposes to do, *more geometrico*, i.e., deductively. But unlike Spinoza Nelson picks no arbitrary point of departure. He finds himself in agreement with ethical common sense. A serious study of the structure and contents of *Ethics* may therefore lead to a reaffirmation of practical reason, and to ethical realism. Its unprecedented consistency alone assures Nelson's *Ethics* an important place in 20th-century ethical

---

* A manuscript translation is available at leading libraries on microcards.

† See Grete Henry-Hermann's incisive analysis and evaluation of the *Critique of Practical Reason*: *"Die Ueberwindung des Zufalls"* in *Leonard Nelson zum Gedächtnis*, Frankfurt, 1953, edited by Minna Specht and Willi Eichler.

literature. A work of this type demands intellectual concentration, though Nelson's presentation is crystal clear: few philosophers are his equal in that respect. A specific element of this clarity is the logical energy with which the central idea of the whole system illumines the argument again and again. This aspect impressively illustrates the agreement between Nelson's *Ethics* and ethical common sense which is concerned with concrete goals for action. Nelson's corresponding abstraction is the idea of an objective task; he uses the whole force of his logic to clarify the concept of the ethical, i.e., the unconditional task, and to determine its contents. Here his thought is in line with Kant's categorical imperative. Yet there is this difference: the categorical imperative is an unconditional task, but not every such task is necessarily (as Kant assumed) a categorical imperative. There may be—and Nelson shows that there are indeed—other important categorical tasks. It is to Nelson's credit that he successfully continues analysis of fundamental concepts beyond mere historicist analysis.

An ethical system which is based consistently on the principle of unconditional tasks—the fulfillment of which is consequently not left to human whims but simply ought to happen—is a system which upholds the independence of ethics. It does not seek other grounds for ethics, either on earth or in heaven. It is, therefore, equally opposed to ethical naturalism and to ethical religionism. Neither psychology nor sociology nor theology is the basis of ethics; it stands on its own feet, on its specific ground of practical reason. "Practical reason," in Nelson's usage, is not one of those mysterious terms pointing to some vaguely conceived meaning but an exact expression taken over from Kant, much refined in significance.

One of those refinements stems from Nelson's consistent distinction between form and content of categorical demands. This distinction is guided by the modern axiomatic requirement of a minimum of presuppositions for deductions. Nelson, founder of a rigorous system of formal ethics with far-reaching implications, never succumbed to the Kantian dogma of ethical formalism. Compared to Scheler's powerful attack * on this grave short-

---

* In *Der Formalismus in der Ethik und die materiale Wertethik*, Berne, 1954. (Formalism in Ethics and the Material Ethics of Values.)

coming of Kantian ethics, Nelson's work convincingly demonstrates the difference between rigorous depth and mere flashes of insight. Where Scheler blurs the relation between ethics and religion and actually abandons the ethics of tasks, Nelson, following Fries and Schiller, gives content to the categorical imperative through the principle of justice and introduces, in addition, the ideals of truth, beauty, and justice, technically called "categorical optatives." Looked at from the vantage point of the history of ethics, Nelson's theory of justice or personal dignity may yet be ranked among the classic systematic treatments of this subject. Nelson makes it clear that justice is not a meaningless term: far-reaching consequences flow from its clarification. They hold not only for ethics in the narrower sense of the term (the "theory of virtues") but for the philosophy of law and politics, for example the theory of property and of social policy. In the same way Nelson's ethics in the wider sense implies important pedagogical consequences.

All Nelson's contributions in the field of ethics have, in addition to the logical vigor of their structure, another important formal factor in common. They combine concepts and principles of categorical demands (imperatives and optatives) with theoretical principles referring to psychological and sociological reality. Ethical demands apply to the spatiotemporal realm of things. Through a methodical device established by Fries, the so-called "formulas of subsumption," Nelson links the demands of practical reason with the laws of nature.

Nelson's *Ethics* successfully overcomes two basic objections to Kantian ethics: its formalism and the vague relationship of its demands to the realities of individual and social life. Furthermore, it overcomes Kantian moralism, i.e., its consideration of duties to the total neglect of other ethical tasks. What Nietzsche and Scheler in vain tried to achieve with their nonrational approach to the realm of values Nelson achieves in fact: a clear outline of those tasks that go beyond duty. These are the goals of service of the true, the good, the beautiful which evoke our enthusiasm because they are the valid ideals of human life. Through his theory of categorical optatives Nelson became the founder of modern Critical Humanism devoted to what he called "the ideal of rational self-determination." Nelson's lucid exposition of this ideal in its formal and material aspects should silence those who complain that the 20th century is lacking in idealist orientation.

Contemporary preachments about the discrepancy between the cultivation of science and technology on the one hand and the neglect of ethical theory and practice on the other often strike a note of insincerity. All too often these admonitions conceal an appeal to maintain or return to outworn theological or metaphysical ways. Yet, unless ethics is imbued with the same open-minded approach that is taken for granted in science, the gap between technology and theoretical morality is unlikely to be closed.

This approach is still sadly lacking. Instead, popular trends and academic fashions, mutually influencing each other, impress themselves on ethics as well. Thus naturalistic ethics—a contradiction in terms—emerges as a strong force. The "natural" is equated with the good, and the evil in the ethical dogmas of National Socialism and Communism is thus justified. Or we get the idyllic pictures of ethical naturalists of humanitarian outlook like Dewey. Still more recently idealism in the pragmatic and utilitarian tradition has been abandoned in favor of a nominalism which either frankly defends ethical skepticism or seeks to replace true ethics by grammatico-logical exercises. As for the existentialist appeal to substitute the decisions of man for the will of God as the basis of our obligations, in what Sartre calls "engagement," it establishes no more than a pseudo humanist authoritarianism. Its practical outcome can be only anarchy or despotism.

These questionable tendencies in ethics find refutation and indeed systematic analysis in Nelson's *Ethics*. Nelson re-establishes the basic logical requirement of an ethical system: the mutual irreducibility of task and fact. In establishing the command of justice and the ideal of humanity Nelson truly functions as a guide to action. Nelson's work neither claims to be nor is in fact perfect. It is, however, an important milestone in the development of ethical theory. Further steps and corrections are needed. But wherever these new steps may lead they cannot be envisaged before the steep and magnificent mountain of Nelson's *Ethics* has been climbed.

JULIUS KRAFT

London—New York
July, 1956

Foreword to the Second German Edition (1949) *

MORE than thirty years ago Leonard Nelson published the first volume of his *Lectures on the Foundations of Ethics,* with which he resumed and extended the work of his philosophic masters, Immanuel Kant and Jakob Friedrich Fries, the critique of practical reason. He offered this study to the public in the middle of the first World War of this century, with the following words:

"To seek to rehabilitate human reason in the present situation scarcely seems a timely undertaking. Yet there may be a few who, even in the face of a whole society laid low, will doubt the reasonableness of that particular order rather than reason itself. In seeking standards of value for a new order they can scarcely avoid penetrating to those sources from which flow all ultimate judgments concerning man's activities. They will thus be inevitably led to examine the capacity for practical judgments in general. Whoever is of such mind will find an undertaking such as is initiated here entirely in keeping with the demands of the times."

We read these words today in the gloom of what has happened since. We stand beneath the ruins of the second World War, amid human and social conflicts that push our lives to the brink of chaos. The naked struggle for power takes the place of wise and humanitarian order. A challenge of inexorable urgency is posed at such a juncture by the question of an order based on wisdom and humanity rather than on the tyranny of whoever happens to be strongest at the moment—an order that will grant men and nations freedom and dignity to shape their own lives even as they honor and maintain the same right for others.

If we would tread that path, we must recall the sources from which alone such an order of human life can flow. Our time is not lacking in calls for such stock taking, though the response is deeply tinged with doubt. For it is not merely a matter of moving from the harsh struggle for existence to a deeper understanding of the meaning and tasks of our lives. Settlement of individual and na-

---

* Except for this Foreword (and a different pagination), the first and the second German editions are the same.

tional conflicts calls for communion as an art. Such an art, alone capable of breaking through the baleful alternative of chaos and tyranny, must be based on the presumption that objective standards can be found by which the common life may be ordered and against which conflict situations may be evaluated. Yet people— and even philosophers—maintain a deep-rooted sense of distrust toward the possibility of finding such standards which all men of good will might accept after proper scrutiny. The time is long past when the great majority of Western nations shared the same *Weltanschauung*, from which they derived common standards for shaping their lives. To communicate today we need a different, scientifically based point of departure—a readiness to transcend differences in viewpoint and outlook, to surmount the weariness and despair borne of doubt and relativism, to seek a common ground from which the problems of our age may be approached.

It is into this colloquy that we thrust the second, unchanged edition of Leonard Nelson's *System of Philosophic Ethics and Pedagogics** as a new test for critical philosophy, in an effort to penetrate to the epistemological foundations of ethical judgments with the weapons of disciplined scientific research and thus derive rules for evaluating human conduct.

The discourses in this volume go back to a course of lectures Nelson delivered in the years 1916, 1920, and 1924. In its final and most mature formulation, the course had to be condensed into a briefer compass than had been at Nelson's disposal before. Hence it lacked a few essential elements contained in the earlier versions. Rather than consult only this last version, it seemed appropriate, therefore, to select the best from all the available protocols. Nelson himself was able to do neither the work of selection nor the requisite editing. He did discuss with his collaborators a few unresolved obscurities.

The editors, basing themselves on these discussions, were faced with the task of reworking a number of passages, while also reducing a text originally intended for classroom delivery to the more concise and precise requirements of book form. The power and beauty of Nelson's own literary style served as natural guides. To

* Only Nelson's *Ethics* is published here.

emulate that lofty model might have seemed the sheerest presumption, but for an unshakable faith that these pages cannot but be permeated by the power of truth.

GRETE HERMANN

MINNA SPECHT

Editor's Note

THIS TRANSLATION of *System of Ethics* was planned and financed by the Leonard Nelson Foundation, Inc., a pedagogic foundation established by friends and students of Leonard Nelson for the purpose of translating his works into English and encouraging interest in Critical Philosophy. It is under the direction of the undersigned, who is responsible for the final text of this translation and the addition of a few footnotes.

The task of translating a learned book, where much depends upon precise shading of meaning, is not to be lightly undertaken and usually must enlist the labors of more than one linguist. The original English rendering of Nelson's *Ethics* was prepared by Norbert Guterman, a scholar and writer in his own right but also long known as an interpreter of foreign literature and philosophy. Mr. Guterman's text was minutely examined and polished by Heinz Norden and myself. My special thanks are due Heinz Norden for tireless and patient labors which, I hope, have born fruit in clarifying obscurities and finding the *mot juste* in many instances. I also owe a debt of gratitude to several philosopher friends of mine who were of help in establishing the proper English terminology.

The goal of the translation has been to give a clear, readable version of Nelson's text. Nelson laid great stress on simplicity of philosophic style. But what is simple and lucid in German is not necessarily so in English. The translator has tried to accommodate the translation to Nelson's individual style but with due regard for good English usage. Even so, the going is at times heavy, because the original text must be served.

Nelson abhorred esoteric technical terminology and used common German ethical terms. The translator faced the usual difficulties with words such as *gut, Recht, recht, Gesetzlichkeit,* etc., and the traditional compromises had to be made. The common English equivalents which were used throughout suffer from similar ambiguities and multiple meanings. However, Nelson generally explains carefully what he has in mind.

Whatever virtues this translation may have are owing to my collaborators.

L. H. GRUNEBAUM

Scarsdale, N.Y.
July 1956

INTRODUCTION

Task and Divisions of Philosophical Ethics

Chapter 1. Possibility of a Scientific Ethics

1. Are Ethical Problems Solvable?

OUR PERIOD of social decline is at the same time one of tremendous advancement in the mathematical and experimental sciences; the tempo goes beyond anything former generations witnessed. Each day we are confronted with new discoveries, often unanticipated by the scientists themselves. The fact of continuing progress in the domain of exact science proves beyond doubt that among the nations prostrated by the late war [1914–1918] intellectual vigor has been preserved intact. If the same intellectual vigor could be applied to ethical problems, we would have good reason to believe that these would be solved, and this despite the many somber prophecies of an imminent collapse of our civilization. In fact, the basic cause of the present social decline is to be seen in our neglect of the problems of ethics.

At this point, however, a question arises: Are ethical problems solvable? That scientific problems are has been amply proved by the unquestionable achievements of science. But our age has displayed little courage or confidence in dealing with ethical problems, and this may be one of the reasons why science has neglected them. Skepticism about the possibility of approaching, let alone solving, ethical problems has become so general and firmly established that the fundamental question as to whether ethical problems are proper matters for scientific analysis is only rarely raised. It is now taken for granted that these problems are unsolvable, and that there is no need to prove this. Profound thinkers, however, have never resigned themselves to such a state of affairs, and have attempted time and again to arrive at a scientific answer to at least the preliminary question as to whether ethical problems can be solved.

A case in point is Henri Poincaré, the great French mathematician. In one of his last essays, *La Morale et la science*, he discussed this question and reached the conclusion that the problems of ethics can never be scientifically settled. He did not

3

content himself with merely asserting this but sought to support his view with proof. Nobody can say that Poincaré's conception of proof was facile or frivolous, and hence it is interesting to examine more closely his argument in support of the assertion that ethical problems cannot be solved scientifically. The idea underlying it is extremely simple and easy to formulate. As Poincaré himself says, it is implied in our very grammar. For if the premises of a syllogism, he argues, are in the indicative mood, the conclusion must also be in the indicative, and thus cannot have the form of an imperative; yet to be part of ethics, it would have to take this form. For ethics deals not with matters that can be expressed in the indicative but only with matters that can be formulated in the imperative—not with what *happens* but with what *ought* to happen. But science, says Poincaré, is always a system of propositions in the indicative; consequently, there can be no scientific validation of ethics.

What can we say about this argument? The contention on which it is based is obviously unassailable: from premises concerned solely with what takes place it is certainly impossible to infer what ought to take place. For concepts which appear in the conclusion of a syllogism must be present in its premises. If such concepts have been brought in by the back door, the syllogism is fallacious.

It is, however, possible to question Poincaré's proof, which is based on an unstated presupposition concerning the nature of science—a presupposition Poincaré overlooked perhaps because of a peculiarity of the French language. The French term *science* has a narrower connotation than the German term *Wissenschaft;* * it denotes, for the French, what "exact science" or "natural science" denotes for the Germans: in French, the term "science" actually stands for a system of propositions in the indicative mood. But if ethics, as has thus been irrefutably shown, cannot be validated on the basis of natural science, we still may ask whether it cannot, despite this, be scientific in form, that is to say, whether it cannot be presented as a system just as rigorously logical in structure as the system of natural science. Poincaré did not even investigate, let alone resolve, the

* This remark is equally applicable to English usage.

question as to whether such a science, consisting only of imperatives, is possible.

Here a new doubt emerges. Assuming that such a science is possible, its very first premises would have to be stated in the imperative; but by establishing ethics on such grounds, are we not begging the question? Some unproved imperative would have to serve as our starting point for another imperative to be deduced; thus we would have only a dogmatic, not a scientifically validated ethics.

But this reasoning proves too much: it could also be applied to natural science. For if the conclusions of natural science have the form of the indicative, this is possible only because they are derived from premises in the indicative. Consequently, if we accepted the argument stated above, natural science too would involve a *petitio principii*, for its system is founded on unproved premises in the indicative, and we would have to conclude that natural science is impossible. But if we refuse to agree with this conclusion, if we maintain that natural science may be developed from unproved premises in the indicative without detriment to its scientific rigor, we have no right to reject ethics on the ground that it begins with unproved premises in the imperative.

Poincaré's argument teaches us one thing, namely that ethics cannot be derived from natural science, that is, from a system of propositions which state matters of fact. It is true that on such a basis ethics cannot be validated.

2. Ethics and Natural Science

Poincaré's argument proves so much, and no more. Today, when we compare the relative merits of natural science and ethics, we take the priority of natural science for granted, without realizing that we do so for historical reasons which are quite accidental. For it is only an accident of history that physics today is a recognized science established on solid foundations; and it is only another accident of history that our conceptions of ethics are changing and controversial, and far from representing the conclusions of a generally recognized science. There was a time when physics, indubitably the pride of our age, was exposed to the same doubts, the same uncertainty, indeed the same uncontested skepticism as ethics in our day. As we all know, it was one of the profoundest thinkers of antiquity and of the whole history of philosophy, namely Socrates, who taught that the striving for a science of nature was doomed to remain forever frustrated; according to him, the gods did not grant man the ability to penetrate the mysteries of nature. And because of Socrates' great authority in ancient philosophy, his opinion became generally accepted, so much so that only the very boldest ancient thinkers ventured to approach the problems of physics. If no one had dared question the authority of Socrates, a scientific physics might not exist today.

Since Socrates a peculiar reversal of roles, as we can see, has taken place. The role that philosophers once ascribed to physics today belongs to ethics, and vice versa. Therefore we may predict that if the current skeptical attitude toward the possibility of scientific ethics were to become permanent no scientific ethics would be developed for millennia to come, just as no scientific physics was developed for several millennia in the past. For it is a characteristic of pessimism that it begets its own justification. No attempt is made to solve problems that are held to be unsolvable: no thinking person tries to do the impossible. Consequently, it is no wonder that wherever such a pessimism becomes established historical experience justifies it. It is a fact that we have no scientific ethics. But the question is, What is the cause of this state of affairs? Perhaps the cause is precisely that up until now a scientific ethics has been regarded as impossible. If so, it would be enough to abandon this skepticism in order to accomplish what was considered to be impossible.

What would be the implications of such an accomplishment? Poincaré discusses this question too in a most stimulating manner. He asks: What are the consequences of the possibility or impossibility of establishing ethics on a solid scientific foundation? How does this affect us practically, i.e., with regard to moral life?

His answer is: It does not affect us at all. The question, he says, is of purely theoretical interest and has no practical significance, or at least no crucial practical significance. Why not?

Would the theorem of Pythagoras, Poincaré asks, and Newton's law of gravitation be less true if Pythagoras had not proved the former and Newton had not discovered the latter? Would the moral law be less observed if it could not be scientifically validated? Poincaré denies this. People do not observe ethical principles, he says, on the basis of abstract reasoning; they do so because they are moved by feelings more powerful than any abstract considerations, even if the latter run counter to the former.

This argument seems at first sight comforting. But if it is scrutinized more closely, doubts arise here as they did before, in this case doubts regarding two points. True enough, even if Pythagoras had not proved the theorem associated with his name, and even if Newton had not discovered the law of gravitation, theorem and law would still retain their full force. It would be impossible to deny that they admit of no exceptions.

But what about the laws of ethics? Ethical laws, if they are valid at all, continue to be so even if men cannot validate them scientifically—this much is as true here as it is in natural science. But we must distinguish between the observance of a law and its validity, as regards the laws of both ethics and natural science. When we say that a law is valid, we refer to its objective status as a law. When we say that a law is observed, we refer to the circumstance that what is stated in the law does actually take place. With regard to the moral law, it may very well happen that it is valid but not observed. Its validity, i.e., its binding character as an imperative, does not depend on the extent to which this imperative is actually obeyed; indeed, the law would remain valid even if it were not observed by anyone anywhere. Its universal validity as an imperative would not be in the least affected.

As regards natural laws, this distinction is of no importance, for here validity and observance are one and the same thing. The very essence of a natural law is this, that if it is valid it admits of no exceptions, whereas the essence of an ethical law lies in the very fact that it may be valid without being observed, that is, without being obeyed. Hence, scientific validation of ethical laws may be quite important if we want them to be observed, even though these laws remain valid, i.e., have an obligatory character, in any event.

How do we stand, with regard to this matter? While the validity of an ethical law does not depend on its observance, its observance may still depend on insight into its validity. For how can we observe a law into whose validity we have no insight? For this, Poincaré says, we need no scientific reflection; the simple feeling suffices. And this feeling, he adds, is a far more powerful lever than the most thoroughly validated science.

Poincaré is partly right: Feeling can secure both knowledge and observance of the law. But what is the nature of moral feeling? If we examine the matter more closely, we discover phenomena that arouse doubts regarding the reliability and overwhelming power of moral feeling. We need only recall that feeling guides some people in one direction and others in another—in fact, in the very opposite direction. Moral feelings can conflict. Sometimes the very thing that one person feels to be worth striving for as the highest, another feels to be deserving only of revulsion. And what is more, we may ourselves be the seat of a conflict of feelings: we may be torn this way and that by contradictory feelings. Which of these shall we follow?

This question could be answered only on the basis of a scientific ethics: for we need a yardstick which lies outside feelings of any kind, and which would enable us to decide which of the contradictory feelings should be regarded as the correct, sound, unperverted, authentic feeling. The mere strength of a feeling cannot supply us with such a yardstick, for it changes from person to person, indeed, it changes from one moment to another within the same person.

When we inquire into the causes of such moral vacillation to which we owe so many inner conflicts and, indeed, about-faces, we discover that one of the most important influences is to be found in ethical doctrines or theories, however fragmentary. It is precisely the dominant influence of doctrines on education and on political institutions that accounts for the shift of feelings from one direction to another. Moral theories determine in which direction the moral feelings of a given individual are steered from childhood on. These feelings vary in character with the nature of the doctrines that governed the education of a given individual, according to whether he was brought up under the influence of an ethics based on man's duties toward God or his fatherland, on his duties toward other men, or toward all of his fellow creatures, including animals. As a glance at history will show us, such doctrines have actually molded the life of nations by their all-powerful influence on developing moral feeling. The theory according to which doctrines are powerless in the field of ethics is itself nothing but another doctrine, and a false one at that, as is proven by history. But if this doctrine, according to which the question of whether ethics can be developed as a science has no bearing on moral life, is false, it obviously cannot be a matter of indifference to us whether, among all ethical doctrines, there is not one which can be scientifically established as the only valid and binding one, as the doctrine that must be victorious when the conflict of opinions is settled by rational argument. The thoughtful man who reflects on such matters, who becomes conscious of the fact that his feelings depend on uncontrolled and uncontrollable forces, and who discovers that one of these forces is the influence of doctrines, can no longer content himself with mere moral feelings. Such a man will try to base his convictions on a deeper and firmer foundation in order to emancipate himself from the rule of accident over the formation of his moral convictions, and by the same token over his moral decisions. Only science can provide him with this foundation.

3. Ethics as Science

How can this be done? Various approaches are possible to this question. We can discuss it abstractly, inquiring into the conditions that determine the possibility of developing an ethical science; but we can also decide it experimentally, as it were, by making an actual attempt to establish such a science and letting the results speak for themselves. I have chosen the latter method in these lectures. Such an experiment cannot be discounted until the impossibility of success has been proven beyond all doubt and by scientific evidence. Up until now, no such arguments have been given; all attempts of this sort have yielded nothing but pseudo proofs.

In choosing the second method, that of experiment, we must, however, put up with a disadvantage. No validation of the principles on which a system of ethics is based can be undertaken here: It is the subject of a critical preliminary investigation which deals with the question of the possibility of a scientific ethics. This preliminary inquiry concerns quite properly the validation of the principles for a systematic development of ethics.* Such a distinction between system and validation exists also in other sciences. When a mathematician develops one of his disciplines, he begins with axioms and erects a system upon them by means of logical reasoning; the highest principles of this system cannot be further accounted for within this structure. No one will for that reason deny the scientific character of the mathematician's undertaking.

4. Ethics as a Philosophical Discipline

We must consider still another difficulty. Our task of evolving a rigorous system requires a special, unusual frame of mind, completely different from the attitude we take toward the realities of life when not approaching them scientifically. These realities, by affecting our feelings—particularly our moral sense —push us now in one direction and now in another, until we have discovered a solid vantage point from which we can judge the realities with scientific objectivity. In other words, it is the practical significance of problems that indirectly induces us to attack them theoretically. To be able to do this we must subject them to the most dispassionate and sober inquiry; that is to say, it is of the utmost importance to eliminate the emotional element, which otherwise is the motive force behind moral opinions. The need for such a sober and dispassionate approach to things that by their very nature appeal directly to our passions, represents an obstacle to the exposition of ethics which can be surmounted only by dint of great effort. This difficulty,

---

* This problem is dealt with in Nelson's *Critique of Practical Reason* (Leipzig, Göttingen, 1917); see footnote p. xiv.

inherent in the subject, will no doubt persist forever, for teacher as for disciple, because it will keep on causing trouble for both. For we must discipline ourselves to maintain the required frame of mind, which does violence to our natural feelings. We must clearly realize in advance that something must be sacrificed; we must either sacrifice scientific exactness, rigor, and clarity for the sake of feeling, or, conversely, put up with a violation, or at least a silencing, of the claims of feeling in favor of scientific thoroughness, rigor, and clarity. Since our aim is scientific, we have decided to make the necessary sacrifice at the expense of feeling, nor shall we swerve from our purpose, no matter what the consequences.

The difficulty disappears more or less when we deal with the applications of ethics, that is to say, when we proceed to subordinate the facts of experience to independently validated ethical theorems. But this will work only once we have established a system of pure ethics, a system in which everything depends on flawless purity and on the abstractness of the principles, eliminating all considerations of their practical application.

In actual fact our concern both for practical application and for scientific system is served by this task of abstraction. To do justice to changing circumstances, the principles of ethics must be arrived at independently of individual instances; otherwise the claim of our propositions to universality would be unjustified since they would apply only in some circumstances and not in others. The universality of ethical principles would thus be violated if they were prematurely adapted to contingent facts of experience, either because one had not pushed abstraction far enough to have discovered the principle independent of the circumstances or because, in investigating the consequences of the principles formulated, one had been induced by one's identification with momentary circumstances to single out a particular consequence without inquiring whether the principle may not admit of still other consequences. These errors lead to doctrinaire and utopian distortions, inevitable when one fails to keep pure theory consistently free of all incidental admixtures. The abstract character of pure ethics is a mark of its philosophical dignity.

Chapter 2. Place of Ethics in a System of Philosophy

5. Ethics as Practical Metaphysics *

ETHICS is a branch of philosophy. Our first question concerns the place of ethics in a philosophical system.

I reserve the term "philosophy" for any type of cognition which can be developed independently of intuitive knowledge by means of pure concepts (though not necessarily on a foundation of pure concepts) and the principles of which, while not themselves intuitive, can be applied to intuitions. A system meeting these requirements merits the title of scientific philosophy.

The whole domain of philosophy is divided into two distinct parts which, following Kant's discriminating terminology, we designate as logic and metaphysics.

This distinction rests upon Kant's discovery of the difference between analytic and synthetic judgments. An analytic judgment, as implied by its name, is a judgment which does not extend our knowledge beyond the concept of its object, but only analyzes this concept. In contrast, a synthetic judgment extends our knowledge beyond the mere concept of its object, and hence requires a source of cognition independent of this concept. For instance, the proposition that every triangle has three sides is an analytic judgment; the proposition that the sum of the angles in every triangle is equal to two right angles, is a synthetic judgment. To be convinced of the truth of the first of these propositions it is enough to know the concept of triangle; to discover the truth of the second, concepts are not sufficient; consequently, this cannot be done by means of logic alone. A system of synthetic philosophical judgments is called "metaphysics"; a system of analytic judgments, "logic."

Because metaphysics consists of synthetic judgments, it re-

---

* This section may be omitted without prejudice to an understanding of Nelson's doctrine. For detailed information concerning the concepts and the nomenclature here employed, see Nelson's *Socratic Method and Critical Philosophy* (New Haven, Conn., 1949), particularly the essay, "The Art of Philosophizing," as well as Nelson's *Critique of Practical Reason*.

12

quires, unlike logic, a source of knowledge independent of the concepts of its objects. On the other hand, because metaphysics consists of philosophical judgments, this source of knowledge cannot be intuitive. Consequently, metaphysical judgments spring neither from mere concepts nor from intuition. They have their ground in a direct, even though originally obscure, cognition.

We are asking here what is the place of ethics in a philosophical system. Now, it is clear that ethics is a part of metaphysics. For in ethics we are concerned not with a mere analysis of our concepts, but with extending our knowledge beyond mere concepts. Our purpose here is not, for instance, merely to study the concept of valuable action; we want to discover what falls under this concept, so that we may be able to decide whether any given action is valuable or not.

The domain of metaphysics is, however, far more extensive than ethics, and we must determine the place of ethics within this domain. Metaphysics is divided into speculative and practical metaphysics; the former deals with the laws governing the existence of things, the latter with the laws governing the value of things. The propositions of the latter cannot, as we have seen, be derived from the propositions of the former, because from that which is we cannot infer that which is worth doing or that which ought to be. Consequently, ethics can be nothing but practical metaphysics.

6. Ethics as Subjective in Contrast to Objective Teleology

Our last proposition was not sufficiently specific, for we may still ask whether its converse is not true, i.e., whether practical metaphysics is nothing but ethics—in other words, whether ethics is the sole content of practical metaphysics. Now, this is not the case. Practical metaphysics deals with the value of things in general, but ethics deals with it only in so far as value determines a task for our action. At this point we must make a distinction, which up until now has not been sufficiently taken into account—an error that is largely responsible for the fact that the scientific development of ethics still leaves so much to be desired. Following Fries,* who was the first to use these terms, we may refer to this distinction as that between objective and subjective teleology.

Teleology deals with the purpose or value of things. Objective teleology is the theory of the intrinsic value or purpose of things, i.e., the purpose or value they have by virtue of their mere existence. It deals ultimately with the highest and most comprehensive purpose of all existence, that of the world as a whole. Subjective teleology deals with values of things *qua* objects of our will. Obviously, ethics does not deal with the purpose of the existence of things in general, but only with that which is required of ourselves, of our will. In other words, ethics can be only subjective teleology.

Even though this distinction is clear, it readily gives rise to the erroneous view that ethics, as subjective teleology, can be derived only on the basis of a prior objective teleology; in other words, that we can determine the goals of our action only if we have first determined what the world goal is.

This view is erroneous were it only because it presupposes that there is such a thing as a scientific objective teleology. If this were true, we would know what the world goal is, and we would have to deduce the goal of our actions from this knowledge. But in fact such knowledge is beyond the powers of human reason.

Consequently, objective teleology can be nothing other than a theory of practical *ideas* (in the Kantian sense), whereas ethics is a practical theory of nature. Any concept of the meaning of the universe is for us only an *idea*, i.e., there is nothing corresponding to it in the entire field of human knowledge—it denotes something that lies outside possible scientific knowledge. We have positive scientific knowledge only of nature. But our knowledge of nature is not a complete whole; it broadens as its boundaries are extended in space and in time. But since space and time themselves extend indefinitely, we can never fix the boundaries of nature in such a way as to be able to say: This

---

* Jakob Friedrich Fries (1773–1843), a pupil of Kant whose philosophy exerted a decisive influence on Nelson. See *Socratic Method and Critical Philosophy*, p. xi; this volume, p. 265.

is the whole of nature, it has such and such a goal. Consequently, the unity and meaning of the world are inaccessible to our cognition of nature. We can conceive of the world purpose as something that is not affected by the incompleteness of nature; but in this way we characterize that purpose only negatively, not by positive concepts. In so far as objective teleology is not content to abide by a merely negative characterization of the world's unity, while still avoiding dogmatic speculations, it must proceed without the armamentarium of specific concepts, i.e., it must fall outside of science. The insights accessible to objective teleology fall within the domain of religion; they are reserved, in Fries' exact formulation, to the faculty of sensing (*Ahndung*).*

Closer scrutiny actually reveals that all positive religious ideas, including those which refer to the purpose of existence, are not scientific but aesthetic in origin. An objective teleological judgment is nothing but an aesthetic judgment; for aesthetic valuation is concerned with the intrinsic value of a given object, independently of its relation to surrounding nature, and hence also independently of its relation to the will of an acting being. When we judge an object aesthetically, we do not compare it with other natural objects, nor do we consider its relation to human will. We ascribe to it a value that characterizes it intrinsically, objectively, and here this means: outside any relation to our will.

At issue here is not the question whether such judgments are valid. What matters is that when we do pass them, we ascribe an objective value to an object. Unless this is done, there is no aesthetic judgment.

In tracing objective teleology back to aesthetic judgment we have by no means reduced it to concepts. For aesthetic judgments cannot ordinarily be passed in accordance with definite concepts, but depend upon feeling, which is not reducible to concepts. They spring from a knowledge that is obscure, and hence cannot assume the form of science. That is why aesthetic judgments cannot be proved, and why there is no system of

* See Rudolf Otto's discussion of *Ahndung* in *The Idea of the Holy*, John W. Harvey, tr. (New York, 1943), p. 150.

aesthetics. For such a system would have to consist of judgments derived from certain general principles by means of logical inferences.

Still another reflection leads us to conclude that even with the help of aesthetic judgments the insights of objective teleology cannot be translated into concepts. We judge an object aesthetically only in so far as we apprehend it intuitively. But only individual objects, not the totality of the world, let alone its meaning, can be apprehended intuitively. Thus aesthetic judgments cannot refer to the whole of the world, nor even to what we presumptuously call "world history." They refer to intuitively determined singular objects, which present themselves to our intuition as unitary wholes, and whose beauty to that extent can become for us a symbol of the world's unity, without thereby enabling us to grasp this unity intuitively, let alone conceptually. It follows that even by means of aesthetic judgments it is impossible to determine a world purpose or to set a purpose for the history of mankind.

Now, it might be pointed out that human actions fall within the domain of aesthetic valuation, and hence that ethics, as a theory of the value of human actions, must include judgments on the aesthetic value of human actions, or on their beauty. To that extent ethics is actually coextensive with a part of objective teleology, namely with that part of it which refers to human action.

But this does not do away with the difference between the two valuations. For we pass aesthetic and ethical judgments on human actions from different points of view. Ethics can do so only from the point of view of subjective teleology, i.e., only in so far as we derive the task of performing a given action from the value of that action, while the objective teleological, and hence the truly aesthetic approach, is independent of this point of view. From the standpoint of objective teleology, the evaluation of human actions is only a part of the aesthetic contemplation of nature. We shall later have occasion to subject this relation between aesthetic and ethical evaluations to a closer and more thorough examination. Here we are merely interested in establishing the fact that ethics can be a science only as subjective teleology, and that it cannot be founded on objective teleology. Its principles must therefore exist independently of all objective teleological considerations.

This does not mean, however, that the goals and purposes with which ethics deals are subjective in the sense that we can choose them at will, that they are arbitrarily formulated and selected. Rather, both subjective and objective teleology contain laws that are independent of arbitrary human choice.

7. Examples of Confusion between Subjective and Objective Teleology

A few examples may show how ethical inquiries have gone astray by confusing the two divisions of teleology, or by attempting to establish ethics on the foundation of objective teleology.

Ethics has often been defined as the theory of human destiny. This formulation clearly reveals a lack of clarity about the relation between the two branches of teleology.

It is possible to speak of human destiny in two senses. First, this phrase may denote the place assigned to man in the whole of the world design; in that case his destiny and the goals he has to pursue are derived from the role he is to assume in relation to the world design. As we have seen, in this sense there is no such thing as a science of human destiny, unless we are presumptuous enough to assert that we can determine exactly what function is assigned to man or to the human race in the task of fulfilling the world goal.

However, the doctrine of human destiny can also be understood in another sense, namely, in the sense of subjective teleology. Then we assume that the goal in question is one that man determines for himself, and we do not investigate purposes and goals assigned to man as a part of the cosmos, but only purposes and goals that he ought rationally to set for himself in his own life and in history. To determine this is the task of ethics, and in this sense alone can human destiny be the object of a science.

Or to take another example, there is an old dispute in ethics between the optimistic and the pessimistic view of the world or of life. According to whether the student of ethics takes one side or the other, he is led to an ethics affirming or negating life. This dispute is based on the same confusion between objective and subjective teleology. We would have to encompass the whole universe in order to know with certainty whether good or evil predominates in it; only then could we establish a scientific ethics on this knowledge.

The confusion is particularly great in what is called the philosophy of history, which exists in many variations. The error I am criticizing here is committed wherever history is approached with preconceived opinions as to its meaning or future course. It can be detected, for instance, in Lessing's famous *Idea for a Divine Education of the Human Race*, and in the fantasies of Schelling's or Hegel's doctrine, which defines history as the gradual self-revelation of God. The same error underlies more recent theories of history, which are presented in a garb borrowed from the theory of evolution or from natural science. Thus an evolutionist ethics has been developed, in which our goal is derived from biology, and a sociological ethics, in which the answer is elicited from sociology or economic history. Another example is afforded in the socialist literature, according to which the inevitable coming of a socialist society is evident from all previous history, and which infers from this that men ought to act in conformity with this historical trend.

There is a philosophy of history of a different kind, which must be carefully distinguished from all such fantasies. This philosophy of history leaves it to empirical investigation to determine the direction of the historical process in the past, and its presumed direction in the future, in so far as experience permits drawing inferences so general in character; in any event, this approach has nothing to do with philosophy. A scientific philosophy of history raises an entirely different question— the question as to the tasks that rational beings ought to set themselves in history. No survey of the actual course of historical development can tell us any more about the nature of these tasks than any presumptive theory of the world purpose. Only ethics as a purely philosophical discipline can inform us about such matters. Philosophy of history in this sense must therefore be regarded as a branch of ethics.

8. Categorical and Hypothetical Imperatives

In order to present more thoroughly and more clearly the relation between objective and subjective teleology, which is crucial for the whole structure of ethics, we shall add a simple reflection based on the previously mentioned distinction between indicatives and imperatives. We have seen that statements in the imperative can never be inferred from statements in the indicative.

There are, however, imperatives of two kinds—categorical and hypothetical. The great reformation of ethics that we owe to Kant rests ultimately upon this distinction. For as long as the difference between categorical and hypothetical imperatives was not clear, the basic difference between speculative and practical metaphysics could not become clear either, let alone the difference between objective and subjective teleology.

A hypothetical imperative is an injunction valid only in respect of a presupposed goal, while a categorical imperative enjoins something irrespective of such a goal.

Hypothetical imperatives are based on natural science; but there is no logical transition from these hypothetical imperatives to categorical injunctions. For instance, the following hypothetical imperatives rest on natural science: If you want to grow a tree, you must provide it with sufficient water. If you want to keep a flame burning, you must feed it enough oxygen. The very word "must" shows that we are not dealing here with ethical, but with natural laws. It is a natural law that a tree inadequately provided with water perishes, or that a flame inadequately provided with oxygen dies out.

Through insight into such natural laws we discover the means required for the attainment of a given end. Whether or not we ought to choose this end the hypothetical imperative leaves entirely unresolved; it merely says that anyone who wishes to attain a given end is compelled to use the given means.

In contrast with this, ethical laws are expressed, for instance, in the following propositions: You ought to keep your pledged word. You ought not to steal another's property. The word "ought" expresses the unconditional character of these injunctions, their independence of any end to be attained by them. This difference between the concepts of "ought" and "must" helps us at the same time to gain a deeper insight into the independence of ethics, as a subjective teleology, from all objective teleology. Even assuming that we knew the purpose of the world, and that we thus had a starting point for the development of a scientific objective teleology, how could we infer from it precepts governing our action?

Let us assume, for example, that the world goal consists in general happiness, or general perfection, or whatever else. Then we could certainly formulate a hypothetical imperative telling us what we must do if we are interested in realizing the supreme good, whatever it be—the world purpose, the divine will, or, let us say, the general happiness. Then we would only need to discover what natural laws govern the increase or decrease of general happiness, and on the basis of these laws, to determine the means we would have to use in order to bring about maximum happiness. But all this would give us only precepts indicating the kind of actions we would have to perform *if* we were interested in furthering general happiness. But why *ought* we to be interested in this? This question would have to be answered *first*, and the answer would have to be established with certainty if our hypothetical imperative were to be of any practical interest to us. Otherwise it must remain a proposition of merely theoretical significance, expressing a mere application of a natural law which may interest us as such theoretically, but which cannot lay claim to any kind of practical significance. It would be practically significant only on the assumption that the furthering of the world goal—whether this goal be general happiness, perfection, or whatever else—is itself worth striving for; in other words, on the assumption that we ought to strive for it.

If all this could be agreed upon, however, if it could be established that we ought to help realize God's purpose in the world —a notion that is highly contradictory and incompatible with divine omnipotence—this finding would for its part be a proposition of subjective teleology, namely, one formulating this task for our will: Do that which contributes to the realization of the divine world goal. This proposition could never be derived from our knowledge of the divine world goal, but would stand quite independently of that knowledge. For how could we—I repeat—infer from the fact that something is God's purpose, the fact that it ought to be or become our purpose? Any attempt to draw such an inference moves in a circle. It presupposes that which is to be proved, namely, that God's will is binding on us, and consequently that it is incumbent upon us to be active in realizing the world goal.

All this will become clear to us and remain clear once we have grasped the difference between categorical and hypothetical imperatives and keep it well in mind. Then we shall not be misled into thinking that ethics, since it is a practical science— practical in the original, narrowest, and most rigorous sense of the term—belongs to anything but practical metaphysics; further, within practical metaphysics, it belongs only to subjective teleology, and hence can be derived neither from the propositions of speculative metaphysics nor from those of objective teleology.

This is not to say that propositions of speculative metaphysics, and hence hypothetical imperatives as well, are completely irrelevant to ethics. In fact, they are of fundamental importance in applied ethics. For if we ask how the precepts of pure ethics can be carried out, we are at once thrown upon natural science, which alone gives us information as to the means required for the attainment of any purpose, including the purpose of fulfilling ethical precepts. Only by resorting to hypothetical imperatives can we derive from categorical imperatives, new categorical imperatives guiding us in the application of pure ethics.

Now, it is only through experience that we can acquire knowledge of the natural laws which we must subordinate to the laws of pure ethics. We cannot discover natural laws by means of mere philosophizing, we must investigate the relevant facts. But since the hypothetical imperatives are taken from experience, the indirect or derived categorical imperatives do not belong to pure philosophical ethics. The theory of derived duties, in so far as it presupposes empirical investigation, cannot be dealt with in pure philosophical ethics.

Summing up, we may say that pure philosophical ethics is a

practical science of nature, as opposed to the practical theory of *ideas* on the one hand, and to theoretical natural science on the other. We are here using the terms "theoretical" and "practical" in the sense in which a cognition is called "theoretical" when it refers to the existence of things, and "practical" when it refers to the purpose or value of things.

Chapter 3. Place of Theory of Virtues in a System of Ethics

9. Individual and Social Subjective Teleology

ETHICS as subjective teleology, i.e., as the theory of the value or purpose of human conduct, formulates: (1) the ethical demands made on the will of the individual, and (2) the conditions governing the value of human society, which are derived from these laws. In the first case we deal with individual conduct as a voluntary ethical task; in the second, with the external forms of human interrelationships, in so far as these forms are determined by ethical norms. Accordingly, we distinguish between individual and social subjective teleology, or, as we may put it, between the practical theories of man's inner and outer nature.

This distinction may also be expressed in the classical terminology. The practical theory of man's inner nature has, since ancient times, been called "ethics" in the narrower sense, or "the theory of virtues" (*Tugendlehre*), as distinguished from the practical theory of man's outer nature, or "the theory of right" (*Rechtslehre*). The theory of virtues * deals with the value of individual conduct, the theory of right with the value of social organizations, i.e., the forms of interaction between individuals. This treatise will deal with ethics in the narrower sense, or the theory of virtues.

In order to gain a deeper understanding of the significance of the theory of the value of individual conduct, we need only to reflect upon its practical importance.

Ethics can be defined as the practical discipline par excellence. For in the true sense, that is "practical" which helps us to make decisions, which guides us in our actions. And, strange as this may seem, practical service in this way can be rendered us by no discipline other than ethics, that is to say, pure philosophical ethics. Only through ethics can any other insight or science acquire practical interest. Indeed, the hypothetical imperatives

* For a discussion of the term "virtue" see sections 11, 12.

23

that are generally regarded as practical are usually theoretical propositions which acquire practical significance only indirectly, through categorical imperatives, that is to say, through ethical propositions.

To have a correct understanding of what has just been stated, we must keep in mind that only the theory of virtues deserves to be called a practical science in the strictest sense. Even the theory of right acquires such a practical interest only indirectly, through the theory of virtues. For even if we know on what the value of a given form of society depends, and even if we know in addition how we can realize that value, we have not yet learned anything of practical interest to us until we know from some other source that we have the task of furthering the realization of this value, namely, right. But this we learn only from the theory of virtues.

The theory of right deals with tasks only indirectly. In itself it determines only the conditions under which a given form of society is valuable, and hence it sets no tasks; for tasks, taken in the strictest sense, refer always to the will of an individual, namely of a being capable of action. But society is not an individual being, and even if it were it would not be a being capable of action, for it has no will which one might charge with tasks. Only the individual has such a will, and can be given tasks: one of these tasks may be that of furthering the realization of a just society. In this sense, the subject matter of the theory of right is included in the theory of virtues.

Thus the theory of virtues and the theory of right are not two different disciplines, dealing with two different kinds of tasks. Only the theory of virtues formulates tasks; strictly speaking, only this theory deserves to be called a practical science.

10. Applications of Theory of Virtues and of Theory of Right

We may throw light on the distinction between the theory of virtues and the theory of right from still another side, by considering their applications and asking what are the underlying principles of each of these applications. This leads us to the distinction between pedagogics and politics. Pedagogics is the systematic guidance of the individual toward virtue; its aim is to make him capable of fulfilling his ethical tasks. Politics is the systematic guidance of society toward a just condition, a condition in conformity with the postulates formulated in the theory of right. Pedagogics presupposes a definition of the goal to which it is to lead the individual: this goal is formulated in the theory of virtues. Politics presupposes a definition of the goal of society: this goal is formulated in the theory of right. Pedagogics deals with the conditions under which virtue is realized in the life of the individual; politics deals with the conditions under which justice is realized in the life of society. The former is based on the theory of virtues, the latter on the theory of right. Thus we obtain a diagram illustrating the divisions of ethics.

	Individual ethics	Social ethics
Pure ethics	Theory of virtues	Theory of right
Applied ethics	Pedagogics	Politics

In what follows we shall deal with ethics in the narrower sense, that is to say, with the theory of virtues.

Chapter 4. Divisions of Theory of Virtues

11. The Call of Virtue

THE GERMAN WORD for "virtue," *Tugend,* is etymologically related to *taugen,* "to serve a purpose," and originally stood for "fitness," or "appropriateness." But we are using this term here in a more specific sense, namely, that of fitness to fulfill an ethical task. Virtue is a quality of mind that we acquire by our own efforts. Only under this assumption can ethics be called "the theory of virtues." Since it is a theory of human tasks, it deals with appropriateness or fitness for a given purpose only in so far as such a quality can be acquired by a man's own free activity. It is in this sense that we shall use the term "virtue," a term that has acquired a somewhat old-fashioned and unworldly flavor. We shall not here investigate the causes of this change of meaning, nor ask whether we have to blame the Philistinism and unrealism of the professional preachers of virtue or the fact that we have lost interest in such profound problems. I shall merely observe that we cannot dispense with this good old word, that we have to defend and rehabilitate it, for we simply have no other term that could serve to denote a concept which we must all clearly understand. We ask, then: What are the qualities of mind that constitute that which we call "virtue," and what is their order of precedence? The same question may also be expressed differently, as: What ought we to do? or, What is proper for us to do? or, What is good for us to do? or, What is worth doing? What has practical interest, practical importance for us?

If we take the terms "ought," "proper," "good," and "worth" in the broadest sense given them in current usage, our question yields a number of answers, which we must carefully distinguish from one another, because each reflects a different interpretation.

When someone asks, What ought we to do?, the answer might be: We ought to do what gives us pleasure; what gives us satisfaction; what prudence counsels us to do; what positive law prescribes; what is required by decency and custom; what is in good taste; or, finally, what morality requires. We thus obtain a number of very different norms; and now we must pass them in review, in order to choose from among them the ones we regard as the proper objects of ethics.

Let us consider each of these norms in turn.

"We ought to do what gives us pleasure." It can be easily seen that this injunction cannot be philosophically determined, and hence cannot, and fortunately does not need to be, the subject matter of a philosophical inquiry. For that which gives pleasure to an individual depends on his particular feeling at a given moment, and no generally binding rules or precepts can be formulated about this. Nor is such a generally valid decision needed here. For we are not confronted with a controversial issue to be settled. The fact that one man finds pleasure in one sort of thing, and another in the very opposite, does not offer us occasion for a difference of opinion: for the first man does not assert anything that the other man has reason to deny; rather, each states something about his own feeling. Pleasure has value for us only in so far as it gratifies our needs. It follows that the question as to what we are required to do in order to have pleasure is not a practical question: it has no bearing upon the tasks we ought to perform, but only on the needs that we actually have. It is a psychological question, a question of fact. Consequently, ethics does not deal with gratification of needs. Such gratification is merely the object of an actual subjective appetite. But ethics does not ask what is actually desired, only what is *worth* desiring.

Gratification of needs can be discussed in ethics only indirectly, in so far as it acquires a value by becoming the condition of that which is worth striving for. But, as we have seen, such conditions are not the concern of philosophical ethics; for their investigation would require a knowledge of natural laws, which can be gained only through experience.

Nevertheless attempts have been made over and over again to derive all ethical norms from the precept of pleasure, even though various theorists have preferred to substitute other words for the somewhat crude term "pleasure"—for instance, "happiness." In this approach, ethics defines the goal of human striving as happiness, i.e., the epitome of what makes man happy. And this is essentially nothing but the gratification of needs. But when the goal in question is put as baldly as that, the presumed coincidence of ethics and happiness carries little conviction. For a man's happiness depends on the intensity and duration of his enjoyment only in relation to the sum total of his needs; and if it were true that only happiness matters, we should have no scruples as to the means toward happiness, provided they do lead us to it.

That is why many champions of the theory of happiness strive manfully to limit the scope of this precept. According to them, we should not be guided solely by the intensity and duration of enjoyment, but rather seek a higher or true happiness— as they are fond of calling it. Thus a distinction is introduced, which takes us beyond the mere intensity and duration of happiness, and which is necessarily based upon a qualitative difference between needs, so that gratification of one kind of need is given precedence over gratification of another kind—even if the gratification preferred affords less pleasure in intensity and duration. In this view, the higher needs would be those *worth* gratifying, or whose gratification is to be preferred to that of other needs.

But if a need is worth gratifying regardless of its relative strength, then its worth must be rooted in something other than the happiness to be acquired through gratification. Thus, if we base ethics on the difference between a higher and a lower happiness, we actually abandon the principle of happiness. We would be guilty of a gross fallacy, to say the least, if we substituted the quantitatively greater for the higher happiness; if we did this, the distinction introduced here would be again erased: we might have spared ourselves the trouble of speaking of the difference between a higher and a lower happiness.

Those who seek to retain this distinction, over and above that between more happiness and less, while still inferring the quantity of a given pleasure from its quality, obviously introduce an additional premise, which is a synthetic proposition. They assume that according to some mysterious law of nature, the higher happiness must also be quantitatively the greater. But such an assumption would have to be proved; we would have to prove that virtue pays and vice does not, that the degree of our happiness is determined by the degree of our virtue, and the degree of our unhappiness or suffering by the degree of our wickedness. Or else we would have to fall back on the excuse that the gratification of the moral instinct, like that of any need, is associated with a feeling of pleasure, in other words, as the saying goes, that a good conscience allows us to sleep the sleep of the just, while a bad conscience poisons all enjoyment of life. But we must still ask whether the gratification of a moral impulse, and hence the fulfillment of the demands of conscience, actually affords us greater happiness than we could obtain if we did not anxiously follow this inner voice, in obedience to which we renounce many a pleasure and put up with many a pain. No matter how willingly we obey our conscience, inclinations remain alive in us which, ungratified under the lash of conscience, produce suffering.

The doctrine of true happiness thus rests on a verbal trick, which should be left to those who, claiming to lead men to virtue, allow themselves to be reduced to such cheap expedients. If we are guided by experience and keep open minds, we must admit that to obey the voice of conscience is not the best way to achieve happiness. With happiness in view, it is far more advisable to do the opposite, namely, to put one's conscience to sleep as soon as possible. This can be achieved precisely by a sufficiently wicked mode of life, for thus one can considerably blunt one's conscience and even silence it completely— certainly the more reliable method of escaping from the "true unhappiness" that is caused by the torment of a bad conscience.

The foregoing remarks also apply, in the main, to the second answer to our question as to what we ought to do—the answer proposing the pursuit of satisfaction.

When we speak of satisfaction, we must distinguish between satisfaction with our condition and satisfaction with ourselves, that is, with our accomplishments. If we seek satisfaction with our condition, we seek something that does not directly depend upon our will. It is something that is determined solely by the extent to which our needs are gratified. For this very reason pursuit of satisfaction is identical with pursuit of pleasure; indeed, there is no way of distinguishing between the two.

Not so satisfaction with ourselves. Here usage affords us a clue: for we ask whether a man has reason to be satisfied with himself or not. Satisfaction with ourselves depends on the judgment we pass on ourselves, that is, on our actions. According as this value judgment is justified or not, our satisfaction with ourselves is also justified or not. Here is a real possibility of a difference of opinion about which we can argue—a difference of opinion as to whether a man is right or wrong in being satisfied with himself. The injunction that we be satisfied with ourselves thus means something different from the injunction that we gratify our needs; we shall state this injunction more exactly if we say that we ought to have a reason for being satisfied with ourselves. Such satisfaction is directed toward a value that is not exhaustively defined merely as actual pleasure. If we now formulate the challenge in question as follows: We ought to strive to have a reason for being satisfied with ourselves; we see at once that we are setting ourselves a goal that is independent of gratification of our needs. For now there arises at once the question *whether* we have reason to be satisfied with ourselves, and here everything depends on whether our action is good—the term "good" denoting here something different from the fact that our action affords us satisfaction. Otherwise we should turn in a circle and never be able to answer the question as to what gives us reason to be satisfied. Consequently, if we were to define the task of ethics by saying that it teaches us how to be satisfied, we would raise a problem without ethical meaning. Such a definition could acquire meaning only in the light of an additional norm of what is worth striving for—a norm by which we would justify our being satisfied.

Let us now ask whether the third answer, which refers us to prudence, provides us with such a norm. Prudence recommends to us the means appropriate for the attainment of our ends. We have seen that its precepts cannot constitute the content of ethics any more than the ones based on the preceding answers. In the first place, the means for the attainment of any end can be determined only on the basis of our knowledge of natural laws, for only these tell us the conditions required to bring about a given effect. Aside from that, all precepts of prudence must themselves be subordinated to a norm from which they derive their validity. For the precepts of prudence inform us about the means to attain a given end, but they do not tell us whether this end itself is worth striving for. The question of the means becomes practically significant only after we have established that the end is worth striving for. But the reason why this end is worth striving for cannot be merely that it is prudent to strive for it: for this would imply that the end in question serves to attain another end, which, for its part, would be arbitrarily chosen, and thus the question would be merely shifted.

Our interest in the means is only derivative: we must first be interested in an end, which we strive to attain for reasons other than those of prudence. Prudence will not help us in the choice of such an end; mere prudence is blind toward differences among ends; one end is as good for it as another. We must first decide what our end is before it makes sense to ask what it is prudent to do.

Let us now consider the mandate of positive law, to see whether it provides us with the desired norm. Positive law, the law of the state, derives its significance from the authority which enforces it, in other words, from the state power. What is in question here, then, is a relation of forces—the relation between our own force and state power. Whether we have a reason to submit to positive law depends on this relation alone, unless some other precept provide us with a further reason to obey the law. In the absence of some other reason for observance, the mere fact of a positive law, i.e., that a statute on the books can be imposed by force, can at best induce us to raise the question of prudence, of whether it is advisable to submit of our own accord. Such, for instance, would be the case if the power standing behind the law made all resistance hopeless. Hence, this precept takes us back only to the question of prudence.

What about decency and custom? Here the situation is essentially the same as with positive law, for decency and custom are observed because of tradition and habit; they merely create prejudgments. Whether we should comply with the verdict of tradition remains a question that is again decided only on the basis of a relation of forces; everything depends on whether we can muster enough strength to assert ourselves against the power behind tradition. Even though the precepts of tradition are seldom backed by naked force as in the case of positive law, they are yet enforced by a kind of compulsion, namely, the psychological compulsion that is generated by our fellow men's judgment on our conduct. In so far as we depend on that judgment, in so far as compliance or noncompliance with this judgment can affect us, it becomes a matter of prudence whether we do well to observe the rules of decency and custom—unless there is a higher norm giving us an additional reason to observe those rules.

Such a norm might be that of good taste. Here the very expression implies reference to a higher norm. For we distinguish, as this expression shows, good taste from bad. Once we recognize this distinction, the question arises: What is good taste? And that only a prior judgment can tell us. But even if we knew what is required by good taste, the question of what we ought to do would not be adequately answered. For even if the requirements of good taste are fulfilled, other and still higher requirements may be violated. What is good with respect to good taste is not necessarily good in every respect without reservation. Yet in the last analysis it is the good in this sense that we seek after.

If we formulate the question in such a way that it refers to what is good in itself and without reservation, we are led to the last of the injunctions listed—the requirement of morality.

12. Theory of Duties and Theory of Ideals

We have eliminated a number of misconceptions which have no place in ethics, although they are only too often included in it; now we must guard against unduly restricting its field. Kant took a great step forward by keeping ethics, for the first time, clear of notions that have nothing to do with it, but he succumbed to an opposite error, namely, he confined ethics to the domain of morality, i.e., to the theory of duties. The idea of duty, as indicated in current usage, implies the idea of a good, pure and simple, a good without reservation. But is the converse of the proposition, asserting that duty refers to that which is good in itself, true? Is it, in other words, correct to maintain that the pursuit of the good is exhaustively defined by the pursuit of duty, and that ethics is coextensive with morality? * We shall see that this is not so. If the precepts of morality are to supply us with a complete answer to our question, What ought we to do? we must determine the concept of morality more accurately; and if we do this, we shall find that the answer can be regarded as a complete solution of our problem only if the term "morality" is taken in the broadest possible sense, namely, as denoting everything that is good in itself, and without reservation. But in current usage the word "morality," just as the word "ought," has a narrower meaning, and in this narrower meaning, the question, What ought I to do? does not encompass the whole of ethics. For the domain of ethics is larger than what is encompassed by the term "ought" taken in its narrower sense, according to which one's duty is what one ought to do.

It will be well if we confine these words to meanings given them in current usage, first, because we would otherwise have to invent new terms to designate the concepts they denote, and second, because we do have other terms to denote the concepts taken in the broader sense. We shall therefore reserve the term "ethical" for the broader concept, and use the term "moral" only in the narrower sense as coextensive with duty.

A distinction has, therefore, to be made in the domain of ethics. Observance of all precepts of ethics is not adequately characterized as "morality." We have another word to denote this broader concept, namely, "wisdom." True, this is also a somewhat old-fashioned word, but we are constrained to use it in order to express the conceptual distinction important here.

"Wisdom" transcends "morality" in the strict sense of this term. Wisdom comprises all ethical norms, not only those ex-

---

* Nelson's important distinction between ethics and morality, not customary in common usage, is made clear in the remainder of this paragraph.

pressed in the form of an imperative, a duty, or an ought, but also those which do not have the form of a rigorous injunction, but which nevertheless express some sort of "should." We may call norms of that second type, "optatives."

We should do not only our duty, but more than that, namely, all that which is worth doing, which deserves to be done, even if we are not duty-bound to do it. We praise some actions and condemn others without always implying that the former are required by duty and the latter are contrary to duty, and that we are morally bound to do the former, and morally forbidden to do the latter.

We do not measure these actions by a norm of duty, but by another norm, for which the term "ideal" is most appropriate. While we shall use the term "morality" to denote observance of the requirements of duty, we shall use the term "culture" for the observance of the aspirations of the ideal. Conformity to what both require, we call "wisdom."

Wisdom comprises everything contributing to the true value of life in so far as man is capable of giving himself such a value. Wisdom is thus that condition which we call "virtuousness," and which is the object of the theory of virtues or of ethics.

These distinctions can be illustrated with a diagram.

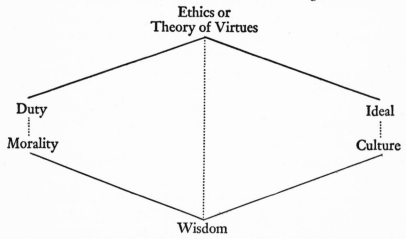

Ethics includes the norms of duty and of the ideal. Fulfillment of duty is morality; fulfillment of the ideal is culture. Morality plus culture is wisdom.

On the basis of the foregoing considerations we may divide ethics into two branches—the theory of duties, and the theory of ideals. Although these branches are co-ordinated, it is worth noting that one of them holds superior rank. For it is important which of the two theories in question is chosen as the starting point in the development of our discipline. Since the concept of duty implies a necessary command, such that unless it is observed no action can have any value, it will be proper to establish the commands of duty before we investigate the broader requirements of the ideal.

Consequently, in developing the theory of ideals, we must take it for granted that the requirements of duty have been met. For the fulfillment of duty is the restrictive condition on which the value of any action depends.

Scientific ethics must strictly observe this division. For if even the basic concepts are not rigorously defined and differentiated, how can we hope to cast light on the more complicated problems that come later?

What we have just said holds for philosophical ethics, which is alone in question here; it is not necessarily true of applied ethics. Indeed—and we are anticipating—to observe the distinction formulated here is important *only* in pure ethics. Applied ethics, the application of the philosophical theory of duties to experience, can be based only on a prior philosophical theory of ideals. For, as will be shown later, it is not possible to establish the content of a given individual duty without taking into account the requirements of culture. This circumstance, however, does not directly affect pure ethics. For the theory of duties, as treated in pure philosophical ethics, does not have the task of deducing specific individual duties; it merely teaches us to recognize the general criteria that must be applied to experience before we can determine our particular duty in a given instance.

13. Formal and Material Theory of Virtues

Each of the two divisions of ethics can be subdivided in still another way.

Each ethical precept, whether it formulates a duty or an

ideal, has two aspects, distinguishable only by means of an abstraction. But we are here concerned with the abstract elaboration of pure philosophical ethics, hence this abstraction is of vital importance. I call one aspect the "form," and the other the "content" of ethical precepts or norms.

The form of an ethical precept comprises those characteristics which are implied in the concept of such a precept, regardless of the specific task it sets us.

The content of an ethical precept is, on the contrary, the specific task that it sets us, or commands us to perform.

Accordingly, each branch of ethics falls into two distinct parts—a formal and a material part. The formal part deals with the form of ethical precepts, and the inferences that can be drawn from their formal characteristics, whereas the material part deals with the content of these precepts, and with the inferences that can be drawn only on the basis of the content of these precepts.

This difficult distinction can best be illustrated by the analysis of a specific ethical norm, say duty.

The concept "duty" underlies the theory of duties but is not sufficient for its development, not even for the development of its purely philosophical side. For even if we know the concept of duty as completely as possible, this knowledge does not help us to determine the content of duty. If we are guided merely by the concept "duty," we can conceive of the most various, indeed, contradictory specific contents of this norm. The concept "duty" is compatible with the injunction, Thou shalt kill, as well as with the opposite injunction, Thou shalt not kill. If we do not go beyond the mere concept "duty," neither of these contradictory propositions can be characterized as correct or incorrect. Thus, if we complied merely with the demand that a given theory of duty be internally consistent, different systems could be developed, each of which would be free from contradiction, but which would contradict one another.

All these theories of duties would have in common those propositions which follow from the concept "duty," and which therefore cannot be excluded without contradiction from any theory of duties. These propositions constitute what we call the formal theory of duties. As against it, the material theory of duties contains those propositions which cannot be determined merely by the logical criterion of consistency, but which can be deduced only on the basis of the content of duty.

A similar distinction exists in the theory of ideals.

This distinction, however, must not be understood to mean that the concepts "duty" or "ideal" must remain problematic in the formal theory of duties (or of ideals), in the sense that nothing can be said about the reality of the concepts in question; in other words, it does not mean that the question as to whether duties or ideals actually exist remains open. Rather, the settlement of this question is the proper province of formal ethics, since it is independent of the determination of the content of the two kinds of norm.

The propositions asserting the existence of something like duties and ideals are, however, the only synthetic presuppositions in the formal part of ethics, and these enable us to go beyond the mere concepts "duty" and "ideal."

It must be observed at the same time that, even though these presuppositions are crucial, formal ethics does not depend on them in its entirety. A considerable part of ethics is independent even of these presuppositions, and hence of any synthetic propositions. On the basis of the mere concept of duty, and the mere concept of the ideal, it is possible to draw inferences so important and so great in scope that it will be worth while to treat this part separately, before bringing synthetic propositions into play.

Thus we shall carry abstraction to the point where we shall even disregard the reality of the concepts in question. How far we can get without assuming these concepts to be real, will be decided experimentally.

A philosophical science deserving of the name is always a whole in which no part is arbitrary, indeed, in which the structure of each separate part must no more be arbitrary than that of the whole. For in a pure philosophical science the structure and the articulation of the whole are clearly prescribed by reason. Any arbitrariness in the division of such a science is a sure

sign that it has not yet reached perfection. Hence it is important
that we should be certain not only of formulating true propositions within this science but above all of carrying out the
construction of the whole in accordance with a strict and unambiguous plan, so that we may gain the firm conviction that
each separate step has been made at the proper place.

Just as the theory of duties precedes the theory of ideals, so
within each of these branches of ethics the formal part must
precede the material. This satisfies the requirement of systematic rigor, according to which we must, in inferring a given
proposition, confine ourselves to a minimum of premises, namely
to those only which are necessary for the deduction of the proposition in question. Therefore we shall begin with the formal
part of the theory of duties, and within it, with those analyses
which do not presuppose even the reality of the concept of
duty.

PART I

Theory of Duties

Chapter 1. Analytic Principles Derived from Concept of Duty

14. Basic Concept of Theory of Duties

THE FOUNDATION of our theory is the concept of duty. It is a basic concept that cannot be reduced to simpler concepts. Consequently, it is impossible to define; for to define something, in the proper sense of the term, is to reduce it to something more elementary. It is, however, possible to characterize the concept of duty sufficiently to distinguish it from other concepts, with which it might otherwise be easily confused.

To make clear what we mean by the concept of duty, we have only to observe that we are here dealing with a so-called categorical imperative. When we say that duty is a categorical imperative we forestall two possible confusions.

(1) The term "duty" denotes a *categorical* demand, i.e., a demand whose validity does not depend on a given goal. This characteristic of the concept of duty is overlooked when attempts are made to replace it with that of the good, and hence to present the theory of duties as the theory of the good. Such attempts lead to a dangerous ambiguity. If the good is taken to mean that which is the morally good or that which duty requires, the concept of duty remains basic to ethics after all, and the idea that it has been replaced by another concept, that of the good, is an illusion. But if, in accordance with current usage, the good is conceived of as something that has positive value, admission to the theory of duties is barred. For no matter what assumptions we make as to the nature of the value in question, they lead us only to hypothetical imperatives: in each case we arrive at a proposition asserting that we *must* perform a given action if we

41

wish to achieve a given goal. But on the basis of this proposition we can make no inferences as to the value of the given action, let alone conclude that the action is required by duty. For even if we know that an action A is valuable, we can never infer from this fact that another action B is valuable, even if we make the additional assumption that unless we perform B, we cannot perform A. In other words, if the realization of a value depends on the fulfillment of a condition, it does not follow that fulfillment of this condition is for its part of value.

(2) The term "duty" does not apply to every kind of categorical demand, only to one in the form of an *imperative*. The word "duty" means a command: it expresses an *obligation*, an *ought*. It follows that even if it were possible, in the manner indicated above, to infer, from the assumption of a good, the value of the action necessary for its realization, we still should not be able to characterize such action as a duty. The value of an action permits no inference that it is required by duty.

The impossibility of such an inference, here again, is masked by the ambiguity of the term "good." For if we conceive of a good action as one that is in conformity with duty, i.e., a moral action, we can, from a judgment that the action is good, infer that it is in conformity with duty. But we can do this only because we covertly imply the attribute of duteousness when we speak of the good. Thus to deduce duty is to move in a vicious circle. For either we assume that the concept "good" already implies conformity with duty—and then there is no use starting from the concept "good" in order to deduce that of conformity with duty; or we do not presuppose that conformity with duty is an attribute of the good—and then we cannot, from the fact that an action is good, infer that it is in conformity with duty. The foundation of the theory of duties is thus the concept of duty, not that of the good.

The term "duty" expresses a practical necessity, just as does the term "ought" or "obligation." A practical necessity denotes here a necessity that restricts the agent's freedom of choice, and hence a *restriction* based upon a *law*. This restrictive law we call "the moral law."

It is not the task of the formal theory of duties to formulate this law: this is left to the material theory of duties. The formal theory confines itself to significant ethical propositions that can be inferred independently of assumptions concerning the content of the moral law; it analyzes the concept of the moral law, and develops the inferences that can be drawn from the assumption that it exists.

15. Task of Analytic Part of Formal Theory of Duties

In accordance with the principle of systematic rigor, we begin with the analytic part of our discipline, that is, with propositions which do not presuppose the existence of a moral law, and which are valid even without presupposing it. Indeed, even those who deny the existence of a moral law will be compelled, by the mere force of logic, to recognize the validity of these propositions.

True, we should not expect too much from this part of our discipline. It falls short of providing us with any moral rules; we must content ourselves with less far-reaching propositions, which, as propositions of a practical science, must meet only the condition that they prove fruitful in practice. Nevertheless they offer an equivalent for a definition of the concept of duty, which, as we have seen, cannot be defined. The system of propositions which I call the analytic principles of the formal theory of duties provides us—to use a mathematical expression—with an axiomatic definition of the concept of duty.

When we consider any proposition expressing an ought, that is, any proposition containing the term "duty" or its equivalent, and disregard the kind of duty it posits, that does not change the inherent ought. In the abstract analysis that follows we shall deal with those specific elements of the proposition by virtue of which it expresses an ought. The analytic principles of the formal theory of duties are confined to the determination of these elements.

An ought proposition is characterized by the fact that it ascribes an obligation to a person, in so far as this person is subject to the moral law. Every ought proposition must therefore contain the following elements:

(1) a reference to the subject of the obligation;
(2) a predicate expressing the obligation; and
(3) an assertion concerning the relation between subject and predicate, in which the subject of the obligation is subordinated to the law.

16. Principles of Moral Universality and Differentiation

Every ought proposition must first of all contain a determination of the subject of the ought and thereby contain a quantitative indication circumscribing the area of its validity. In this way we arrive at an analytic principle that refers to the form of the subject.

Each ought proposition presupposes a general rule determining what ought to happen. It follows that the subject of such a proposition cannot be determined individually, but only generally, i.e., on the basis of a concept under which it is subsumed, or as the member of a class.

Each ought proposition is thus generally valid, i.e., it refers directly to a class of individuals, not directly to single individuals as such. Consequently, the subject of the ought can be determined only on the basis of a concept, i.e., on the basis of a general characteristic. When we say of a given individual that he ought to do something, when we ascribe a duty to him, this statement is meaningful only if we can specify a characteristic of this individual, which is that of the class of individuals who are liable under the law in question.

Thus there is no moral distinction independent of the law, no distinction that could not be derived from the law itself. In other words, no one carries an individual moral tag that says what he alone ought to do. Everyone must qualify by displaying a trait enabling us to say that he owes the duty in question. It applies to any other individual with the same trait. All individuals who have the same qualitative traits are liable to the duty in question. This is the principle of moral universality.

This principle does not imply, however, that there are no moral distinctions between individuals. We must distinguish here between the validity and the applicability of a law. In so far as the law links an obligation to specific circumstances, its applicability depends on the presence of these circumstances, which, in relation to the law, is fortuitous. If these circumstances should occur only once, only one individual might be subject to the obligation in question, but he would be subject to it on the basis of the law, not independently of the law. All of which shows that the universality implied in the concept of duty does not imply uniformity in the application of the law. The unity of the law does not exclude that diverse duties may be derived from it: it postulates only the same obligations under the same circumstances. But since the law links different obligations to different circumstances, the duties themselves will change with circumstances. With the occurrence of one circumstance or another, one duty or another will arise on the basis of the law. Hence we can supplement the principle of moral universality with another principle, which I shall call "the principle of moral differentiation." According to this principle, the lawfulness implied in the concept of duty still leaves room for different duties with changing circumstances and for variations in the frequency with which specific duties occur.

This dependence of duties on changing circumstances and conditions does not imply, as one might suppose, a negation of the categorical character of duty. For the conditions conceded here affect only the application of the command, not, as is the case with the conditions of hypothetical imperatives, its coercive character. The conditional character of a hypothetical imperative rests on the presumption of a goal from which the binding character of the command is derived in the first place; if this condition is dropped, the command itself falls. Hence, a hypothetical imperative cannot have the form of an obligation; for no obligations can result from a mere fact such as that we pursue specific goals. An ought proposition, on the contrary, does have the form of an obligation. The necessity it expresses has its source in a practical law; the circumstances named in the conditions determine only the area of application of this law.

The proposition, If you have promised to do something, you ought to do it, has the form of a hypothetical proposition, but this does not mean that it has the form of a hypothetical imperative. For the condition stated here is not a goal, and the necessity expressed here is not that of a must but of an ought. Hence it cannot be derived from the reality of a goal, but only from a practical law given independently of it. This law is not to be found in the condition stated in the proposition; for this condition merely describes a state of affairs to the incidence of which the law links the obligation in question.

17. Principles of Moral Autonomy and Objectivity

The subject of an ought, required in every such proposition, is always determined according to the principles of moral universality and moral differentiation: this means that someone is liable only in so far as he belongs to the class denoted by the law. The condition under which the law is obligatory for a person or for a class of persons is formulated in the principle of moral autonomy, according to which the law can be binding only on someone capable of comprehending it; for the law in question here is not just any law, but the moral law, and as such it refers to the actions, or more accurately, to the will of a rational being. But the will can be made answerable for the fulfillment of its obligations only if it knows them. Consequently there can be no obligation which the person under obligation cannot recognize as such. This is the principle of moral autonomy.

Let us analyze the significance of this principle.

If we ask what we ought to do, there is no higher court to answer this question than our own insight. Let us assume that the highest court were another person who informed us that something was our duty. Such a communication is certainly possible; but when we say that a given person tells us what we ought to do, we merely record a fact, an occurrence that can be empirically verified. This need not convince us that an obligation has been imposed on us; for someone to say that to perform a certain action is our duty is one thing, and for it really to be our duty is another. And since we can never infer the existence of a duty from facts, we cannot infer it from the fact that someone else declares something to be our duty. Indeed, if all men unanimously declared that we are duty-bound to do something, we still could not infer the existence of an obligation from this fact.

On the basis of this simple analysis we may answer the question of whether duty can be founded on the command of some authority. If by authority we mean someone who can impose an obligation on us, authoritarian morality is a morality that bases obligations on orders. An order is the expression of some other person's will or judgment concerning what is alleged to be our duty. The fact that someone wants us to do something does not obligate us. To regard such an order as binding, we must be convinced that the person issuing it is an authority for us, i.e., that his orders create an obligation for us. But we can ascertain this only when we compare the order in question with our obligation; for how else can we recognize the person issuing the order as an authority? In this way, however, we are obviously turning in a circle: to recognize that someone is an authority we must know in advance what is our obligation. But authoritarian morality traces obligation merely back to the orders of an authority.

Despite the simplicity of this argument, the principle of autonomy has often been misinterpreted. How can such a simple truth be so obscure, the subject of so many controversies? The reason for this lies in the fact that moral cognition itself is originally obscure; it becomes clear only through systematic reflection in the course of which errors may occur. If moral cognition were self-evident, errors and conflicts among moral judgments would be impossible. Nor could there be in such a case a conflict between the judgment of the agent and that of the authority, for the problem of an authority would not exist at all. The analytic principle of moral autonomy is in itself a truism, but it is important to state it because moral judgments can be conflicting.

According to this principle, the agent's own moral insight is the court of last resort when he has to decide upon what he ought to do. But moral insight is possible only if the content of the moral law is unambiguous and objective. For moral insight is nothing but knowledge of this content. Thus the principle of autonomy presupposes that the moral law has a content. We are not asking here what this content is; but it is worth noting that the fact that it has content follows from the mere form of the moral law. The concept of a law without a content is self-contradictory. The principle asserting that the content of duty exists objectively, that is, independently of one's conviction of duty, may be called "the principle of moral objectivity." This principle forestalls a misinterpretation of moral autonomy, namely, the view that the agent's own conviction of duty is sufficient to determine duty, that the correctness of the conviction is unimportant, and that in fact there is no valid distinction between true and false conviction. The principle of moral autonomy emancipates the agent from the will of an authority; at the same time, rather than leaving him to his own fortuitous judgment, it commits him to his moral insight, which, in accordance with the principle of moral objectivity, means his unprejudiced knowledge of duty.

18. Principles of Morality of Attitude and of Moral Readiness

The foregoing reflections concern the relation between the agent's insight and his obligation. But what is ultimately important is not the fact that we know our duty, but that we do it, that is, the relation between the law and the agent's will.

The fact that the moral law is addressed to a will which is commanded to fulfill it, is inherent in its mere form. It is a practical law, i.e., a law that bids one act.

An action is an event that depends on a will. The moral law does not refer to an occurrence as such, to the event that takes place through an action, but to the action itself, i.e., to the occurrence precisely in so far as it depends on a will. Hence it is not sufficient for the fulfillment of the law that the willed occurrence should conform outwardly with the content of the law; for such a conformity may be fortuitous in relation to the will. The crucial question here is whether conformity with the law would have been secured even if the action had not resulted from some other motive, for instance, a mere inclination. Even when our inclination does not conform with our sense of duty, that is, even when inclination is opposed to duty, we ought to do our duty; and this is possible only if our insight into duty is the determining motive for the action. The moral law, as a law that is directly addressed to a will, can be complied with only through actions whose conformity with the law is secured by the agent's attitude (*Gesinnung*). The principle expressed here is that of the morality of attitude.

A man's attitude is characterized by the direction of his will, i.e., by the object to which his will is directed. The important thing here is not *that* he wills it, but *why* he wills it, what makes him will it, or the motive determining his will.

An action is moral if its determining motive is consciousness of duty, or, in the words of Kant, if it is performed out of mere respect for the law. An action is immoral if it is performed in violation of respect for the law, or in contempt of the law. This does not mean that an action is always either moral or immoral, or, to put it differently, that there is a duty always to act morally. In addition to moral and immoral actions, there are actions that may be called "amoral." They may be in conformity with the agent's sense of duty without being motivated by it. This is the case whenever inclination coincides with duty, whenever we deal with an inclination that duty does not forbid us to follow. This is also the case whenever consciousness of duty happens to be altogether absent: it is easy to see that an action performed under such circumstances can be neither moral nor immoral. It follows that there can be no duty always to act morally, that is, from a sense of duty.

The same conclusion can be reached on the basis of purely logical reasoning. Let us assume, for the sake of argument, that there is a duty always to act morally, i.e., to perform every action out of respect for the law, out of the knowledge that the action is required by duty. It would follow that whenever an action is required by duty, this would create a second duty, that of being motivated by consciousness of duty to perform that action. Similarly, this second duty would create a third one, that of fulfilling the second duty out of consciousness of duty; the third would create a fourth, and so on, *ad infinitum*, and in this series of duties no duty could be fulfilled without violating the duty derived from it.

The following analysis is less abstract. If we were duty-bound always to act morally, we would necessarily also be duty-bound to have a consciousness of duty: such a consciousness would then be indispensable to provide us with a motive determining our action. But only actions, not convictions, can be commanded, for convictions do not depend solely on our will. The moral law is a law governing actions, and hence there can be no morality imposing upon us the duty to act morally. Accordingly, the principle of the morality of attitude must be supplemented by the principle of moral readiness, under which the moral law, rather than demanding that each action be moral, makes this demand only when moral action alone can satisfy duty.

19. Principle of Moral Rigorism

The predicate of each proposition expressing a moral imperative denotes an ought, an obligation. It is an essential characteristic of such a practical obligation that it cannot be subordinated to a goal to be realized by the action; on the contrary, it subjects every possible goal to the condition of conformity with duty. This is the principle of moral rigorism.

Moral rigorism is opposed to what we may call "moral libertinism," according to which the obligatory character of duty may be restricted in favor of a given goal. Moral rigorism says merely that there can be no such restriction. If we assumed that duty could be restricted by a goal, the concept of duty would become nullified. As before, the reason why this proposition needs to be expressly stated is that moral knowledge is not self-evident.

The principle of moral rigorism, however, lends itself to misinterpretations that must be avoided. The practical necessity to subordinate inclination to the demands of duty does not imply that we ought never to gratify our inclinations, but only that we ought to disregard them when they are contrary to the demands of duty. If the principle of moral rigorism is interpreted as an injunction not to gratify our inclinations, we arrive at either an ascetic morality hostile to pleasure or a moral libertinism, which surrenders the necessity inherent in the concept of duty. The traditional distinction between remissible and irremissible duties implies such a surrender.

Here we can see the advantage of separating the theory of duties from the theory of ideals. Unlike the concept "duty," the concept "ideal" does not imply necessity. The ideal denotes goals worth striving for, even though it is not certain that they are attainable in every case. Disregarding the difference between these two ethical norms leads either to a violation of moral rigorism or to a denial of ideal values.

Distinguishing between the two concepts rids us of the quandary of having either to admit the existence of unfulfillable duties or abandon the idea that duty is obligatory. To confuse duty and ideal is to be exposed to the danger of sacrificing the principle of rigorism on the ground that it cannot always be applied.

Only by separating the theory of ideals from that of duties do we dispel the illusion that violation of duty may be justified on the basis of an ideal, for instance, the ideal of love, i.e., on the basis of a value which, it is thought, makes up for the disvalue inherent in the violation of duty. Duty is the sole requirement that restricts every goal inconsistent with it. But the realization of an ideal may be subject to restrictions. There is a rigorism of duty, but no rigorism of ideals.

20. Moral Valuations

In discussing the place of ethics in the system of philosophy we have characterized it as subjective teleology, i.e., as the theory of the value of human actions. At the same time we have established a line of demarcation as against aesthetic values. On the basis of the analytic principles so far established we may now formulate a criterion enabling us to recognize the specificity of moral evaluation.

The moral value of an action can spring only from the relation of the action to the moral law.

According to the principle of moral objectivity, the content of the moral law is unequivocal and objective. It follows that it is possible and necessary to evaluate actions in terms of their conformity with the content of the law, i.e., we must ask whether what the law requires is actually carried out. This evaluation, which we call "lawful" (*rechtlich*), deals with the rightfulness (*Rechtlichkeit*) or lawfulness (*Legalität*) of a given action, but does not inquire how the action has come to be in conformity with the moral law.

According to the principle of moral attitude, however, it is not a matter of indifference whether conformity of action with moral law is or is not accidental in relation to the agent's will. This principle calls for an evaluation of the action different from the lawful one—it calls for a moral valuation. We evaluate an action morally according to the relation obtaining between the agent's will and his consciousness of duty. It might be objected that this valuation, being merely subjective, must be excluded from ethics, on the ground that it replaces the objective moral law underlying lawful valuation with the individual's subjective consciousness of duty. This objection leaves out of account that, even though moral valuation refers to the relation obtaining between the agent's will and consciousness of duty, it is not based on subjective consciousness of duty: rather, moral valuation, like its lawful counterpart, is founded on the law itself, indeed its necessity springs from the very concept of duty. Hence this valuation too is objective, even though one of the elements on which it is based is subjective conviction of duty.

Now, the moral law does not by any means require moral actions only. An action may be in conformity with our sense of duty without being motivated by it. The conformity of an action with the agent's sense of duty has a value that we call its "subjective lawfulness." In determining such a value we are guided by the agent's subjective judgment, not by the objective requirements of the law. The agent's judgment of the lawfulness of his action may contain an error. Then the action corresponding to this judgment would remain subjectively lawful, but lack lawful value proper.

All these principles of valuation receive their real significance for the theory of duties only through the principle of moral rigorism.

It is a specific characteristic of duty that the action it bids us do gets preference over any other that might be performed in its place. When we say that an action deserves preference over any other possible action, we assert that there is no equivalent to the value of that action, i.e., that among all things we can do there is nothing valuable enough to offset the negative value implied in the omission of that action.

This state of affairs permits of various interpretations. It might be said that the value of doing one's duty is such that it surpasses the value of any other possible action. This would mean that fulfillment of duty has an infinite positive value; for only such a value could exceed any other possible value. Has fulfillment of duty such positive value? According to the principle of moral rigorism, it has not; for a moral action is not valuable because of any positive value attached to it. It derives its value not from the fact that through it some goal is achieved, but only through the fact that it is required by duty. But from the fact that an action is required by duty, we cannot infer that it is sufficient for the realization of a value, but only that a negative value, which our action would otherwise have, is excluded by the fulfillment of duty. We may say that any value that an action might otherwise have is entirely destroyed, indeed, changed into a disvalue, if this action is contrary to duty. From this follows the common characteristic of the moral valuations here derived,—what I call their "negative character." We do not say that moral action has value, but that immoral action has negative value.

This negative value, however, is not merely relative; if it were, a violation of duty would reduce the value of our action to zero, so to speak. In reality, violation of duty represents an absolute disvalue. We judge it as guilt. This term denotes the absolute negative value inherent in a violation of duty. Indeed, this disvalue is infinite; it cannot be compensated for by any positive value, however great. The disvalue we call "guilt" does not have its counterpart in any positive value, any merit arising from the fulfillment of duty. Consequently, fulfillment of duty is preferable to any other possible action not because there is any special positive value attached to it, but because violation of duty represents a negative value.

Chapter 2. Moral Imputation

(Analytic Principles Derived from the Notion That the Moral Law
Applies in Nature)

21. Concept of Nature

SINCE ETHICS is a practical theory of nature, its norms are
designed to govern our actions in the natural world. The moral
law, by definition, postulates actions, i.e., events that are caused
by a resolve of the will. Consequently, the concept of moral law
presupposes that of cause, and by the same token, that of natural
law: for the link between cause and effect rests always upon
natural law. Actions are possible only if they are part of the
great process governed by natural law; in other words, they are
possible only in nature.

It follows that the analytic part of the formal theory of duties
cannot be confined to the analysis of the purely practical concepts of ought, duty, etc. From these concepts we have derived
the analytic principles so far established. Now we must consider
those principles which can be derived from the notion that the
moral law applies in nature. For this concept too is presupposed
by the moral law.

At this point let us once again recall that all the propositions
deduced in this section are analytic propositions. We make no
claims regarding the reality of the concepts we have investigated. This also holds for the concept "nature," which we have
just introduced. We analyze the concept "nature," but we leave
open the question whether there is such a thing as nature. Consequently, our propositions will be valid regardless of whether
nature exists or not.

In analyzing the notion that the moral law applies in nature,
we come upon the last subject one would have expected to find
in this part of our theory, namely, the subject of moral imputation. It is true that a complete theory of moral imputation can
be developed only on the basis of empirical investigations, and
thus it goes beyond not only the formal theory of duties but

54

the philosophical theory of duties as a whole. It is not possible to develop fully a theory of imputation without the use of psychological data. But the *foundations* of such a theory—and these alone are in question here—are philosophical, and even purely analytic. We seek to formulate only the logical conditions of the possibility of imputation, and for this purpose it is sufficient, as an analysis of the concept of imputation will show, to inquire into the conditions under which the moral law is applicable in nature.

We impute something to a man when we ascribe to him an action as one to be judged under a law. The possibility of imputing something to someone implies two things: (1) an action which is ascribed, and (2) a law under which this action is ascribed. This statement says nothing about the kind of law we apply when we judge the action. What is in question here is only moral imputation, that is, imputation according to the moral law. We ask: What are the general conditions of the possibility of moral imputation? Or: Under what conditions can the moral law be applied to actions taking place in the realm of nature?

22. Problem of Choice

It is an analytic proposition that the notion of duty can apply and, indeed, have meaning only within a frame of reference of natural law. The laws of nature, which govern the existence of things, do not conform to the moral law. What ought to take place does not necessarily take place in nature, and conversely, what takes place in accordance with the laws of nature is not for that reason always what ought to take place. Only because the precepts of the moral law are neither necessarily observed nor necessarily transgressed in nature, is the statement that they ought to be observed, meaningful. This implies that there are beings who have a choice between obeying or disobeying the moral law; it is only to such beings that we can morally impute anything.

The possibility of choice, which is in question here, and which is a condition for the application of the moral law, must not be

misinterpreted in the sense that it postulates complete freedom
from natural law. Rather, it postulates only an independence
of the following extent: when the moral law associates a given
set of circumstances with a given result, that same result (or its
opposite) must not flow inexorably by natural law from the
same circumstances. Consequently, the actions of a being that
has freedom of choice do not take place outside of laws, or, as
we say, without grounds, but are unequivocally determined by
circumstances, in accordance with natural law. What is postu-
lated is only this, that there is no law of nature that would make
it theoretically either necessary or impossible for the agent to
observe the moral law.

The foregoing discussion may be clarified by an analogy
from another field. Some persons think that the weather depends on the phases of the moon, and that a change of the moon
determines a change of weather. Those who disagree with this
view, arguing that changes of weather only accidentally coincide with changes of the moon, do not thereby assert that changes
of weather are not determined by laws; they rule out only a
specific cause of those changes, namely, the phases of the moon.

Our contention can also be made clear as follows. A law determines that a phenomenon occurs necessarily only on the basis
that it belongs to a certain class of phenomena; only by assign-
ing it to such a class can we say that a given phenomenon occurs either necessarily or accidentally. When someone says that
changes of the moon necessarily cause changes of weather, he
assigns the phenomenon of meteorological change to a specific
class of phenomena, namely, the class of phenomena which occur simultaneously with the phases of the moon. But those who
deny the natural law in question imply that meteorological
changes, however inevitable, are not determined by virtue of
belonging to the class of phenomena which coincide with phases
of the moon.

Our case is similar. Freedom of choice, whether we obey or
disobey the moral law, does not postulate action independent of
natural law; it requires only that our action in fulfilling or violating the moral law do so on some ground other than that of
belonging to the class of actions through which the moral law

is fulfilled or to the class of actions through which it is violated. This is all that need be said here on the problem of choice as it presents itself in the theory of imputation.

23. Relation of Angelic, Human, and Animal Will to Imputability

The analytic principle of the possibility of choice implies that actions can be morally imputed only to beings that are capable of envisioning the moral law, as well as of experiencing subjective impulses or inclinations. For only in so far as a being is susceptible to a sense of duty, can it direct its will toward the fulfillment of duty. And only in so far as it is susceptible to inclinations, i.e., impulses which influence the will in accordance with whatever strength they have—regardless of whether the object of these impulses is ethically desirable—can it decide to ignore the moral law. For a being not susceptible to inclinations would by its nature have to prefer the action that is morally desirable, and thus would have no possibility of eschewing its duty.

There is no internal contradiction in the idea of beings that are susceptible to impulses of only one kind, whether determined by moral law or by inclination. We can conceive of a being that might be induced to act by sheer insight into the moral value of the action. Such a being would have to act morally by its very nature. Its will would be angelic, as by its very nature it would do what is ethically valuable.

Furthermore there is no contradiction in the notion of a being whose will is determined only by inclinations and that is completely incapable of insight into the ethical value or unworth of its actions. The will of such a being we call an "animal will." Actions cannot be morally imputed to beings whose will is angelic or animal.

The human will stands midway between the angelic and the animal will. Human is the will of a being that can be moved to act by moral impulses on the one hand, and by inclinations on the other—in other words, a being that can be motivated by both types of impulse. Only such a being can choose between following its moral consciousness and its inclination. Thus only the human will can decide whether to obey or to disobey the moral law, and actions can be morally imputed only to such a will.

24. Intention, Accident, and Purpose

The principle of the possibility of choice provides us not only with a criterion for deciding to *whom* something can be imputed, but also with a criterion for deciding *what* can be imputed. Only that can be attributed to a being upon which it can decide freely, i.e., only what is determined by its intention and not by external circumstances independent of its intention. We refer to this restriction when we call what we impute to someone, his "act."

What do we designate as an act? An act is not merely something that has taken place as the result of volition: it must be the object of such willing, and someone's will must be directed toward bringing it about. The actual result of an action may not be identical with the object of the decision; for the fact that a man wills to accomplish something does not yet mean that he will succeed in accomplishing it. An outside power may prevent him from carrying out his resolve or his own error may cause him to fail and may cause him to achieve, through his action, something different from what he intended. To impute an intended occurrence to someone it is not sufficient, or necessary, that it actually occur as the result of his willing; but the occurrence is imputable if he has willed it, if it is the object of his will, if he does what he can to achieve it. Consequently, that which he has resolved to do is to be attributed to him. When we impute something to someone, we are interested only in whether he willed it, not in whether he succeeded in carrying out his resolve. An action that does not achieve its purpose is called a mere "attempt." It follows that (1) the mere attempt deserves to be imputed, and (2) an unintended result may not be imputed.

Here we come up against the difference between intent and accident—a distinction familiar to us in everyday life, although its theoretical determination involves a number of difficulties. The result of an action is called an "unfortunate accident" when we do not wish to impute it to the agent; and we call the nonoccurrence of a result "mere luck" when we nevertheless impute the intention of bringing the result about to the agent. Thus the correct definition of what is called an act will exclude unfortunate accidents from the range of this concept, but will include attempts. This is done in our definition. For both the nonoccurrence of the intended result and the occurrence of the nonintended result are accidental in relation to the will. They are accidental in the sense that they do not have their source in the agent's will or in his intention but in something else, for instance in an external circumstance or in an error.

The concept of intent, however, requires a more detailed examination. As we have seen, we must define the concept "act" narrowly enough to exclude accident from its range. At the same time it must be sufficiently broad so that what we designated as the intended result—namely all that the agent resolves to do—falls under the concept because it is all imputable to him as his act. It is important to note here that the intended result denotes more than merely the purpose of an action, i.e., what the agent is directly concerned with in making his resolve, for the sake of which he resolves to act.

The term "purpose of an action" is here taken in its most general sense in current usage: it designates what the agent has in mind when he undertakes a given action.

The concept "intended result" is broader in range than the concept "purpose." In addition to the purpose we include under "intended result" every condition and effect of the action the agent has in view, in so far as he knew them. For in so far as the agent knew that a given event would take place as a consequence of his decision to act, he intended it; otherwise he would not have made the resolve. Everything he could anticipate as a condition of his action is included in the object of his decision, or is "co-intended."

The truth of this assertion, namely, that the agent co-intends every anticipated condition or effect of his action, can be seen in the light of the following consideration. We are able to will something only in so far as we conceive of it as at least a possible consequence of our resolve. For it is impossible for us to decide to do something that we think cannot be done; we cannot even intend such a thing. But if we know that the event we have in view is linked with some other event (which may be a condition or a consequence of the first), we also know that the first event cannot take place unless the other event, which is the condition or the consequence of the first, also takes place. Hence it is impossible to will a purpose without co-intending the anticipated conditions or effects of its realization. It follows that we must impute to the agent each event which he knew would occur as a condition or a consequence of the purpose he had in mind.

The fact that such a co-intended effect may not be desired by the agent is of no importance here. We must impute to the agent even the least desired effect of his action just as we must impute to him his purpose—if, that is, the former was anticipated as a condition or effect of the latter. For the agent co-intended it no matter how little he desired it, and this is enough for it to be imputed to him.

Furthermore, a given result, which is a condition or effect of the purpose the agent has in view, is not necessarily co-intended by him, even if it actually takes place, unless he knew that it would occur. On the other hand, if the agent conceived of a result as a condition or an effect of the purpose he had in view, if he anticipated it as at least a possible consequence of his resolve, it must be regarded as part of his intention even if it does not actually take place.

We have thus defined the concept "act." Now we need only add a few words concerning omissions—for omissions too can be acts.

An omission is something that might have occurred but does not occur because someone wills it not to occur. But the failure of an event to take place can be regarded as an act only if we presuppose a will excluding the event in question, and, needless to say, it is irrelevant to ask whether the event would not have taken place even without the intervention of that will. Unless such a will is present, there is no act of omission. An act always presupposes a will; it is not enough for someone not to will something to take place, rather he must will it not to take place. Thus even the nonoccurrence of an event can be intended and properly imputed.

25. Concept of Negligence

The foregoing considerations will enable us to decide a question which has always presented one of the greatest difficulties in the theory of imputation and which has not been resolved to everyone's satisfaction to this day. For if, as we have just established, only the intended result of an action is imputable, we are confronted with the following problem: How is it possible to impute a nonintended result? Yet seemingly we do just this whenever we blame someone for being remiss.

We speak of negligence under the assumption that the result of an action, even though it *was* not foreseen, and hence could not be intended, *could* nevertheless have been foreseen by the agent. The meaning of this statement must be carefully analyzed. In the light of our previous discussion, this much is certain: since imputation presupposes intention, a result stemming from negligence can be imputed, if at all, only if we can classify it as an intended result. Under no circumstances must we establish two parallel classes of imputable results—intended results on the one hand, and effects of inadvertence on the other. On what basis, then, is it possible to impute results of laxity?

A second difficulty arises because in addition to cases in which we impute the result of an action despite the absence of intention, we also have converse cases, in which we do not ascribe consequences although intention was present. If there are cases in which we cannot impute the result of an action to someone despite the presence of intention, it would appear that not even intention is sufficient to make imputation possible. Such cases occur when we deal with mental incompetence.

Let us first examine the question of negligence. As I have said, a result is brought about by negligence when the agent did not intend it although he could have foreseen that it would occur as a consequence of his decision or his action. Thus negligence is nothing but the failure to foresee a result that occurs in cases when the agent could have foreseen it. We have to deal here with two questions: (1) What is meant when we speak of possibility of foresight? and (2) How is it possible to impute results stemming from negligence?

As for the first question, we must guard against taking it too lightly. For we must sharply distinguish between the possibility of foreseeing a result, and foreseeing the possibility of a result. When we foresee the possibility of a result, the result is intended, and no true case of negligence arises. Consequently, cases when the possibility of the result is foreseen present no difficulty; a difficulty arises only in cases when the possibility of foresight is in question. The second group of cases cannot be reduced to the first.

Now, what do we mean when we speak of the possibility of foreseeing a given result of an action? This question is difficult because it might be said that actual lack of foresight is in itself proof of the impossibility of foresight, so that the possibility of foresight is ruled out; after all, everything that happens is necessary in so far as it is governed by specific natural laws. Therefore, something different must be meant when we blame someone for being remiss on the ground that he could have foreseen the result of his action even though in fact he did not foresee it. What is meant can obviously be only this, that an agent can achieve insight into the consequences of his action only if he reflects upon them; he must deliberate to some extent in order to realize the foreseeable consequences of his action. The fact that this deliberation is lacking shows that it was ruled out by natural law, but we still have to ask what natural laws make deliberation impossible. If deliberation is absent for reasons independent of the agent's intentions, we say that he is incapable of it. This is the case, for instance, when he altogether lacks the knowledge required in order to be able to foresee the consequences in question. But the agent's failure to deliberate may also have been caused by the fact that he was not inclined to reflect on the consequences of his action. In this case, deliberation was possible for him: for he would have overcome his disinclination to deliberate if to do so had been in conformity with his intention. Thus, when we speak of the possibility of deliberation in this case, we mean that its absence was not independent of the agent's intention, but rather, that he failed to foresee the consequences of his action only because of his disinclination to envisage them. Even in this case, of course, his failure to deliberate was necessary in the trivial sense that everything that happens is necessary. But the cause of the necessity lies here only in the fact that the agent had no inclination to institute the proper deliberation.

On the basis of the foregoing we can also answer our second question, that is, the question of how it is possible to impute a result of negligence. The answer to this question is: Even though an unintended result of an action cannot be imputed as such, omission of the deliberation that would have enabled the agent to anticipate this result, must be imputed to him. Only when there is such an omission may we blame him for being remiss. This also makes it clear that since we ascribe to the agent not the effect of his negligence, but his negligence itself, the latter cannot be judged automatically on the basis of the result that actually occurred, perhaps accidentally. Rather, remissness must be imputed to the agent on the basis of the results that he could have anticipated from his knowledge of the circumstances. Consequently, the agent's level of education will affect the degree to which negligence is imputed to him. We must impute to him his lack of reflection, in so far as he was able to institute an adequate deliberation, and in so far as he could know that because he omitted it his action might produce objectively reprehensible results. Carelessness, for the very reason that it dispenses with the deliberation required to estimate the possible results of an action, is a rightful ground for condemning a course of conduct. Whenever we may assume that a man is aware that careless action may lead to unlawful consequences, and hence that reflection is needed to insure lawful action, and whenever we may furthermore assume that reflection was within the power of his will, the carelessness he evidenced and its foreseeable results should be imputed to him as his guilt.

26. Criterion of Responsibility

Now we shall have no difficulty in answering the question still remaining as to whether and in what circumstances it is improper to impute to an agent the results of his action, even though intention was present. We cannot impute the consequences of his conduct to a man when he is in a condition that makes him incapable of anticipating these consequences. We call a man responsible when he meets the conditions required to make imputation possible, and we say that he is incompetent when he does not meet these conditions.

Another question arises here. We have defined the concept of responsibility; but we still have to establish a usable criterion of responsibility. We must ask: How do we recognize whether the condition of responsibility is present or absent? We say that a man is responsible when he is capable of instituting the deliberation required to foresee the results of his action: the criterion of responsibility is thus given in the possibility of deliberation. Jurists define incompetence as a condition in which the agent cannot reach decisions by his free will. But again, freedom of will does not imply that the agent's resolve is independent of natural law. Rather, this freedom implies only independence from the domination of instinctual impulses influencing the will and excluding conscious control. Consequently, it would be false to say that someone who acts thoughtlessly could not have acted thoughtfully, on the ground that actual thoughtlessness is sufficient to prove that reflection was impossible. For reflection to be possible, it is sufficient that the agent be in a condition which does not as such preclude reflection. Thus we are led back to the question as to whether and to what extent the fact that the result of an action was intended is insufficient to make the action imputable. The condition that must be met if such a result is to be imputed, is the presence of responsibility, i.e., of the possibility of thoughtful action. The agent must be capable of sufficient reflection to achieve insight into those consequences of his action which are relevant to the moral law, and to let himself be governed in his resolve by this insight. For deliberation is required to safeguard the result of the action against chance. In securing or forestalling such a result, reflection alone, by intervening in the mechanism of the impulses, achieves emancipation from the relative strength of the various impulses that happen at the moment to be working on the will. In other words, the will must be able to control the interplay of the impulses, to guide them freely—by directing attention toward or away from one object of the impulses or another—in order to make the decision conform to the presupposed general rule of priority value.

Thus a man cannot be regarded as responsible merely because he is independent of external compulsion, merely because he is able to choose an arbitrary and positive course of action. When we say that a man is able to choose a given course of action we imply only that the action is dependent on himself, that is, on his will. But to act arbitrarily in this sense is by no means the same thing as to act with deliberation; for it is possible to act arbitrarily even in a state of incompetence. Arbitrary action is deliberate only when the agent's will, rather than being moved to it by direct instinctual impulses, in turn reacts on the impulses through reflection in order to modify them in accordance with a general rule against which the possible actions are checked. Freedom of will thus means the possibility of emancipating one's resolve from instinctual impulses through the intervention of reflection in the mechanism of the impulses.

Now it may well happen that a man acts carelessly, even though thoughtful action is possible, his carelessness being solely due to his disinclination to institute the required deliberation. Consequently, to determine whether he is responsible, the important thing to consider is not his action in a particular case but whether the cause of his thoughtlessness may not lie in a condition that cannot be influenced by the will. Only if the cause of his thoughtlessness lies in such a condition—then, and only then, do we say that he is incompetent. But if the cause lies in the agent's disinclination to institute the required deliberation, we say that he is responsible. Hence, when there is doubt as to whether the agent is competent or not, we need only ask

whether he would have failed to make a deliberate decision even
if a preponderant inclination could have been gratified only by
such a decision.

In the light of the foregoing analysis, it is clear that the
criterion of responsibility admits of degrees, for the condition
of responsibility can pass gradually into the condition of irresponsibility; hence we rightly speak of degrees of irresponsibility, short of outright incompetence. In each individual case the
question is how strong the reflection-requiring element in an
inclination must be, barely to bring about such reflection, or
how strong are the preponderance and power of instinctual
impulses that hamper reflection. The more they obstruct reflection, the less the responsibility.

All this naturally does not mean that we cannot blame someone for his irresponsibility. Irresponsibility is a fault when it is
intended, even when it is only brought about by negligence, a
result of an action committed or omitted.

It must be noted here that imputation of irresponsibility admits of degrees according to the agent's level of education. The
question is always: To what extent could a given person foresee that his irresponsibility would produce certain results. The
greater a person's insight into this matter, the more we must
blame him for his irresponsibility. Irresponsibility is a state
in which the will is determined by the spontaneous strength of
its impulses. When an agent is irresponsible, the object toward
which his impulses are directed depends only on circumstances
that are accidental in relation to his will. In so far as these circumstances cannot be foreseen, it is impossible to know in advance what a man will do when he is in a state of irresponsibility:
for we have assumed that the things he will do in this state depend on unforeseeable circumstances. A man who deliberately
puts himself in such a state cannot know what he will do in it,
but he must know that he will not be able to know this. Consequently, assuming that he has sufficient insight, he foresees the
possible consequences of his conduct in such a state, and to that
extent these consequences must be imputed to him. If such
consequences nevertheless are not produced, this fact is accidental in relation to his will; then too he must be considered

guilty of irresponsibility, and his guilt is measured by all the possible consequences of his irresponsibility. Every person with sufficient intellectual experience must know that he is responsible for the foreseeable consequences of his conduct, and he acts against his insight if he fails to reflect upon these consequences.

27. Criterion of Imputability

We must keep in mind that the agent's responsibility is not a sufficient but only a necessary condition for imputing to him the consequences of his actions; even when a man is responsible we can impute the consequences of his conduct to him only in so far as he intended them. At the same time we must not forget that imputation presupposes responsibility.

Thus we must combine the two—responsibility and intention —to obtain the conditions to justify imputation. It is useful to designate with a new term the concept of the conditions sufficient to justify imputation, and the most appropriate term for this purpose seems to be "imputability." Thus I shall call the result of an action "imputable" if the conditions sufficient for its being imputed are met. These include: (1) responsibility, and (2) the intentional bringing about of a given result.

Hence, we may say that the result of an action is imputable if it was intended by a responsible being.

28. Degrees of Imputation

The foregoing considerations show that when we impute something to someone as his guilt such imputation admits of degrees. It is important to distinguish between two aspects when we establish degrees of guilt. To impute an act we must evaluate it by the law under which we impute it. Under the law, a result is characterized as wrong by these two criteria: it must have been brought about in contravention of the law; and it must be the act of a rational being. The degree of guilt is determined by both.

Accordingly, the degree of guilt can first be established objectively, on the basis of the relation of the act to the law. When we say that an unlawful act is wrong, we may distinguish various degrees of unlawfulness, so that we may speak of a greater or lesser wrong. Whether a wrong admits of such differences of degree, depends upon the content of the law. Since we do not here wish to make assumptions regarding the content of the law, we cannot indicate any rules by which the degree of guilt could be objectively measured; indeed, so far we cannot even assert that there are objective degrees of wrong. The question of whether wrong admits of gradation can be discussed only in the material theory of duties though we must even now take into account the possibility of such degrees. The fact, already demonstrated, that any violation of duty represents an infinite disvalue does not rule them out. The idea that degrees are possible even within the realm of the infinite is not self-contradictory.

There is also a subjective gradation of guilt, which rests upon the fact that imputation admits of degrees. Here we do not measure the result of an action objectively, by the law, but subjectively, by the agent's intention. In doing so we must determine, on the one hand, to what extent the result in question was intended and, on the other, to what extent the agent can be held responsible. Here we consider not the effect of the agent's will but only its object, and hence the result of his action only in so far as it was anticipated as a consequence of his decision. We thus obtain degrees of imputation corresponding to the degrees of probability with which the agent anticipated a given result of his action. We can impute to him a result of his action only to the extent to which he anticipated it. This he can do only according to the degree of his knowledge or insight. Upon this insight depends the extent to which the result may be regarded as intended, and hence, to what extent it can be imputed to him.

29. Moral and Lawful Imputation

The foregoing considerations apply to moral imputation in general; they do not take into account the distinction between moral and lawful imputation. In moral imputation we are not immediately concerned with the relation of an act to the moral law; here the act must be measured against the agent's subjective sense of duty. For in judging an act morally we do not ask whether it conforms or is contrary to the objective content of the law, but rather whether it conforms with or is contrary to the agent's sense of duty. Only to the extent to which the agent is conscious of committing a wrong, can we impute it to him as guilt. Thus we are guided here by the degree of clarity of his consciousness of duty. The agent's realization that his act is unlawful, not the fact that his act is unlawful, determines his moral guilt.

In questions of lawful, as distinguished from moral imputation as such, we completely disregard the agent's insight: we ask whether an act is in conformity with the objective norm of the law, not whether the agent regarded his act as lawful.

Consequently, the fact that an action is subjectively right is not sufficient to make it objectively right. An action may be objectively lawful even though the agent is under the delusion that he is committing a wrong and, vice versa, an action may be objectively unlawful even though the agent believes it to be lawful or even moral. In lawful imputation we disregard the agent's ideas on law; we must not, however, disregard his evaluation of the consequences of his action. For even in lawful imputation we are concerned not with the actual consequences of an action, which may be fortuitous, but with the intended result. The agent's factual errors must be taken into account in both lawful and moral imputation. In questions of lawful imputation we ask only whether the intended result of an action is lawful or unlawful; but we may impute an unlawful result to the agent only on the assumption that he anticipated it. We need not assume, however, that he had knowledge of the unlawful character of this result: such knowledge plays a part only in moral imputation.

Here we conclude the analytic part of the formal theory of duties. To carry our system further we shall have to resort to synthetic presuppositions.

Chapter 1. Imperative of Character

30. Fundamental Synthetic Proposition of Formal Theory of Duties

THE SYNTHETIC PART of the formal theory of duties must be founded on a practical synthetic proposition. This fundamental proposition or principle must be completely independent of the content of the moral law—if it were not, it would not belong in the formal theory of duties. At the same time, however, it must go beyond the mere *concept* of the moral law—if it did not, it would not be a synthetic proposition. The new element we add to our previous presuppositions is the assertion that there actually is something that is denoted by this concept, an assertion which we formulate as follows: "There is a moral law."

This principle meets the conditions stated above. It is, to begin with, a practical proposition, i.e., a proposition of ethics, although its form might mislead us into regarding it as a proposition of the theoretical science of nature. The illusion that our principle is a theoretical proposition, i.e., a judgment concerning something that "is" or exists in the manner of a law of nature, rests upon the fact that it does not express the moral law. This is true: it does not express this law, and should not express it, for otherwise it would have to refer to its content and it would transcend the formal theory of duties. Our principle asserts merely the reality of this law, but the reality in question is a practical one, for although the moral law is unconditionally valid, it is not unconditionally observed in nature. Thus our principle asserts the practical reality of the concept of duty.

Furthermore, our principle is a synthetic proposition: for the mere concept of duty does not imply that there actually is such a thing as duty. The negation of our proposition does not involve self-contradiction.

70

Our principle is, however, the only synthetic proposition to serve as a foundation of this part of our discipline. However poor its content may seem to be, it has practical significance, because with the help of this proposition which itself expresses no imperative, it is possible to deduce an imperative, and this without resorting to other synthetic presuppositions. This procedure may seem paradoxical, but it will be justified by its results.

31. Minor Premise of Formal Theory of Duties

It is true that the imperative in question cannot be deduced from our major premise alone: we also need a minor premise. This raises a difficulty. Where shall we find this minor premise, since we may add neither synthetic propositions derived from experience, nor synthetic propositions referring to the content of the moral law?

We do not have to resort, however, to such auxiliary propositions. All we need is to recall that the existence of the moral law does not imply that it is obeyed; indeed, our insight into the practical significance of ethics as a whole depends on the validity of this observation. The contrary assumption, that is, the assumption that the moral law operates with natural necessity even involves a logical contradiction. For the very form of the moral law implies the possibility of a conflict between what does take place and what ought to take place.

All that is needed to obtain the imperative in question is to take this analytic principle asserting that natural law can diverge from the moral law, as our minor premise, and to combine it with our major premise. In view of the logical importance of this principle for the structure of the formal theory of duties, I call it "the subsumption formula of the formal theory of duties." It says that there can be no natural law according to which the moral law either must be or cannot be observed in nature.

The importance of this proposition for the deduction of the imperative in question becomes clear when the concept of action in nature is examined more closely. Our action in nature is determined by forces present in nature; it is not determined directly by what we ought to do. Natural forces are distributed independently of their positive or negative value, and, more particularly, independently of their relation to the moral law. If we call the forces acting upon the will, "impulses of the will," and the impulse that determines the will, "the determinant of the will," we may say that this determinant does not depend on whatever objective factors may entitle a given action to preference, but depends on whatever predominant impulse happens to be acting on the will. This is implied in our subsumption formula.

We may also express it as follows: The moral value of an action is not self-evident. The term "self-evident" is taken here in the sense of *practical* evidence. The moral value of an action would in this sense be self-evident if our knowledge of it were immediate, and if insight into the practical necessity of an action directly determined our resolve. If the moral law were practically evident, the fact that an action is in conformity with duty would be sufficient to make us prefer this action to any other, and to carry it out; thus there would be—in contradiction to our minor premise—a natural law according to which that which ought to take place does necessarily take place. There can be no such natural law, and hence moral necessity cannot be self-evident. And in actual fact, whether we realize the moral necessity of an action, and whether our realization is sufficient to make us carry out this action, depends on the development of our reflection: for it is only through reflection that we can gain insight into moral necessity, and only if this insight is sufficient to overcome subjective inclinations can it bring our resolve into conformity with duty. The extent to which our reflection is trained and developed is fortuitous in relation to the moral law. The moral law does not directly determine what we do; rather, we observe it only to the extent to which our reflection is sufficiently developed for this purpose. This is only another way of saying that the moral law is not self-evident.

It is essentially to this circumstance that scientific ethics owes its unique practical interest. If ethical cognition were self-evident, no reflection would be required to raise it to the clarity of consciousness and to observe it. Concern with scientific ethics would then be superfluous for all practical purposes; for a science is nothing but the perfect reflective form of a domain of knowledge.

32. Concluding Proposition of Formal Theory of Duties

With the aid of the two premises we have introduced we can proceed to formulate our imperative. Since these presuppositions are valid a priori, the imperative to be deduced from them, which is the concluding proposition of the formal theory of duties, will also be valid a priori. Under the subsumption formula, it is a matter of accident whether a given subjective inclination of a being acting in nature is in conformity with the requirements of the moral law; on the other hand, the practical necessity of the moral law implies that its fulfillment may not be a matter of accident. For a law expressing a practical necessity, even though it is not a natural law, nevertheless postulates that it be necessarily valid in nature, i.e., that it be valid as though it were a natural law. But observance of the law would be a matter of accident in the sense referred to here unless it were secured by the will. For the moral law demands that it be fulfilled by a will; if the law is fulfilled by events independent of the will, this fulfillment is accidental in relation to the law. Hence, if there is such a thing as a moral law at all, it imposes on every rational being in nature the imperative to insure its observance independent of any contingencies in nature by which such observance happens to coincide with some predominant impulse directed toward the objectives of the moral law. It follows that we are under the injunction to make fulfillment of duty the object of our will. I call this injunction "the imperative of character."

The imperative of character, the concluding proposition of the formal theory of duties, is the pivotal point of this part of ethics. A proper understanding of this imperative requires above all to keep clearly in mind the method by which we have deduced it. For we are confronted here with a special difficulty: the imperative of character seems to be incompatible with the subsumption formula. According to the subsumption formula,

the relative strength of the impulses, which is fortuitous in relation to the moral law, determines whether what ought to take
place does take place in nature. But the imperative of character
demands independence from random strength of impulses; in
other words, it demands that fulfillment of duty not be left to
chance.

Whether we do or do not obey this command, our action is
governed by natural law. Consequently, the only possible way
of securing dutiful action is to make the sense of duty the preponderant impulse. It follows that the will itself must determine
by which impulse it is to be governed, i.e., which impulse is to
become preponderant. Although in nature a decision depends
only on the relative strength of the impulses, this relative strength
must nonetheless depend on our will; consequently, we ourselves
must have the power to choose the impulse which determines
our action. Such a capacity to determine through our own will
which impulse shall determine our will seems necessarily to transcend all bounds of nature.

How this paradoxical capacity can be accounted for, is a speculative problem with which we must not and need not concern
ourselves here, however important its solution may be in itself.
For our purpose it is sufficient to know that we have such a
capacity. We know this on the basis of the proposition that
there is a moral law. The reality of this law implies that we can
do what the law commands, and hence that we can eliminate
accident from the operation of our impulses, which, if left to
itself, is determined by the fortuitous interplay of the impulses.
The presupposition which constitutes the major premise of our
discipline is ultimately sufficient to establish the existence of
such a capacity, whatever may be the solution of the relevant
speculative problems. We call this capacity to free ourselves
from subjection to the impulse which happens to be the strongest at a given moment "freedom of will."

Chapter 2. Conditions of Character

33. Meaning of the Term "Character"

FROM THE RESULT just obtained important inferences can be drawn concerning the conditions of character.

The term "character" is used in a broad and in a narrow sense. In the broad sense, when the term denotes a person's mental constitution, character can be qualified as good or bad. In the other sense, the term already carries a praiseworthy connotation, and we need not add the adjective "good" since the expression "bad character" would be self-contradictory.

In the preceding chapter we used the term "character" in the latter sense. We ascribe character in this special sense to a man who has resolved to fulfill the moral law, so that fulfillment of it is no longer a matter of accident for him. We say a man has character if he makes his sense of duty the preponderant impulse of his will; it is such action that initiates or lays the foundation of character and constitutes the duty imposed on us by the imperative of character. To perform it is our duty, whatever the content of the moral law may be: no element of that content can be incompatible with the imperative of character.

Now, character in this narrower sense presupposes character in the broader sense. We say that a man has character in a broader sense when he does not act blindly, when he does not merely drift along, but acts in conformity with resolutions; and we say that such a man has a good character when the resolutions according to which he acts aim at fulfillment of duty.

In other words, character in the broader sense, as a condition of good character, designates that quality of a will which seeks to emancipate its actions from accidental influences.

This definition does not take into account what kind of rule the will adopts as the result of its decision; for a man to have character it is sufficient that he subject his action to some sort of norms, whether these derive from the moral law or not. Character here consists in the will's independence of whatever impulse happens to be the strongest one operating at a given moment. This independence can be achieved only if the will subjects the impulses to control in conformity with a general rule, and modifies them when they do not conform to this rule.

For the sake of brevity and convenience, I shall designate an impulse that determines the will in a direct and spontaneous manner, as an "emotional impulse," and a corresponding decision as an "emotional decision." Then we may say that character signifies the will's independence of emotional motivations, i.e., motivations that determine the will without the mediation of a deliberate resolution. Since the rule by which we judge the value of an action is not self-evident, and since we can apply this rule only through the intervention of reflection, we may also define character in positive terms, as control of reflection over impulses.

When the impulses do not directly and spontaneously determine the decision, when the decision is reached only through the intermediary of reflection, after the various impulses have been judged by the rule of value, we say that the decision is deliberate. The rule of value which underlies a deliberate decision is referred to as a resolution, a maxim, or a practical principle. Accordingly, we may also describe a nonemotional decision as a deliberate action or an action in conformity with a resolution. For the time being we shall not ask by what specific rule a given action is chosen in preference to another; it is enough that some such rule should guide the decision. The content of the rule applied has no bearing on character in the broader sense; what matters is only the *form* of the action, i.e., the fact that it is an action determined by practical principles, as against actions determined directly by spontaneous impulses, or emotional actions.

34. Strength of Character

On the basis of the foregoing we may formulate a condition of character which I shall call "the postulate of strength of character," i.e., the requirement that our action be independent of affects. An affect is a violent emotional impulse. Strength of character implies above all independence of affects.

We ascribe strength of character to a man whose will is not a plaything of affects which happen to assail him at a given moment. Affects for their part depend upon the impressions which happen to influence a man. In other words, affects reflect circumstances more than they do character; for a man's character consists in his ability to control his affects. His strength of character is in direct ratio to the effectiveness of this control. The stronger an affect can become without bending the will, the greater the strength of character.

Strength of character may assume various forms. It is manifested negatively, by omissions, when the will does not yield to the assault of affects; and positively, by actions which involve the mastering of affects. In either respect we may make a further distinction, according to whether strength of character is revealed in an individual decision or evinced in carrying out a decision once taken, in adhering to it against the continuing onslaught of affects.

We thus obtain different virtues as manifestations of strength of character. To find a proper name for each of these without doing violence to current usage presents some difficulties. I propose to call "self-control" the negative virtue of omitting emotional actions to which we are driven by affects. Self-control is thus a man's ability not to be carried away by affects assailing his will. It is distinguished from "resoluteness," which designates a man's power to act in a certain way although his affects drive him to act in an opposite way. The virtue that manifests itself in the ability to take decisions in the face of contrary affects, I shall designate as "presence of mind," and distinguish it from the virtue of "steadfastness," which consists in adherence to decisions once made and ability to repel continually renewed assaults of affects.

It will now be relatively easy to name the four virtues that can be obtained by combining the qualities mentioned above, and that together constitute strength of character. Self-control plus presence of mind is moderation; self-control plus steadfastness is patience; resoluteness plus presence of mind is courage, and resoluteness plus steadfastness is fortitude. At least this is how we can best name these virtues in conformity with current usage.

	Self-control	Resoluteness
Presence of mind	Moderation	Courage
Steadfastness	Patience	Fortitude

For the correct understanding of these terms, we must keep in mind that each of them denotes a virtue, or a quality of character. We must, however, guard against confusion. Strength of character must not be taken merely as the ability not to be carried away by affects. Under certain circumstances this requires no character—namely, when no affects arise. A man insensitive to affects will not be carried away by them, and yet we cannot say that he has strength of character. For this consists in one's ability to control affects, and we can speak of control only where there is something to be controlled.

Corresponding remarks may be made about all the virtues we have listed. When Goethe wrote, in his *Faust*, "And above all, cursed be patience," he had in mind not patience, but submissiveness, which is the opposite of patience—indeed, patience implies nonsubmissiveness to affects. Nor must the virtue of courage be confused with fearlessness. A fearless man does not have to be courageous, just as an apathetic man does not have to be moderate. The virtue of courage consists in the mastery of fear. More generally, character is manifested only where inclinations are actually overcome, and only where such mastery is the work of the will and rests upon a decision, not upon an accidental inclination. A man is not courageous if he happens to be the kind that is undeterred by obstacles, or even finds pleasure in fighting obstacles, from a desire for battle or adventure, or because he wishes to gratify his vanity or other inclinations. Hence the kind of mastery that is the hallmark of character is rightly called self-mastery, which always requires a resolve—the resolve not to be swayed by one's own inclinations.

35. Spontaneity of Character

The second condition of character consists in what is best called "spontaneity of character." This term stands for the will's independence of the power of habit. Habit denotes a uniform mode of conduct, which results from the automatic operation of impulses that have become permanent. When such permanent impulses, such inveterate habits, attain a certain strength, they are designated as passions.

Current usage presents us, here too, with certain difficulties. For the term "passionate" is used to characterize a man easily swayed by affects. But here I am concerned with the distinction between affects and permanent impulses, and for these I find no better term than "passions."

Just as strength of character postulates freedom from the influence of affects, so spontaneity of character postulates freedom from the influence of passions. It requires that we be perpetually ready to act against our habits, and to break them whenever we are commanded to do so by the moral law. In this sense, spontaneity of character may also be designated as the virtue of inner freedom.

Here again we must guard against confusion. What I call spontaneity of character is something entirely different from what is called a man's vivacity. The latter quality signifies responsiveness to external impressions, and hence susceptibility to affects and passions. The postulate of spontaneity neither includes nor excludes such susceptibility. Passions are part of a healthy and rich life. Indeed, where passions are absent, spontaneity of character cannot be put to the test, just as strength of character cannot be put to the test where affects are lacking. But spontaneity of character implies control of passions, not their intensity. The stronger the passions, the more pronounced the spontaneity of character: for it is measured precisely by the maximum strength of the passions which the will can master.

It is clear now that character is not a matter of habit, as is often maintained. On the contrary, character calls for freedom from the tyranny of habit. Where habits rule, an essential condition of character, namely, spontaneity, is lacking. Spontaneity of character asserts itself through special resolves—*new* resolves—and thus can never be replaced by habit.

A man of character acts in accordance with principles, he acts deliberately. Deliberate action is different from action that is guided merely by one-sided and permanently predominant impulses. The two kinds of action, however, may be easily confused because each of them results in a certain constancy or uniformity of conduct. Character postulates constancy in action, i.e., subjection of the diversity of possible actions to the unity of principles. But constancy of action does not always result from what we call character; it may also result from natural traits so that impressions produce uniform effects. Thus natural traits may result in a mode of conduct similar to that resulting from character. Uniformity of conduct can, moreover, rest upon the mere constancy of the circumstances that influence the agent; but it can also rest upon the fact that the impulses directed by the will are themselves uniform. In each case we must ask whether constancy in action is merely the result of uniform circumstances, particularly those circumstances which can be accounted for in terms of traits, or is the result of principles. If it is not the result of principles, what appears as character may be due merely to the fact that the agent had no opportunity for acting differently.

This brings up the question of the difference between character and temperament. Temperament is not a characteristic of the will; it refers to the nature and strength of a man's instincts, affects, and passions. These may be so constituted that the mode of conduct they determine is internally consistent. But then the quality of his conduct is accidental, i.e., it does not depend on the agent's will. Uniform dispositions that produce effects similar to those produced by character are not for that reason virtues; they might at most be called virtues of temperament. Such virtues are qualities that superficially resemble traits of character, but are not necessarily associated with true character. Indeed these qualities may occasionally reveal weakness of character, for instance, when character calls for an action contrary to one's disposition—we can never be sure that such a situation will not arise. Consequently, we must distinguish between uniformity of conduct, which results from uniform dispositions, and constancy of action, which is a manifestation of character. This distinction is practically important, because if a man's actions are in conformity with a practical principle, this conformity may be purely accidental as in the former case.

No virtue of temperament can be relied upon to result necessarily in actions consistent with the moral law. We must rather be prepared for exceptions: for in the case of deliberate action, consistency of conduct does not rest upon immutable traits but upon firm principles. Such principles call for equal actions only under equal circumstances—according to the principle of moral differentiation which we must take into consideration when applying the moral law. Firm adherence to principles does not by any means mean uniformity of conduct; on the contrary, it may require us to break through habit, to deviate from uniform conduct. What we called "spontaneity of character" is precisely a man's readiness, out of his loyalty to his principles, to deviate from a mode of conduct that has become habitual. Strength and spontaneity are the necessary and sufficient conditions of character in the broader sense, or character in so far as it is manifested in deliberate action. They are necessary conditions of character in the narrower sense.

36. Purity of Character

What, then, are the qualities, which, together with strength and spontaneity, constitute character in the narrower sense, i.e., moral character? A man has character in the broader sense when his conduct is guided by principles, whatever these principles may be. But in order to define moral character, we must specify the kind of principles that determine a man's actions. An action may be fully deliberate, yet the practical general rule or principle that governs it and by virtue of which it is deliberate, may be completely arbitrary. The maxim to which a deliberate action conforms may even be morally reprehensible. In such cases, the impulse has a subjective cause, and the maxim of action is not an objective rule of value, but a subjective inclination which has been raised to the status of a maxim through the intervention of reflection, and which determines the action in the form of a maxim. A moral resolve is always deliberate, but the converse is not true: a deliberate resolve is not always moral.

We can now readily formulate the additional condition that must be satisfied if deliberateness is to be a moral quality. I call this condition "purity of character." It is fulfilled when the content of the maxim governing an action is put beyond accident, i.e., beyond merely fortuitous coincidence or discrepancy with the objective rule of value.

If we dispense with this condition and look at character only in the broader sense, even the worst criminal may often possess character to the most marked degree. He is a criminal by virtue of the kind of principle he has chosen as his guiding maxim, by virtue of the circumstance that the content of his maxim is determined not by the content of duty but by an extramoral impulse. When a man is dominated by impulses that pit principle against duty, that very conflict may make him a criminal. Thus, principles are possible without purity of character; but purity of character is impossible without principles.

Purity of character requires us not only to eliminate the accidental influences of inclinations on our conduct, but also to eliminate such influences in favor of the rule of value that the command of duty imposes on us. Strength and spontaneity of character, which are necessary to eliminate accidental influences on action in general, are also necessary to eliminate accident from observance of duty. Our sense of duty is not necessarily clear enough to determine the will. Consequently, it cannot determine the will through an emotional impulse, but only through the intervention of reflection in the mechanism of impulses, or through strength and spontaneity of character.

Purity of character is thus the quality of that man who subordinates his impulses to his sense of duty, who makes fulfillment of duty a necessary condition of his actions. Purity of character, we may say, is nothing but moral readiness; indeed, it is the very foundation of moral readiness.

What is important here is that we correctly combine two truths. We start from the fact that purity of character calls for fulfillment of duty as the necessary condition of action. According to the principle of moral readiness, this cannot mean that we are commanded to follow the moral impulse to the exclusion of all others. Purity of character does not require of us to deaden all inclination in favor of a moral resolve.

At the same time we must keep in mind that readiness to observe the moral law even when we are not inclined to do so cannot be a matter of mere accident, but must be based on a special decision—the decision to fulfill our duty even when we are not inclined to do so. We must always be prepared for such a situation, because no natural law guarantees that our inclinations will always be in conformity with duty. Thus a separate decision is actually required here—the decision through which alone moral disposition is created in man. Even if the imperative of character does not explicitly require us always to act morally, it nevertheless implies that moral readiness includes the resolve to act morally whenever the occasion arises, namely, whenever we are not inclined to do our duty. In other words, whenever necessary we ought to act out of mere respect for the law.

We cannot say a priori how often we shall have occasion to do our duty from purely moral considerations. Hence a man's morality cannot be estimated by the number of his moral actions. Whether or when he finds himself in a position to act morally depends on circumstances, and provides no indication as to his character.

There is, however, one moral action whose practical necessity can be demonstrated a priori, namely, the very action through which the imperative of character is fulfilled. It is possible to fulfill this imperative only through a moral action: for it would be self-contradictory to assume the existence of an inclination which could determine us to make the decision to act, when necessary, against any possible inclination, even the strongest. Yet this very decision is called for by the imperative of character. No inclination, but only our sense of duty can get us to do this, and this is the only moral action whose practical necessity we can demonstrate a priori.

Further investigation of the conditions of purity of character shows that they include two virtues. Purity of character requires that inclinations be subordinated to sense of duty. But the sense of duty can control the will only through the intermediary of reflection. Consequently, moral insight is the first condition that must be satisfied if purity of character is to manifest itself. The second condition is a sense of duty that is capable of moving the will. We say of a man to whom we ascribe purity of character that he acts to the best of his knowledge and conscience. In the light of the foregoing, we may say that a man acts to the best of his knowledge when he reflects upon his duty in order to achieve clarity about it, and that a man acts in accordance with his conscience when he subjects his will to his insight. In the first case we refer to deliberateness in the narrower sense; in the second, to the moral sense, the attitude.

We thus obtain the virtues of moral clarity and of moral attitude. The opposite of moral clarity may be designated as moral obtuseness, or an impaired sense of duty, that is, a sense of duty blunted by affects or passions. But even extreme moral clarity may be associated with extreme weakness of will. That is why a moral attitude calls for, in addition to moral clarity, the subjection of inclinations to the sense of duty, and hence, moral readiness.

Both moral clarity and moral attitude are virtues, i.e., qualities of the mind that we evaluate in moral respects. But we cannot regard them both as duties: we cannot correlate each of them with a corresponding duty. Moral clarity cannot be the object of a duty, because it is not dependent on the will. But even though a man's insight does not depend on his will alone, we may say that he is duty-bound to strive for moral clarity, to do whatever depends on his will in order to attain clarity. This is what I designate as the duty of moral truthfulness. It enjoins us to strive for the possession of that insight which is needed to arrive at a sufficiently clear sense of duty. But this duty as such is only a consequence of the duty of moral readiness. Moral truthfulness, i.e., the striving for moral clarity, is a condition of a moral attitude. This imperative is the only duty that we deduce directly in the formal theory of duties, and all other duties mentioned in this theory can be derived from this one. With this we have reached the end of this part of our discipline.

At the same time, however, we already see clearly outlined the path leading to the material theory of duties. For we need only to ask *what* are the insights that make for moral clarity, what ideas about the content of duty we can form with moral clarity, in order to formulate the problems of the material theory of duties in so far as this theory can be developed by philosophical methods. The task of the material theory of duties is to determine the content of the moral law, and to formulate the consequences that can be drawn from it.

SECTION 2. MATERIAL THEORY OF DUTIES

Introduction

37. Transition to Material Theory of Duties

AT THE CONCLUSION of the formal theory of duties we were led to ask what is the content of the moral law—a question that is dealt with in the material theory of duties. But at the very threshold of this theory we are confronted with a difficulty which is inherent in the very formulation of our task. We have found that all that matters in moral evaluation is the agent's sense of duty, regardless of whether his ideas about duty are true or false. Yet our purpose in the material theory of duties is precisely to discover a criterion of what is true duty. Here, all that matters is the content of duty, and that very factor is of no importance whatever when we evaluate an agent's morality.

The resolution of this difficulty is implicit in the final proposition deduced in the formal theory of duties—the proposition asserting that we are duty-bound to strive for knowledge of the objective content of duty, and hence that we have the task of developing the material theory of duties. We are no longer concerned with formulating criteria of morality, but only with developing criteria of rightness. The conditions of morality are fully developed in the formal theory of duties: there are no conditions other than those of purity of character. But these include the striving for moral clarity, and hence for insight into the content of duty. Thus, the task of the material theory is directly connected with that of the formal theory: the material theory provides us with the information about duty, which the formal theory enjoins us to strive for.

That we are bound to undertake the new task and that this task is compatible with the formal theory of duties will also be evident from the following consideration. We could deduce the imperative of character without determining the content of the moral law; but at the same time we found that the very form of the moral law implies *that* the moral law has a content. The imperative of character does not provide us with that content; rather, it logically presupposes the existence of another imperative, which has a specific content, and which provides us with the criterion of rightness.

Now, it is worth noting that the formal theory of duties not only compels us to attack the problem of the material theory, but actually assures us that this problem can be solved. For it provides us with the principle of moral autonomy, according to which there is no duty that cannot be discovered through the agent's own insight. Whoever recognizes the imperative of character thus cannot deny without being inconsistent that there is an objective moral law, and that he can determine the content of this law through his own insight. However great the difficulties involved in determining this content may be, we cannot doubt that the problem is solvable.

In establishing the moral law my method will be to characterize its content in progressive steps by propositions, so that each proposition will serve as a premise for the next, in the same way as the propositions of the formal theory serve as the necessary premises of the propositions of the material theory. We shall introduce new propositions only after drawing all possible consequences from the preceding ones.

Chapter 1. Restrictive Character of the Moral Law

38. Proposition Asserting Restrictive Character of the Law

THE FIRST ESSENTIAL CHARACTERISTIC of the moral law is what we call its "restrictive character." I maintain that the moral law in itself is only a negative command: it directly enjoins only *omissions*. To be sure, omissions are actions—a mere failure to act is not an omission—but omissions are actions of a specific kind. The proposition asserting the restrictive character of the moral law says that the moral law rules out, i.e., forbids certain actions toward which an impulse is directed. Thus the moral law is directly applicable only in *prohibitions*, and in each case an impulse must be present to make application of the moral law possible. This law in itself does not tell us how we ought to act in a positive sense, or what ends we ought to pursue; it intervenes restrictively only on the assumption that we are pursuing given ends.

This proposition must not be confused with a proposition formulated earlier, which asserts the negative character of moral valuation. This earlier proposition was implied in the very definition of duty: to assume a positive moral valuation involves a logical contradiction. But a moral law expressing a positive command is not self-contradictory. Propositions such as "Thou shalt honor thy father and mother," and "Thou shalt kill if thy superior order thee to do so," are certainly free from logical contradiction. The proposition asserting the negative character of moral valuation would remain valid even with respect to a law expressing a positive command. We should ascribe no positive value to an action carried out in obedience to such a command: such an action would not be meritorious. Consequently, the proposition asserting the restrictive character of the moral law introduces a new element, which is an essential characteristic of the content of the moral law.

39. Impossibility of Moralism

That the proposition asserting the restrictive character of the moral law introduces such a new element can also be seen from the fact that we can draw from it an important practical consequence, which goes beyond the principle of negative valuation. This consequence is that moralism cannot be valid. I call "moralism" a system of normative moral principles sufficient for the positive regulation of life. In other words, moralism excludes the possibility of morally indifferent actions. According to it, every action must be characterized as either fulfillment or violation of duty. Thus no room would be left for norms other than those deriving from the moral law. If the moral law were of such a nature, if it were sufficient completely to regulate life, it could not be restrictive in character. For a restrictive moral law leaves open the question of whether the agent is obliged to perform a specific action or is free to choose between various morally permissible actions. Thus, the proposition asserting the restrictive character of the moral law implies the repudiation of moralism.

We must, however, guard against carrying our new assertion too far. Rejection of moralism does not imply that there is such a thing as a morally indifferent action, but only that the moral law per se leaves scope for morally indifferent actions, and hence, if there are no such actions, that this is due to circumstances independent of the moral law. In rejecting moralism, we merely reject the theoretical assumption that there is no margin for morally indifferent actions, but we must admit the possibility that such a margin is actually eliminated. For we cannot decide a priori, on the basis of the moral law alone, how wide is the scope for morally indifferent actions. Consequently, we cannot a priori rule out the possibility that this margin may be insignificantly small.

The objection that the moral law can be applied only if extra-moral impulses exist, and hence must leave scope for these impulses in any case, is beside the point. For we cannot infer the necessity of extramoral *actions* from the existence of extramoral *impulses*. Conceivably a moral law may forbid all actions through which extramoral impulses are gratified, so that the agent can fulfill his duty only by following a moral impulse.

Chapter 2. Formal Character of the Moral Law

40. Proposition Asserting Formal Character of the Law

THE NEXT ESSENTIAL CHARACTERISTIC of the moral law I designate as its "formal character." I call the action required by duty in a given case "the material content of duty," and I maintain that the content of duty cannot be logically derived from the content of the moral law. This is precisely what the proposition asserting the formal character of the moral law says. I use the term "formal" for lack of any better word, although I have previously used the same term in a different sense. In the sense the word has here, a given determination can be more or less formal, according to the amount of empirical data required to make it applicable. Since the moral law is formal in character, it determines duty in an incomplete manner: in itself it is not sufficient to establish specific duties.

It might be objected here that the proposition asserting the formal character of the moral law contradicts the analytic principle of moral objectivity, and hence is itself contradictory. This objection rests upon a confusion between the material content of duty and the content of the moral law. It is true that, according to the principle of objectivity, the moral law must have a content: it must provide us with an adequate criterion of what we ought to do in a specific instance. But this does not mean that the law must directly designate the action which we ought to perform in a given instance, and which is thus the material content of duty in that instance. The question whether the moral law designates the material content of duty in this sense cannot be answered on the basis of logic. It is answered only by the synthetic proposition asserting the formal character of the moral law. According to this proposition, the criterion of duty cannot be discovered directly as the characteristic of an action, which would indicate to us whether this action is or is not dutiful, but we must instead apply the criterion to the given circumstances, and only on the basis of our empirical knowledge of these circumstances can we determine what is our duty. Only depending on the nature of the circumstances can anything become the *material content* of our duty. But the *criterion* that we apply to the circumstances, and that is given us directly by the moral law, is established independently of the circumstances.

41. Impossibility of a Moral Code

From the proposition asserting the formal character of the moral law we infer directly that it is impossible to formulate a moral code, i.e., a systematic catalogue of duties, which would tell us how we ought to behave in each given situation. For according to this proposition the content of duty cannot be deduced a priori from the moral law; indeed, it cannot even be stated a priori. What the material content of duty is depends on circumstances that can be only empirically discovered from case to case, so that the influence of circumstances cannot be limited a priori. Knowledge of these individual circumstances, which characterize each case, can never be replaced by any rule of conduct, however detailed. For no matter how many circumstances are enumerated and taken into account in such a rule, we can never be sure that a given case will not be attended by further circumstances, which deserve to be taken into account according to the moral law, and by virtue of which our rule of conduct may become unrightful. Such a possibility could be excluded only if the rule in question were limited by the negative condition that no such further circumstances are present. But then we would be compelled to subject each case to a special examination in order to find out whether disturbing circumstances are not present. Our rule of conduct would thus fail to fulfill its purpose, which is to spare us the trouble of examining the circumstances.

The moral law, by virtue of its formal character, requires that we ourselves undertake this examination; any attempt to free the individual agent from this obligation leads to a violation of the moral law. Whoever foregoes the trouble of examining the circumstances essential to the determination of his duty, and resorts instead to a general catalogue of rules, cannot to that degree act morally. Even if he happens to choose what is objectively right in a given case, his observance of the moral law does not rest upon his own insight, but only on his compliance with instructions emanating from another's will, i.e., on a heteronomous morality.

The need for a moral code, which has manifested itself in all ages, springs from want of confidence in the power of our understanding to give us adequate information about the material content of duty.

From the foregoing considerations, however, it follows that even a moral code would not remedy such a deficiency: for the fact that an action conforms to a moral code can never have moral value. Such conformity would not result from the agent's own moral insight, but from another man's rules, which are accidental in relation to the agent's moral insight. A chained criminal is just as unworthy morally as a free criminal, even though his fetters consist in a psychological compulsion—for instance, a compulsion based on a moral code to which he submits. Indeed, there is no greater threat to genuine morality than such timorous restraints of the agent's own moral judgment. They imply abrogation of the principle of moral autonomy. Only by banishing from ethics all attempts to formulate a moral code do we gain the freedom of mind consistent with the conditions of a moral life.

42. Impossibility of a Conflict of Duties

A further consequence of the formal character of the moral law is the proposition asserting the impossibility of a conflict of duties.

As a matter of fact, the impossibility of a conflict of duties can be proved even on the basis of the formal theory of duties. For what would a conflict of duties be? It would consist in this, that we had the duty to perform a certain action under specific circumstances, and at the same time to omit that action under the same circumstances. Duty would thus call for something contradictory, and thereby cancel itself.

If, however, we ask why this doctrine of conflicting duties has continually re-emerged in ethics and has gained a foothold in it, we find that the root of the matter is a failure to appreciate the formal character of the moral law. If one falls into the error that duties are determined a priori, independently of the individual circumstances, one easily supposes that an action required in a given situation on the basis of one moral rule might be forbidden on the basis of another rule, i.e., that a conflict of duties is possible.

There will be no justification for making the illogical assumption of the possibility of conflicts of duties, once we have summarily rejected the idea of any catalogue of moral rules; and, as we have seen, the inadmissibility of such catalogues is a consequence of the principle of the formal character of the moral law. Whoever has grasped the meaning of this principle, will decide on the content of duty only on the basis of an appraisal of the given circumstances, and apply a given moral judgment to another case only if the situation thus appraised is repeated in all its particulars.

The logical problem involved here can be made even plainer. Let us assume that the situation to be appraised is characterized by the circumstance C_1, and that, on the basis of the moral law, we have found that a certain action A_1 is required by duty in this situation. In another situation, characterized by the circumstance C_2, we would be required by duty to perform another action, A_2. Now, let us assume a situation in which both circumstances C_1 and C_2 are present. This circumstance, i.e., the simultaneous presence of C_1 and C_2, we shall designate as C_3. Now, it may happen that the duty required by C_1 is incompatible with the duty required by C_2; that is to say, we may be faced with the alternative of performing either the action A_1 or A_2, since each excludes the other. For instance, in one case our duty may be not to kill, and in the other case, not to lie. Now, under C_3, we may have a case in which we must lie in order not to kill, or vice versa. Whoever concludes that this is a case of conflict of duties assumes tacitly that the duty in the situation characterized by C_3 is obtained mechanically by the addition of duties A_1 and A_2. But there is no principle justifying such an assumption, which would be incompatible with the formal character of the moral law. For C_3 is not characterized merely by the presence of C_1 and C_2, but by their *simultaneous* presence. This simultaneous presence is a new circumstance that calls for a separate appraisal. Only on the basis of such an appraisal can we establish what is our duty in this new situation.

43. Duty of Inner Truthfulness

The foregoing considerations lead to another significant inference. To attain insight into what is our duty, and hence to be able to do our duty, we must take into account the circumstances of each given case. In other words, we know a priori that, according to the proposition asserting the formal character of the moral law, we cannot determine a priori what the content of our duty is in a given case, and that to discover it we must undertake an empirical investigation. But if we know this, and know it a priori, we know also that we are duty-bound to acquaint ourselves with the circumstances in question and to obtain the necessary knowledge of the facts. This is what I call "the duty of inner truthfulness."

We established a similar duty in the formal theory, namely, the duty to strive for that which we called "moral clarity," i.e., clarity about the moral imperative of duty. The duty of moral clarity could be inferred from the mere form of the moral law. The duty of inner truthfulness goes further. For the absence of such a duty would not be logically incompatible with the form of the moral law. Unless we asserted the formal character of the moral law, we might admit the possibility of an exactly opposite duty, which might be formulated as follows: Deceive yourself concerning the facts—even though not concerning the actually valid duty. Even such a duty, to deceive ourselves about the facts of our existence, could be fulfilled only if we had sufficient moral clarity concerning the content of duty. On the basis of the mere form of the moral law, we can assert the reprehensibility of moral self-deception, but not of self-deception concerning the facts. To be able to do our duty we must be clear about its content; but this does not yet mean that we must also be clear about the circumstances under which we act. The impossibility of a duty to deceive ourselves concerning the facts can be inferred only from the proposition asserting the formal character of the moral law. One of the consequences of this proposition is the duty not to deceive ourselves concerning the facts, but to strive for increasing our knowledge of those facts which may influence us in our judgment of what our duty is in a given case. No limits can be set a priori to the extent of this influence.

Chapter 3. Dignity of Person

44. Principle of Personal Dignity

ON THE BASIS of the proposition asserting the formal character of the moral law we have determined the content of that law as a criterion of duty. But so far we have not formulated this criterion itself; to do so we need additional synthetic propositions.

We have found that the moral law directly expresses only a restrictive principle: it subjects our actions motivated by extramoral impulses to a certain condition. Of this condition we have so far learned only that it is formal in character. What, then, is this condition by which the moral law restricts our action?

Our conduct depends on what we prefer and what we condemn; in other words, we are guided by the values that we ascribe to things. The faculty of ascribing positive or negative values to things, I designate as the faculty of interest. Now, our action is free from moral restriction when it affects only our own interests. A restriction is imposed on it only when it affects not only our own interests, but also the interests of others, that is to say, when we deal with beings who have interests. Such beings we call "persons."

Aside from the moral law, the value of an action is determined for each person by his own interests. If a given action affects the interests of several persons, these persons are not necessarily at one in judging the value of the action; rather, we shall be confronted with various judgments concerning the value of one and the same action whenever the interests of the persons involved are in conflict.

The moral law is directed against this diversity of judgments. Its significance is that it restricts the practical possibility, or permissibility, of a given action, and hence the satisfaction of a given interest, by the condition that this action must be compatible with a regard for the interests of others affected by the

97

action. Regard for the interests of others is what restricts our freedom of choice, in keeping with the moral law. The fact that we attach greater value to a given action than to another possible action is not sufficient to make this action permissible, i.e., not forbidden to us; we have first to ask how this action affects the interests of other persons, the interests of those who are the objects of this action. The object of my action is anyone whose interests are affected by my action.

Thus the moral law restricts us in our actions in so far as other persons are the objects of these actions. We ascribe dignity to whatever the law protects from our discretion. Consequently, the dignity of the person is the condition to which the moral law restricts our action. Subjection of our will to the condition that the dignity of the person must be upheld is what we call "respect." Hence, we may express the condition we have just established in the form of this imperative: "Respect personal dignity!" I call this postulate "the principle of personal dignity."

45. Moral Law as Law of Right

On the basis of the principle of personal dignity each person is entitled, by virtue of his interests, to restrict the will of others. We call such a title a person's "right." The moral law is thus a law of rights, i.e., it determines the content of our duties by rights.

We must sharply distinguish this proposition, which asserts that the content of duty is determined by rights, from the proposition formulated earlier, which asserts that the content of the moral law provides us with a criterion of lawfulness. This earlier proposition is analytic: for lawfulness denotes only the conformity of conduct with the requirements of the law. The present proposition is synthetic: it answers the question as to what is the actual content of the law or of the criterion of lawfulness. This criterion is provided by the concept of right.

46. Subjects of Duties and Subjects of Rights

According to the principle of personal dignity, every being that has interests, in other words, every person, has a claim to respect for his interests. This claim is the person's right. Thus every person is a subject of rights; for he is, by definition, a subject of interests. True, a person's right is in question only when he is affected by the actions of another person, namely, a person subject to the moral law, or what we call a "subject of duties." To secure correct application of the principle of personal dignity it is therefore important to distinguish sharply between the concepts "subject of rights" and "subject of duties." We shall see that the extension of the term "subject of rights" is greater than that of the term "subject of duties."

Only a person can be a subject of duties, but not every person is necessarily a subject of duties. For only those persons can have duties, and thus be subjects of duties, who (1) are capable of action—for duty refers to a person's will, and a person without will cannot be subject to any duty—and (2) are capable of having a sense of duty, that is, are rational beings. For no one can be subject to a duty, who is incapable of grasping the idea of duty. On the other hand, any being capable of having interests can be a subject of rights. Consequently, someone may very well be a subject of rights without being a subject of duties.

We see that the concept of interest is crucial for the distinction between subjects of duties and subjects of rights. This concept must be carefully differentiated from that of impulse and that of purpose or end. Every impulse presupposes an interest, for an impulse is possible only when a valuation takes place. But the converse is not true, namely, that every interest already constitutes an impulse. An interest becomes an impulse only when it influences the will. Thus a being can have interests without having impulses.

It follows that a person who is a subject of interests is not necessarily a subject of ends. To be sure, an end is always the object of an interest; but not every object of an interest is thereby an end, indeed, not every object of an impulse is an end. An end is an object the idea of which is the determining

ground of an action, and which is conceived of as the effect of
the action. But we can conceive of something as an effect of our
action only by means of a judgment—a judgment by which we
conceive of the object of our will as the effect of our will. Only
rational beings are capable of such judgments. Thus, ends can
be the objects of interests only of rational beings. For beings
incapable of judging cannot grasp the concept of effect and
hence cannot pursue ends.

To subsume a being under the concept of person, it is sufficient that this being be capable of experiencing pleasure and
pain: for pleasure and pain designate those interests of which
we are conscious independently of any judgment, and which
do not necessarily operate as impulses of the will. Any being
that can feel pleasure or pain is therefore a subject of rights,
and has dignity in the sense defined above.

What is the actual extension of the concept "person" thus
characterized is a question that cannot be answered philosophically but only on the basis of experience. For whether a
given being possesses or lacks the quality required to be classified as a person can be decided only on the basis of an empirical
investigation, not by mere reflection. Nor can we decide a priori
whether the subjects of rights that we encounter in actual life
are also subjects of duties: for this depends not only on whether
they have interests, but also on whether they are rational beings capable of action. Per se the extension of the concept
"subject of rights" is broader than that of the concept "subject
of duties," i.e., every subject of duties is necessarily a subject
of rights, but a subject of rights is not necessarily a subject of
duties.

47. Rightfully Necessary and Unrightful Interests

A person has dignity by virtue of his claim to respect for his
interests by others: the moral law protects him against being
subject to the discretion of those whose actions affect him.
This does not mean that *all* of a person's interests deserve to be
respected: only some of these interests do. Hence there arises
the question: Is it possible, without introducing a new proposi-

tion, to determine whether a given interest deserves to be respected or not?

The answer to this question is in the affirmative. First of all, we can say that no interest may be regarded as worthy of respect if gratification of it violates the moral law. I shall summarily call such interests "unrightful." An interest is unrightful when it involves an action violating the moral law; to satisfy such an interest is reprehensible. It can never be worthy of respect: for if it were, its bearer would have the right to satisfy it. But since this is forbidden him, it would be self-contradictory to say that he has a right to satisfy it.

It is also clear that interests which the moral law bids us satisfy are always worthy of respect. I shall call such interests "rightfully necessary interests." We apply this term to an interest in an action which is itself rightfully necessary or which the moral law bids us perform. Such an interest is always worthy of respect. For if it were not, this would imply that its bearer has no right to satisfy it, and we would be led to make the self-contradictory assertion that he has no right to fulfill his duty.

48. Principle of Abstraction from Practical Error

It is possible, however, to go even further, and this without resorting to new presuppositions, in determining what interests deserve to be respected according to the principle of the dignity of the person. So far we have distinguished between interests that are satisfied in conformity with duty, and interests that are satisfied in violation of duty. But independently of this distinction we can also ask whether what a man is interested in is truly in his interest or not. For what someone is actually interested in may be more or less in his interest. The reason is that he may be mistaken as to what is in his interest—namely, to the extent to which he must use his judgment in determining what is in his interest. This determination can be influenced by his judgment in many respects, so that he is exposed to various errors. Hence we must distinguish between interests which I shall call "putative" and interests which I shall call "true."

To begin with, it is clear that if something is in someone's interest, he also has an interest in fulfilling all the conditions necessary to satisfy his interest. In other words, fulfillment of these conditions is itself in his interest. But whether he is actually interested in fulfilling these conditions, depends on specific circumstances, above all, on whether he has sufficient insight to form a correct judgment of the conditions necessary to satisfy his interest. For only if he has such insight can he discover the means he must use in order to satisfy his interest. Furthermore, whether he actually uses these means depends on whether his judgment determines him to act, that is, on whether his insight is sufficient to arouse in him a sufficiently strong interest in using these means. For in order to fulfill the conditions necessary to satisfy his interest, it is not enough that he know them; this knowledge must also be capable of moving his will. We may call the interest in the means of satisfaction of a given interest, an "indirect interest," since the interest in the means arises only on the basis of the interest in the end. Such an interest is always a derived interest; it is related to its object only indirectly. It is clear, then, that our indirect interests may enter into conflict with what is truly in our interest, namely, when we are incapable of sufficient reflection to evaluate correctly the means of satisfying our direct interest, and when we are incapable of being moved to act by our knowledge. There is no doubt that in such a case putative and true interests may diverge, and an error as to the true interest becomes possible. Such an error rests upon a deficiency in the theoretical use of reflection. For the judgment by means of which the error might be discovered refers to a natural law, which determines the conditions under which the given interest can be secured. We must know this natural law to discover the means of satisfying our interest, and to use them. Thus, the judgment in question is theoretical, not practical.

The actual and the true interest may diverge for still another reason—one that rests on a deficiency of reflection not in its theoretical, but in its practical use. Errors are possible not only in existential, but also in value judgments. Even a direct interest, i.e., an interest related to its object without the mediation of another interest, is not necessarily directly conscious, i.e., is not necessarily an interest of which we are conscious independently of reflection. To raise to consciousness what is in our interest, may require reflection; and the judgment we make in the process may be erroneous.

Not all interests spring necessarily from what we call "pleasure" or "pain." Pleasure and pain are direct interests, of which we are conscious directly, that is, without the intermediary of a judgment. In the case of pleasure or pain, therefore, no error is possible as to what is in our interest. To say, in this case, that something is in our interest, is to say merely that it gives us pleasure. Whether it does or does not, we know directly. The answer to this question does not depend on a judgment, and for this reason no error is possible here.

But no logical contradiction is involved in assuming the existence of an interest which, although it is directly related to its object, does not directly reach our consciousness, but requires a judgment to make us conscious of it: thus we can assume an interest which becomes clear to us only in the form of a judgment concerning the value of its object. The case here is different from that of pleasure or pain, in which the judgment merely repeats a valuation of which we are conscious independently of judgment. Hence we can also say that no contradiction is involved in assuming the existence of direct interests of a kind different from pleasure or pain. It is entirely incidental to the concept of a direct interest whether we are directly conscious of the interest. But if there are interests of which we become conscious only in the form of reflection, i.e., of a value judgment, we are exposed to the possibility of error in our consciousness of these interests, and this error is then not a theoretical, but a practical one, namely, an error in a judgment concerning not the existence, but the value of things. Practical errors are thus possible when we deal with interests which, although they are direct, are not directly clear, or, as we may also put it, are not self-evident. Such direct interests, which are not clear per se, but which become clear only in the form of value judgment, I call "originally obscure interests."

Now, I maintain that the duty to respect the interests of persons affected by our action in accordance with the principle of dignity, does not include putative but only true interests. In other words, we have to make allowance for the interests in question as they would manifest themselves if we supposed them free from error; we have to judge them not by the degree of strength with which they actually happen to manifest themselves, but by the weight they would have if they had been sufficiently reflected upon, that is, freed from error. Only to that extent are we duty-bound to respect them.

From the foregoing we can draw two inferences. First, our duty extends beyond regard for the actual interests of the person affected by our action: we must also make allowance for those interests which such a person may not actually have, but which he would have if his actual interest coincided with his true interest. Second, our duties are restricted in so far as we do not have to respect those interests which are not true, but merely putative, and which the person in question actually has, but which he would not have if he were not caught in error as to what is in his interest.

Consequently, before reaching a decision on the matter of duty on the basis of interests actually present, we must make a mental correction. To make this correction, we suppose the given interests free from practical error; thereby we eliminate those interests which rest only upon a practical error, and add those which are absent only because of such an error, and which would be present if sufficient reflection had been applied. The proposition just stated, I call "the principle of abstraction from deficiencies of reflection or from practical error."

According to this principle, a person's actual interest is not per se sufficient to make it an object of respect for us, but it commands our respect only if it is that person's true interest. At the same time, a person's interest does not have to be an actual interest in order to be an object of respect; to be such an object it has only to be a true interest, regardless of whether it is represented by an actual interest.

The principle of abstraction from practical error will prove to be very fruitful. Strictly speaking it is not a new proposition, but only a clarification of the implications of the principle of personal dignity. In deducing that principle we started from the observation that the value of an action is not unequivocally determined by the interests involved. Each person affected by the action evaluates it from the point of view of his interests; it is therefore only a matter of accident if different persons reach the same conclusion, and different evaluations are possible. The principle of personal dignity provides us with a standard for an unequivocal evaluation of an action, in that it calls for consideration of the interests of the persons affected. Only what is in the interest of the persons affected has to be considered, not what they are actually interested in. In determining what is in their interest, we are guided by our judgment concerning the truth of the interests actually present. Needless to say, this judgment must be a correct judgment if it is to lead us to a correct determination of the subject matter of duty, and hence, in determining the subject matter of duty, we must abstract from practical error.

49. Impossibility of Duties to One's Own Dignity

The principle of abstraction from practical error leads to an important consequence when it is combined with the proposition asserting the restrictive character of the moral law. According to this proposition the moral law can mean only that certain other interests—extramoral interests, as we may call them—are ruled out as motives of action. According to the principle of personal dignity, we rule out satisfaction of such an interest only in consideration of other interests which conflict with it. For, according to this principle, the person with whom we are in conflict is an object of respect for us, in so far as he has a claim to consideration of his interests, and by virtue of this claim restricts the satisfaction of our interests.

Now, one might ask whether we could not find ourselves in the position of a person affected by our action, so that the dignity of our own person would constitute to ourselves a ground of duties. In fact, a moral law that would admit of such duties is logically conceivable. For by satisfying an actually preponderant interest we can injure another interest of our own, and if that other interest had a claim to be respected, we would be required, in consideration of this interest, to disregard our actually preponderant interest. To disregard this interest would then be a duty in respect of our own personal dignity.

This case may conceivably occur in two forms. First, we may, by satisfying a present interest, injure a preponderant future interest; such an action would result from a deficiency of prudence, from the fact that our reflection is not sufficiently developed to enable us to recognize the means of satisfying our own future interest, or to use these means in accordance with our knowledge. Second, a duty to our own dignity is conceivable in so far as a direct true interest, of which we are not conscious with sufficient clarity, may come into conflict with an actual interest of ours. In this case we would be led to injure our true interest not because of a deficiency of prudence, but because of a deficiency of culture.

Now, it is my contention that neither consideration of the means of our advantage nor direct consideration of our present true interest can provide a ground of duties for us. For if we assume that we have applied the principle of abstraction from deficiencies of reflection, and that our actual interest is free from practical error, our actually preponderant interest will be identical with our true interest, and we shall then inevitably give preference to those actions which meet the requirements of prudence as well as those of culture; for a violation of the precepts of prudence or of culture is possible only if reflection is inadequately developed. Consequently, we need only to abstract from the deficiencies of reflection to make our true interest actually preponderant, and thus to make it determine our action. Once this correction has been made, our action is no longer restricted by the principle of personal dignity, for no interest remains that this law could exclude from the motives of the action. For if our actual interests are identical with our true interest—and this is what we have assumed to be the case—consideration of the latter cannot restrict the former: the possibility of such a restriction arises only when our actual interests do not coincide with our true interest. Consequently, if all duties spring from the restrictive principle of personal dignity—and this is our contention—considerations of prudence or culture cannot impose on us any duties to ourselves. There is no duty to respect the dignity of one's own person; there can be only a duty to respect the dignity of other persons. Our dignity can become a ground of duties only for persons whose actions affect us, just as their dignity is for us a ground of respect for their interests. For the principle of personal dignity is applicable only to those cases in which our freedom of action is subject to restrictions even after elimination of the deficiencies of reflection. This principle can therefore be applied only to actions by which persons affect each other; it cannot be applied to actions by which the agent affects only his own interests.

50. Impossibility of a Valuational Criterion of Duty

From the foregoing we can draw an interesting consequence, which casts a new light on the problem under discussion. If our own dignity were a ground of duties for us, we would be duty-bound to prefer that action which, assuming that our reflection is sufficiently developed, we would in any event prefer to any other possible action; in other words, it would be our duty to perform that action to which we ascribe the greater value after abstracting from practical error. We would be duty-bound always to prefer the more to the less valuable. In short, value would be the criterion of duty. By denying the existence of duties to one's own dignity, we have rejected such an assumption in advance. The assertion that there are no duties to one's own dignity implies the assertion that value cannot be a criterion of duty.

We must clearly distinguish this conclusion from a proposition formulated earlier, namely, from the analytic proposition asserting the impossibility of a valuational morality, according to which the fact that an action conforms to duty is not based on any value created by the action, whether this be the value of the action itself or of the result of the action. This proposition asserts that the concept of value cannot be the *foundation* of a theory of duties. Now we have deduced an assertion of far greater import, namely, the assertion that value is not the *criterion* of duty. The proposition asserting the impossibility of a valuational morality is compatible with a theory of duties, in which value is a criterion of duty without being the foundation of the theory. In such a theory we would not infer logically that an action is dutiful from the fact that it is valuable, but we would, on the basis of the moral law, judge the dutifulness of an action by its value. Whether something of the sort is compatible with the moral law can be decided only on the basis of a synthetic proposition: for this question concerns the content of the moral law. We have answered it here by asserting that under no circumstances can value be a criterion of duty. Thus not only is the concept of dutiful action different from the concept of valuable action, but in addition, different objects are subsumed under each of these concepts. These concepts differ not only in intention or content, but also in extension.

51. Duty to Develop Practical Knowledge

A further implication of the principle of abstraction from practical error is a proposition that determines more closely the duty of inner truthfulness. If the content of duty can be discovered only after elimination of the practical errors committed by the person affected by our action, we must, in order to discover the content of our duty, be free from such practical errors ourselves.

It follows that the duty of inner truthfulness is considerably broader than the duty to develop theoretical knowledge: for the former duty also bids us develop our practical knowledge, i.e., we are duty-bound to develop not only our knowledge of facts, but also our knowledge of values. We have said earlier that, in accordance with the formal character of the moral law, an adequate knowledge of the situation is required to determine the subject matter of duty. Now we see that knowledge of the facts essential to the situation is not sufficient for this purpose: we must also have knowledge of the true interests relevant to the action in question. Ascertainment of the actual interests involves a theoretical judgment—a judgment concerning the facts. But when we judge that something is a true interest, we imply that it deserves preference over other interests, and this implication is for its part expressed in a practical judgment. In so far as this practical judgment influences the moral decision, the determination of the content of duty, it must be a true judgment: it may not rest upon an error. Therefrom follows the duty to develop our practical knowledge.

Chapter 4. Principle of Equality of Persons

52. Equality as Rule of Restriction of Interests

THE PRINCIPLE of personal dignity subjects our freedom of action to the condition that we respect the true interests of persons affected by our action, but does not provide us with a rule by which we can determine the degree of this respect. That we have no such rule can be seen from the fact that the principle as we have formulated it clearly admits of different possible contents of the moral law without logical contradiction: in other words this principle does not determine to what extent we ought to restrict the realization of our own interests in favor of conflicting interests of others. We are thus still lacking a rule governing the reciprocal restriction of the interests of persons affecting each other by their actions. Only on the basis of such a rule can we fully determine the content of the moral law.

The moral law, as we know, is a law of right. As such it grants each person a right, namely, the right to have his interests respected by rational beings. But we still have to determine what interests are associated with such a right. On the basis of the foregoing, the only answer to the question, What is duty? is: The safeguarding of right. But for the time being we have no answer to the question, What is the extent of one person's right vs. another person's right? To obtain an answer, we need a new proposition. This proposition is the law according to which the command to respect that right receives its content from the command of justice. We have already learned that the moral law commands us to respect the dignity of the person; now we can define that law more closely as the command of justice, or as the law that commands us to safeguard the equality of persons.

The command of justice may be formulated as follows: Each person per se has equal dignity with every other person. Although this formulation does not directly express a command, it clearly adds to the content of the moral law an element that has so far been lacking, namely, a rule enabling us to determine to what extent one person's interests may be restricted by another's.

Equality of persons is opposed to subordination of some persons to others, a relationship which implies that some persons are given preference over others. Unless we recognize equality as a criterion of justice, we are confronted with a choice between two extremes—the principle of egoism, which subordinates the person affected by an action to the agent, and the principle of altruism, which subordinates the agent to the person affected by his action. If we designate the realization of a person's interests his "welfare," we may say that egoism calls for the unrestricted furthering of our own welfare, without regard for other people's welfare, and that altruism calls for the unrestricted furthering of other people's welfare, without regard for our own welfare.

Neither egoism nor altruism can be the foundation of a moral legislation. If we try to conceive of a state of affairs in which moral legislation is based on the principle of egoism, we fall into a logical contradiction. Moral principles must be universally valid; if they are valid at all, they must apply equally to all rational beings. Consequently, should egoism be the principle of moral legislation, each man would be duty-bound to gratify his interests ruthlessly at the expense of the interests of all others. Each man would be duty-bound to further his welfare at the expense of the welfare of all other men, and all other men to further their welfare at his expense: this is self-contradictory.

Any moral legislation based on altruism would demand that each man confer benefits on others without accepting benefits from them—a situation which is likewise inconceivable. For it is self-contradictory to speak of conferring benefits that cannot be accepted. There is a legend about the monk Macarius who lived with his fellow monks in a desert, and was in danger of dying of thirst. A friend sent him a bunch of grapes. Macarius, an altruist, passed the grapes on to another monk, who passed them on again, and so on, until the grapes were returned to

Macarius who then ate them, in violation of his altruistic principles. For if he had been a consistent altruist, he would have
passed on the grapes again to make the round, until they were
shriveled and inedible.

53. Principle of Abstraction from Numerical Determination of Person

To forestall possible misinterpretations of the principle of
equality just formulated, we must keep in mind what this
principle does *not* imply:

1. Equality of persons must not be taken in a theoretical
sense: it does not denote equality of actual personal characteristics. Whether or to what extent persons are equal in this respect, is a theoretical problem that does not concern us here.
For we do not ask what is each person's situation, but only
how each person ought to be treated.

2. Equality of persons does not imply equality of personal
value. We do not inquire after the value of persons, but only
what duties they have toward each other. The value of a person is determined in positive terms by considerations other than
the moral law. The moral law is not a principle of positive valuation of persons, but only a negative principle, according to
which a person's value is subject to the condition of fulfillment
of duty. We do not assert that all persons are equal in value,
but only that they are equal in dignity, that is to say, in their
right to restrict the freedom of action of other persons whose
actions affect them by the condition that these other persons
respect their interests in accordance with the principle of equality of persons.

3. The principle of equality does not imply the right of each
person to equal treatment. The principle in question says: Each
person *as such*, i.e., only in so far as we abstract from his individual qualities, has a dignity equal to that of every other person. A difference in individual qualities may well justify a difference in treatment. Equality of personal dignity does not
rule out such a difference: the moral law merely subjects it to
a specific condition. It forbids the agent to favor his own in-

terests as against those of the person affected by his action if he does so solely on the ground that he is the agent rather than the person affected by the action; in other words, it permits the agent to favor his interests only on the basis of a difference in the situation or in the qualities of the persons involved.

It is easy to see why the moral law cannot unconditionally forbid us to favor one person over another. As we know, the moral law refers to cases of conflict of interests between an agent and the person affected by his action, that is to say, to cases characterized precisely by the fact that only the interests of one of the conflicting parties can be satisfied, so that under any circumstances one of these parties must be preferred over the other. Thus the moral law cannot possibly mean that we are forbidden to favor one person over another; rather, the command of justice is a rule governing such preference. By this rule, the person affected by the action ought to be preferred over the agent, if that person's interest is the preponderant one. The interests of both ought to be weighed against each other without regard for any distinctions between persons *qua* persons, i.e., as the agent would weigh them if the interests of the person affected by his action were also his own. A preference given to an interest because it is the interest of the agent and not of the person affected by his action—a preference of that kind only—is forbidden by the moral law.

In the light of these considerations, the criterion of duty expressed in the principle of personal equality can be formulated as the principle of abstraction from the numerical determination of persons. An object can be characterized on the basis of its qualities or of its numerical determination. Qualitative characterization refers to its nature, but on the basis of it we cannot single out an object as a specific, individual object: the various attributes which distinguish it from other objects define its nature, but no matter how far we may carry such a conceptual determination, we do not in this way define a specific object, but only a *class* of objects. The same attributes may apply to a number of objects. Therefore it is not possible to establish the individual identity of a given object by stating its qualitative characteristics. This individual identity of an object, which cannot be established by stating the concepts under which the object can be subsumed, is what I call its "numerical determination." It can be perceived only intuitively.

Now, the moral law says that we should abstract from the numerical determination of persons affected by our action. It rules out any preference solely contingent upon a person's numerical determination, a preference that would have no basis if we assumed that the persons involved no longer differed numerically. If we suppose that all interests affected by our action are those of a single person, if we suppose, in other words, that the interests of the person affected by our action are ours as well, we would favor the preponderating interest regardless of whether it is our own or that of the other person. The possibility of injuring another person's interest that is contrary to, but of greater weight than our own interest, would then automatically vanish. Such a possibility exists only by virtue of numerical differentiation among persons. Consequently, the moral law forbids only a mode of conduct that would be impossible under the assumption that persons do not differ numerically. To put it differently, the moral law insists that a given action shall retain its claim to preference even after abstraction from the numerical determination of persons; thus the preference given to an action is made dependent only on the qualitative characteristics of the circumstances, i.e., on all of the interests affected by the action, regardless of whose they may be.

We may express the same criterion in another way. Instead of abstracting from the difference of persons, that is, instead of picturing the interests distributed among different persons as attaching to one and the same person, we may also put ourselves in the place of one person and then of the other, and suppose that we are successively in the situation of both, but that we can realize our own interest only in one of these situations. For this is inherent in the conflict of interests, which is the sole premise for applying the law in question. If we now ask whether we should like to see our interest realized in the first rather than in the second situation, it is obvious—provided our decision is taken after deliberation and abstraction is made from practical error—that we shall give preference to the preponderating interest, and consent to injure the other interest, in order to avoid a greater injury of interest, which would otherwise be unavoidable.

Our criterion may also be expressed as follows (once again assuming that we abstract from practical error): In deciding how we shall behave toward another person, we should act as though there were a natural law under which our own mode of action would inevitably be turned on us, whenever we become its object instead of its subject. It is of course presupposed here that we shall find ourselves in the position of the person affected by our action. This corresponds to the Kantian formula, "Act as if the maxim of thy action were to become by thy will a universal law of nature." For what this formula actually implies is that we should, in place of the actual choice confronting us, which is a choice between two specific actions, make another, mental, choice between two natural laws. We ought to choose that action, which we would also choose if the maxim in favor of which we decide is thereby raised to the status of a natural law.

Let us assume, for instance, that we are confronted with the question of whether we ought to help a man in distress through no fault of his own, who depends on our help, even if by doing so we deprive ourselves of a pleasure. In accordance with the principle of abstraction from the numerical determination of persons, we are in this case required to weigh the interests involved without differentiating between our own interests and those of the person affected by our action—in other words, to make just as much allowance for the affected person's interests as we would if they were our own interests. Obviously we shall prefer occasionally to forgo a pleasure rather than to forgo help should we ourselves fall into distress through no fault of our own. We arrive at exactly the same conclusion if we apply the Kantian criterion. We suppose the specific action we have in mind to be replaced by a general rule of action, i.e., we suppose that we are confronted not with a choice between helping the person in distress and gratifying our pleasure, but with another choice, between a natural law under which a man in distress through no fault of his own must always be denied help so that another man's pleasure be secured, and a natural law under which the man in distress is helped while the other man's pleasure is sacrificed. If we now assume that the chances of our falling into the situation of the first and of the second man are equal, we shall obviously choose that natural law under which the man in distress through no fault of his own is helped. This shows that Kant's criterion of natural law, if interpreted correctly, is nothing but our principle of abstraction from the numerical determination of persons, which rules out any preference that would automatically lose its basis after such an abstraction had been carried out.

54. Negative Character of Principle of Justice

With the analysis of the principle of equality of persons, we round off our description of the content of the moral law. There still remains the task of testing whether the fundamental principle thus deduced satisfies the conditions established with respect to the content of the moral law.

It is easy to see that the principle of equality of persons is a restrictive principle. It does not determine the value of an action in positive terms; it says no more than that we ought to give preference to a given action only if we would still do so after abstracting from the numerical determination of persons. This principle rules out as motives only those interests that would never serve as motives of action if we did not differentiate among persons. This clearly shows that the law is restrictive in character.

Hence justice does not require us to make the interests of other persons our own in a positive sense, but only to refrain from injuring them in contravention of the principle of equality. A duty to satisfy actively the interests of others can arise only indirectly, for example, to redress an inequality when others, unlike ourselves, are unable to satisfy their interests themselves. Whenever they are able to do so, we incur no duty to satisfy their interests. Such a duty would imply arbitrary preferment of these persons, and would thus be contrary to the principle of equality. But whenever others are unable to satisfy their interests, while we are able to satisfy ours, an inequality arises, restricting our right to do so; for if we were in their situation, we would surely not consent to being left helpless, i.e., without any possibility of satisfying our interests.

To avoid fallacious conclusions, however, we must in each case decide whether a man's inability to look after his interests is due to an unfortunate accident or to his own deliberate actions. If a man voluntarily puts himself in a position in which he cannot look after his interests, other persons have no duty to help him; for his claim to such help would then rest on disregard of the interests of others, and violate the principle of equality. He would thus forfeit his right to have his interests respected.

55. Formal Character of Principle of Justice

It is also clear that the principle of justice is formal in character; for the law we stated does not tell us what the subject matter of duty is in each case, but only gives us a general indication as to how we can determine our duty in each given case. The moral law thus admits of unlimited variations in the content of duty, because under this law we base our decision as to what duty is on the circumstances of each case, and we are required only to rule out considerations resting upon the numerical determination of the case. Each application of the principle thus involves an extramoral decision, on the basis of which we judge whether our intended action deserves to be given preference. The moral law subjects us, with respect to this decision, to only one condition: we are required to ignore the numerical determination of the given case, or not to differentiate among the persons whose interests are involved.

56. Inalienability of Right to Realize True Interest

In the course of our elaboration of the moral law we formulated a principle asserting that the required appraisal of interest is to take place after abstraction from practical error. We must keep this principle in mind if we wish to avoid erroneous applications of the principle of justice. For the principle of abstraction from practical error here leads to a far-reaching consequence. The principle of justice holds regardless of whether the interest it protects is or is not represented by an actual interest of the person affected by the action. Consequently, the content of duty cannot be determined by a mere comparison of the actual interests of the persons involved; we must first abstract from the deficiencies of reflection, that is, from practical error.

It follows that in weighing the interests affected by a given action, we should not base our judgment merely on those interests which the persons involved regard as preponderant. If one of these persons is willing to renounce realization of an interest on the basis of an error, he does not forfeit the right to realize this interest, and we are still duty-bound to respect it. The fact that a man actually consents to a violation of his interest is not sufficient to legitimize such a violation. Only if his consent is compatible with his true interest can he renounce the right in question.

The possibility of error regarding one's own interest thus compels us to assert that some rights can be inalienable, in contradiction to the maxim, *Volenti non fit iniuria*, "no wrong is done to the consenting party."

It must be noted that we assert merely the possibility of inalienable rights; we have not said what such rights are, nor can we say it at this place. To do this we would first have to determine what is the content of a true interest—a task that is beyond the scope of the theory of duties, and that can be dealt with only in the theory of ideals. Here we must confine ourselves to the statement that the right to realize one's true interest, if such an interest exists, is inalienable.

57. Objective Measure of Wrong

We are now in a position to decide a question that arose in the formal theory of duties, but that we could not answer there. In discussing moral imputation we ascertained that it admits of degrees. We established the existence of subjective degrees of guilt, corresponding to the degrees of imputability of an act. But there still remained the question whether guilt also admits of objective degrees, that is, whether an action can represent a greater or less wrong, regardless of the extent to which this action can be imputed to someone as having been intended by him.

We could not answer this question in the formal theory of

duties because it cannot be answered on the basis of the mere *concept* of wrong. Now we can answer it, and this answer must be affirmative: there are objective differences of degree in possible wrongs. The criterion of duty directly implies this. For according to this criterion, a wrong consists in a deviation from the principle of equality of personal dignity. Consequently, the greater this deviation, the greater the wrong. Its magnitude is determined by the extent to which the agent unrightfully gives preference to his own interest, or by the magnitude of the unrightful injury he inflicts on the interest of the person affected by his action. The magnitude of this injury provides us with an objective measure of guilt.

Chapter 5. Duty of Justice

58. Principle of Equity *

THERE ARE two possible situations—each of them involving a conflict of interests between the agent and the person affected by his action—which call for application of the principle of justice. The first of these situations arises when the agent is duty-bound to refrain from injuring the other person's interests. The second arises when this duty has been violated. For then we are confronted with the question, What are the consequences attached to such a violation of duty? We shall begin with a discussion of the first situation.

The principle of justice commands us to refrain from actions injuring any interest of another person unless our own interest in such actions is preponderant. This command covers all our interactions with other persons. I designate it as "the law of adjustment," or "the principle of equity." It may be formulated as follows: Never act in such a way but that you could assent to your conduct if the interests of those affected by it were also your own. In order to apply the criterion of equity we must therefore regard all the interests involved as attaching to a single person. When we do this, and provided that no practical error is made, we necessarily give preference to that action which is the upshot of the interest that deserves to be preferred.

The application of this criterion may cause certain difficulties when we are confronted with a situation in which the conflicting interests balance, that is, when we find, on weighing the interests in question, that neither is preponderant, or, which amounts to the same thing, when we are unable to decide which party's interests are preponderant. What does justice require in such a case? Or shall we say that in such a case no decision can be reached?

In reality, our principle of equity enables us to reach an un-

* Literally: "The Law of Fair Adjustment (Just Adjudication)" (*Das Gesetz der gerechten Abwägung*).

equivocal decision even in cases where the conflicting interests are in equilibrium. For what does this principle require? It forbids the agent to accord precedence to his own interest unless this interest outweighs the conflicting interest, in other words, unless his interest is still entitled to preference after abstraction from the numerical determination of persons, that is, when the conflicting interests are regarded as attaching to a single person. Let us now apply our law to a case in question, let us suppose that two conflicting interests are of equal force and are attached to a single person. Then we have no preponderant interest in favor of which the decision can be made. Consequently, neither of the two persons involved in the conflict is permitted to give preference to his own interest, for such an action would violate the condition that the interest of the person affected may be injured only if the agent's interest is preponderant. It must be noted here that the moral law does not forbid one or the other or even both parties to renounce satisfaction of an interest in favor of realization of another's interest—unless such renunciation is ruled out by consideration of the interest of a third party. But whether renunciation is permitted or not, neither party is obliged to renounce satisfaction of his interest.

When we ourselves have two conflicting interests of equal force, neither one nor the other can determine our decision: neither of them is preponderant. But in such a case there arises a third interest—namely, an interest in realizing at least one of the two conflicting interests, since it is impossible to realize them both. Which of the two is to be realized remains undetermined, for neither outweighs the other. Under our assumption, the decision as to which of the two interests is to be realized cannot be determined by either of them, precisely because they balance. The decision that we are interested in bringing about can therefore be determined only by a factor which is fortuitous in relation to the two conflicting interests. We have a preponderant interest in such a factor which provides us with a basis for a decision.

If the conflicting interests of equal value are divided between two persons, each of them is interested in satisfying his interest as far as this is possible in his situation. Consequently, each party is duty-bound to respect this interest of the other, that is, to make just as much allowance for it as for his own conflicting interest. Although the principle of equality forbids either party to give preference to his interest as against the other's, it is compatible with a decision according preference to one of the conflicting parties, if that decision lies outside the free choice of these parties. In other words, the decision must lie in a circumstance that is fortuitous inasmuch as it cannot be foreseen by either party. Such a decision we call "a decision by lot."

It might be contended that a contest could serve as a means of decision equivalent to a decision by lot. This may be granted with the reservation previously mentioned that no considerations of a third party's interests demand the avoidance of such a contest, and on the further condition—which is of special importance here—that the issue of the contest shall be equivalent to a decision by lot, i.e., that it is a matter of accident. Only if the chances of being victorious are equal for the two parties does a contest have the character of a decision by lot. But even then there is no reason for preferring it to any other form of decision by lot, unless we think that unnecessary violence is something to be desired.

It is often objected that a contest is precisely a means for proving that the victor's interest is preponderant on the ground of his superior strength. It is actually conceivable that in the absence of better criteria of preferability we have reason for leaving the decision to a contest, for instance, a competitive struggle in economic life. But this does not answer the question concerning us here, namely, the question of what has to be done if there is no way of ascertaining which of the conflicting interests deserves to be given preference; moreover, the objection is sophistical in that it ignores the assumption under which our question has to be answered. For this objection proposes a method of deciding which of the two interests is preponderant, while we have assumed that these interests are of equal value. Consequently, a contest cannot in this case represent a decision by lot.

59. Law of Just Retribution

Our analysis of the principle of equity needs to be supplemented by a discussion of the situation that arises as a result of a violation of this law. Such a violation implies that someone satisfies an interest he has no right to satisfy under the law of equality of persons. In order to restore equality, the unfair advantage thus created has to be compensated for; this can be done only if the person who has taken unfair advantage is made to suffer an injury equal to the one he has unjustly inflicted on others. He is thus deprived of his right to realize his interests in the same measure as he has deprived others in violation of equality. On the basis of the foregoing we may formulate "the law of just retribution."

It can be expressed as follows: You ought to assent to a disregard of your interests equal to the disregard you have shown for the interests of others. For it is clear that according to the principle of equality of personal dignity, which asserts that all persons as such have an equal claim to satisfy their interests, no one has the right to better treatment than he accords others in a similar situation, hence that he forfeits his claim to satisfy his interests in the same measure as he has unrightfully injured the interests of others. The unfair advantage he has taken in violation of the principle of equity demands just retribution in accordance with the principle of equality of persons. This retribution consists in his suffering an injury to his interests equal to the one he has unrightfully inflicted on others.

To be convinced of this we need once again only apply the principle of abstraction from the numerical determination of persons, that is, to suppose that the various interests affected by the action are attached to a single person. For then we are at once compelled to conclude that a man who unjustly injures the interests of others ought to suffer an equal injury to his own interests. For if he abstracted from the numerical determination of persons, he would be able to envision his own action only if he assented to an equal injury to be inflicted on himself. Thus just retribution inflicts on him only what he should have had to will to perform his action. Justice enjoins him to assent to something which he otherwise could not have willed, namely, to a just retribution for the offense he committed.

An injury to interest which is the rightful consequence of a wrong committed is what we designate as punishment in the narrow sense of the term. The law of just retribution establishes the measure of rightfully required punishment.

For its correct application, it is necessary to keep in mind the following points:

1. According to our argument, which deduces this law from the law of equality of persons, just retribution requires equality in respect of the magnitude, but not of the kind of the injury in question. On the basis of the norm of justice, we cannot demand equality in *kind* in the satisfaction of an interest, i.e., satisfaction of identical interests, but rather only equality of *degree* in satisfying interests, whatever interests may be in question. Consequently, just retribution does not depend on the kind, but only on the magnitude of the interest unrightfully injured.

2. The interest, which, according to the law of just retribution, forfeits its claim to satisfaction, is not identical with the interest satisfied through the unrightful action. The interest unrightfully satisfied, or the unrightful interest, has no claim to satisfaction in any event: otherwise it would not be an unrightful interest. Liability to punishment as a consequence of an offense is quite different from the mere forfeiture of a claim to satisfaction of an interest unrightfully satisfied by the offense. That an unrightful interest may be violated, even if it actually outweighs all other interests involved, is an obvious consequence of the principle of equity. But liability to punishment means that the offender forfeits his claim to satisfy another interest. Punishment is not an injury to an unrightful interest, i.e., an interest that violates the principle of equity, but an injury to another interest, which otherwise would have a claim to be realized, according to the principle of equity.

For instance, the right of self-defense, defined as the right to foil an intended, unrightful injury to our interest, and hence to prevent someone from satisfying his unrightful interest, is a direct consequence of the principle of equity. But the right to punish is something entirely different. This is the right to injure another interest that in itself (aside from the law of just retribution) deserves to be respected—provided that such injury serve to restore the equality of the dignity of persons.

3. Punishment must be distinguished from mere revenge. Revenge consists in gratifying a subjective desire, namely, vengefulness, and its demands and extent are determined by fortuitous subjective interests: a man motivated by desire for revenge does not ask whether the injury done to his interests deserves to be punished, nor even whether it was rightful or unrightful. Punishment, on the other hand, is an injury to interests which does not itself serve to satisfy a subjective interest, but to fulfill an objective requirement of the law. Hence punishment is something entirely different from revenge, just as it is something entirely different from an injury to interests effected for reasons of social expediency. Punishment serves neither directly nor indirectly to satisfy interests, whether they be the interests of the person who has been injured or the interests of the majority of a given society: it serves exclusively to fulfill the law.

These two laws together, the principle of equity and the law of just retribution, constitute the entire content of the imperative of justice and, by the same token, of the moral law.

Chapter 6. So-called Duties to Ourselves

60. The Indirect Nature of All So-called Duties to Ourselves

ALL NORMS that express real duties and not merely arbitrary demands must be deducible from the command of justice. Because of the formal character of this command, however, no specific duties can be derived from it by purely philosophical methods. Hence there arises the question of what problems remain to be solved in the material theory of duties after the principle of justice has been established. As a matter of fact, all this theory has to offer from this point on is additional arguments in support of the proposition that our sole direct duty is to act justly. There is no general consensus that this is so. Time and again moral philosophers have attempted, on the one hand, to formulate duties that would rank with the precept of justice, and to restrict the scope of that duty, on the other. We still have to come to grips with doctrines of that kind. We shall show, by specific examples, that the arguments in support of such doctrines are untenable. They cannot disprove the proposition that all norms derivable from the principle of justice are duties. As for the so-called duties that are allegedly of other origin, either they are not duties at all, or can be traced back to the principle of justice. In the light of this methodological remark, let us first examine the so-called duties to oneself.

My contention is that these duties, in so far as they really deserve the name of duties, are indirect, and can be derived from duties to other persons. As we have seen, it is impossible, from the principle of the dignity of the person, to infer the agent's duty to respect his own dignity. The assumption that there is such a duty would, moreover, be incompatible with the restrictive character of the moral law. For if there were a direct duty to realize one's own interest—one's preponderant interest, of course —if, in other words, we were always enjoined to pursue our own preponderant interest, we would have to affirm the principle of moralism, which, as we have seen, is incompatible with the restrictive character of the moral law.

If we drop the assumption that there is such a duty, it still seems possible to assume the existence of a duty to realize our own interest when it conflicts with the interests of others—the duty, that is, always to give preference, in such a conflict, to the preponderating interest, even if it is our own. But we have shown that the mere circumstance that our own interest is preponderant is not sufficient to impose on us the duty to satisfy it; and if this circumstance is not sufficient, the further circumstance that we would injure the interest of another cannot obviously impose on us the duty to satisfy our own interest. For then we would not be duty-bound to respect the interest of the person affected by our action, but rather to injure it. This simple reasoning suffices to show that even in this narrower sense there is no duty to prefer one's own preponderant interest.

Those who assert the existence of duties to oneself may try to escape from their dilemma by claiming that certain interests have a special value, and that to respect such interests is a duty of that kind. Particularly high value is attached to life; and since antiquity ethical doctrines have been advanced according to which man is duty-bound to preserve his own life, and forbidden to commit suicide. Let us investigate whether there can be a duty to preserve one's own life, regardless of whether this affects the interests of other persons: for it is only in this sense that duties to oneself are in question here.

It is generally granted that there is no unconditional duty to preserve the life of another person, and occasionally we may be permitted and even commanded to kill another being. Thus, it is impossible to see why we should be duty-bound to preserve our own life under any circumstances.

Such a duty is sometimes justified on religious grounds: it is argued that life is a gift granted us by a higher power and that we have no right willfully to relinquish it. It is obvious that such an argument proves too much: for if it were true, all actions by our own will would be forbidden as infringements of the rights of Providence. If there is no general prohibition to act by our own will, there is no reason for denying us the right to decide as we please regarding our life. On the contrary, if life were the work of God, and if everything God did were good, all human actions would be good, and no actions could be forbidden. Thus it would be possible to reason the other way round: God granted us the freedom to make decisions regarding our life, hence everyone has the right to make use of this freedom.

Equally threadbare are all arguments according to which duties that cannot be derived from ethical principles are justified on religious grounds. Whoever seeks to derive a specific duty from a divine decree must at least have some knowledge of God's will: otherwise the injunction to fulfill God's will would be meaningless. If it is argued, for instance in justification of the prohibition of divorce, that men may not dissolve a marriage, since man ought not to put asunder what God has joined together, one could reply with equal justification that man ought not to join together what God has put asunder. The situation is the same in all other cases. Moreover, the injunction that we fulfill the will of God presupposes, if it is to be meaningful, that the divine will can remain unfulfilled—a presupposition that directly contradicts the assumption of divine omnipotence, and is therefore quite questionable on purely religious grounds.

Again, duties that we would deduce in the manner just discussed would not, strictly speaking, be duties to oneself, but duties to God. Consequently it is impossible in this manner to deduce a direct duty to oneself.

The method of surreptitiously introducing alleged duties to ourselves as duties to others assumes still other forms. Where no duties to God are invoked, it is argued for instance that the individual has a duty to society. Thus, in connection with the prohibition of suicide, it is said sometimes that an individual enjoys the benefits of living in society, that this imposes certain duties on him in relation to society, and that he must not for that reason dispose of his life at will.

It is clear, however, that such considerations justify a duty to preserve one's own life only for those who do enjoy the benefits of society. Whoever departs from society—and the suicide does this—renounces its pleasures, and by the same token no longer owes the duties that are directly based on these pleasures. Even less can we assert that a man who shuns society altogether owes such duties. Thus it is certain that no generally binding duty can be deduced by this method. Whether a man who voluntarily puts an end to his life thereby injures the rights of society depends on circumstances—and only respect of such rights may indirectly impose on him the duty to preserve his life.

Aside from the consideration of rights of others, his action might be foolish. For instance we would have a plain case of foolishness if a misfortune caused a man to be so unreasonable as to lose sight of the values he might still give to his life. Or one might say that a suicide reveals lack of self-control and courage; but this too implies no violation of duty.

Nor must we deceive ourselves as to the fact that under certain circumstances it is not suicide, but failure to commit suicide that manifests lack of courage, and that such a lack of courage may even result in a violation of duty. Then suicide is not only permitted, but even morally required. Such would be the case of an incurable invalid who realizes that by living on he imposes a burden on others because he prevents them from making a more valuable use of their energies. But we need not go so far as to question the right to live of an incurable invalid: there are other, more frequent cases in which the right to live is forfeited. For instance, a man who seeks only pleasure at the expense of others ought to say to himself that he forfeits his right to live by refusing to work, and hence, in so far as he refuses to work, that he should renounce his life, because only in this way can he free himself from his duty to work.

In the light of impartial scrutiny, the grounds usually adduced to justify the prohibition of suicide prove inadequate, indeed, in part they are highly hypocritical. Alleged duties to oneself always serve as a ready excuse for shirking duties owed to others. It is essentially this dialectics of interests that accounts for the popularity of duties to oneself, a popularity that duties owed to others do not always enjoy to an equal extent. What we have said holds true of all other so-called duties to oneself, such as the duty to be temperate, the duty to develop one's capacities, etc. My contention is not that there are no such duties, but that they are not direct duties to oneself. In so far as such duties exist, they can only be indirect, that is, derived from duties that we owe directly to other persons.

It might be objected that we previously deduced certain duties which seem to be duties to oneself, since we arrived at them without reference to any duties we owe to others. Such are for instance the imperatives of character and of inner truthfulness, which we deduced independently of the imperative of justice. But it does not follow that these imperatives constitute duties to ourselves in the same sense in which justice imposes on us duties in relation to other persons. The fact that the imperatives in question can be deduced without reference to the content of the moral law has no bearing on the question to whom we owe them, indeed, whether they are duties in relation to any persons at all. The imperatives of character and of inner truthfulness follow from the practical necessity of safeguarding the fulfillment of the moral law against accidental influences. Since justice is the content of the moral law, the imperatives in question are valid only in relation to the duty to act justly, and hence only in relation to duties we owe to others. This does not conflict with the fact that the duties deduced in the formal part of our theory would remain valid even if the moral law had a content other than the principle of justice.

61. Why There Can Be No Duty Not to Use Oneself as a Mere Means

Moral philosophers who uphold the doctrine of duties to oneself in the strict sense of the term are inevitably led to question the determination of the content of the moral law, and to contend—as has actually been done—that the dignity of one's own person is the ground of duties to oneself just as the dignity of the person affected by our action is the ground of duties we owe to others. Thus, the duty to uphold one's honor is sometimes regarded as being of the same order as the duty to be just. This duty to uphold one's honor, it is alleged, enjoins one directly not to lower oneself to the level of being a mere means, just as the duty to act justly forbids us to degrade other persons by using them as mere means to serve our own ends.

To clarify the nature of such a duty, we must ask what the expression "to use something as a mere means" signifies. The answer to this question is: "to use a thing only in relation to an end, not as an end in itself." To use a person as a mere means would then signify to make him serve an end that is not his own end. In the light of this definition we can see at once that it cannot be our duty never to use ourselves in such a way that the end of our action is not our own end. Such an injunction would demand of us either too little or too much. For the end we pursue when using ourselves as a means in a given action is the end of our action, and hence our own end. If we take the injunction in this sense, it demands too little of us, because we could not possibly violate it; in this sense, then, it is impossible for anyone to use himself as a mere means.

If, on the other hand, we take the injunction to mean that in pursuing a given end we ought not to act contrary to other ends of ours, it demands too much of us. It may certainly happen that we treat ourselves in a manner to which we could not agree if we took all our other ends into account; for it may be that by achieving our present end we may deprive ourselves of the possibility of achieving other ends that we might wish to pursue at some future time. In this sense, we can use ourselves as mere means and act against our own preponderant interest.

An action contrary to our preponderant interest, however, involves a practical error: it would be impossible if our actual interest were identical with our true interest. To act against one's own well-understood or true interest is foolish or ignorant, but not criminal: such an action is not a wrong. A duty to uphold one's honor that would forbid us every action contrary to our own true interest would demand too much of us, for it would forbid us to injure our own true interest and would enjoin us always to satisfy our own true interest, so that no room would be left for morally indifferent actions. We would then again fall into moralism, which we have already rejected.

62. Why There Can Be No Duty to Prevent Others from Using Us as a Mere Means

Even granting that there can be no duty to uphold one's honor in the sense defined above, we might assert the existence of a duty to prevent others from using us as a mere means, or a duty to resist disrespect of our interests. This would be the duty not to tolerate any violation of our own right. Can there be a duty to uphold one's honor in this sense? Can such a duty be regarded as a duty to oneself, i.e., one that implies no indirect reference to duties owed to others? If a man allows another to disregard his dignity, and to injure his rightful interest, he thereby assents to this injury. But he can do so only for his own ends, in which case the other no longer uses him as a mere means. He may assent to such an injury of what would otherwise be his right; perhaps in return for a promised reward. To secure this reward is then his end—an end for the sake of which he renounces the satisfaction of an interest that is in itself justified.

Now, it may happen that the other man's action is nevertheless contrary to duty—this is the case, for instance, when the assent in question is not sufficient to alienate the right of the man who gives it, i.e., when he assents to a violation of an inalienable right, and when the actual assent rests only on a practical error. Then the other man's action does not injure the first man's actual, but rather his true interest, and consequently wrongs him. But this does not mean that the first man's assent is a wrong. To renounce one's right—whether or not this gives another man the right to injure the interest in question—is not to violate one's duty.

The other man's action is also a wrong when the first man assents to an injury to his interest only because resistance to this injury would result in an injury of a superior interest. Yet even such a renunciation of resistance is not itself a wrong; indeed, the existence of such a duty to uphold one's honor as a duty of the same order as that to be just would lead to a gross injustice. For then we would not merely have the right to resist an unrightful aggression, and thus to injure the aggressor's unrightful interest; we would indeed have the duty to do so; persistent malevolence on the part of other persons would then impose ever new duties upon us, and end up by depriving us of any opportunity for satisfying our own preponderant interests.

As we have said before, all this does not mean that in some cases it may not be contrary to duty to allow others to slight our dignity, and thus to tolerate injury to our right by others. Our contention is only that there is no direct duty to uphold our right, and that such a duty, in so far as it is valid, can be deduced only from other duties.

It is easy enough to show that such a deduction is possible. For a man who tolerates an injury to right contributes thereby to undermining the security of man's rights in general, by encouraging others to violate their duties; he thus becomes co-responsible for injuries to rights committed by them. Therefore it is actually our duty to resist injustice, unless we are required to act differently because of special circumstances.

63. Why There Can Be No Separate Duty to Uphold One's Honor

A final effort to maintain a direct duty to uphold one's honor is made when the term "honor" is taken in a broader meaning, as the condition for self-respect. Morality is obviously a condition of self-respect, i.e., acknowledgment of our own dignity; we fulfill this condition when we freely subject ourselves to the moral law. Hence, if we interpret the obligation of honor as the duty to fulfill the condition of self-respect, we arrive at a general injunction to do our duty, but we do not arrive at a specific duty different from, and of the same order as the duty to act justly. Rather, the obligation of honor would then include all duties, and merely impose them on us under another name; it would not isolate a specific class of actions as duties. Thus, all duties would be duties to uphold one's honor, whether they be duties we owe to others or not; at the same time, no specific duty would be a duty to uphold one's honor as distinct from the duty to act justly. For the mere injunction to do one's duty leaves it undetermined through which conduct duty is fulfilled or violated. Consequently, it is impossible in this way to establish a separate obligation of honor as a duty to oneself.

To forestall misunderstandings, we recall that we are dealing here only with *duties*, not with ethical norms in general. Even though there is no specific duty of honor, it may be ethically desirable to uphold one's honor.

64. Duties to Oneself and Duties Owed to Other Persons

Granting that the assumption of duties to oneself involves difficulties, a fundamental objection may be raised against the theoretical rejection of such duties. The doctrine of duties to oneself, which has been prevalent so far, seems to be thoroughly consistent with the principle of equality of persons, while this principle seems to be violated when duties owed to others are given special prominence. For do we not in this way give precedence to the interests of the person affected by the action over those of the agent? In other words, does not our position imply surreptitious adherence to the principle of altruism, which is incompatible with the principle of equality of persons?

This suspicion can be removed by proof that it rests upon a misunderstanding. Let us assume for the sake of argument that there is no moral law, and that the relations between people are governed solely by natural law. Then the agent's interest will have precedence over the interest of the person affected by his action, for under natural law the agent's will is determined only by his own interest, and not by the other person's, even when the latter interest is the preponderant one. This is true even in cases in which the agent is motivated by sympathy, for sympathy is an interest of the agent's. A man who acts from sympathy does so on the basis of his own interest, and consequently from regard for himself. At the same time, there is no natural law guaranteeing that each interest of the person affected by the action, no matter how strong this interest may be, is matched by an interest of the agent's.

The moral law, however, is valid, and by the same token, so

is the principle of equal dignity of persons. In order to apply this principle, we must nullify the agent's advantage which he has under natural law. We can do this only by placing him under the moral obligation to give precedence to the other person's interest, whenever it preponderates over his own. There are no duties other than those in relation to other persons. The existence of these duties rests upon the fact that under natural law alone, i.e., aside from the moral law, the agent's own interest always has the advantage when it conflicts with other persons' interests. It is precisely the law of equality of persons that requires this advantage to be nullified.

Chapter 7. Duties to Animals

65. Subject of Duties and Subject of Rights

ALL SO-CALLED DUTIES to oneself, in so far as they deserve the name of duties, are indirect, and as such presuppose duties to other persons. With this finding we are safeguarded against the error of fallaciously extending the scope of our duties. But an opposite error is possible, that of fallaciously restricting the scope of our duties. If we designate a being in relation to whom we have duties as an "object of duties," we may say that only other persons can be objects of duties. In addition, we assert that *all* other persons, in so far as we affect them by our actions, are objects of duties for us. For every person, being a subject of interests, has rights, i.e., has a claim to respect of his interests under the law of equality of persons.

Failure to understand this leads to the above-mentioned false restriction of the scope of duties—a dangerous error far more prevalent in ethics than the opposite error of fallaciously extending the scope of duties. If we assume the existence of more duties than there actually are, we at least do not directly violate any duty; but if we assume that there are fewer duties than we actually have, we are directly led to such a violation. The proposition asserting that all persons can be objects of duties is therefore of greater practical significance than the proposition asserting the nonexistence of duties to oneself.

To recognize the full import of the former proposition, we must sharply distinguish between the concepts "subject of duties" and "subject of rights": for we cannot rule out a priori the possibility that some subjects of rights are not subjects of duties. Under the moral law, all beings who have interests are subjects of rights, while all those who in addition to having interests, are capable of grasping the demands of duty, are subjects of duties. Only rational beings are capable of such an understanding. Accordingly, we may classify all duties remaining after exclusion of duties to oneself into duties in relation to rational and to nonrational beings. If we designate as an animal a being that is a subject of rights, but is by its nature incapable of attaining rational self-determination, and as a man a being that is a subject of rights and at the same time potentially endowed with reason, we may state briefly that duty is always either to an animal or to a man. It is my contention that we have duties to animals, and that these duties are direct, i.e., that they are not derived from duties to men, or rational beings.

66. Duties to Animals

Moral philosophers, even those belonging to the Critical School,* have often represented duties to animals as indirect duties to oneself or to other men. For instance, maltreatment of animals is forbidden on the ground that it encourages cruelty, that is, a disposition that obstructs fulfillment of duty. Now, maltreatment of animals may have just that effect; nevertheless the argument in question takes no account of the whole . truth. For according to this argument, maltreatment of animals is reprehensible because of the incidental effects it has on the character of the agent or of other men. Where the effects are not harmful, maltreatment of animals would thus be permitted.

If we examine the arguments on the basis of which the existence of direct duties to animals has been denied, we are compelled to conclude regretfully that most of these arguments are sophistical—indeed, they are so threadbare that we find it surprising that they could be advanced by people who claim to be schooled in scientific method. The treatment this problem has received in ethics would be devastating testimony to the limitations of human understanding, if it were not clear that interest rather than error accounts for it. To eliminate all possible excuses for such a treatment, and to clear the way for an objective study of the problem, we shall here go beyond the boundaries of philosophy, and subject the arguments in question to a close scrutiny, although they are advanced on purely empirical grounds.

The first of these arguments is based on the contention that

* The followers of Kant and Fries.

we cannot know whether animals really have interests. We may observe, to begin with, that such a contention is irrelevant here, since we have defined animals as carriers of interests, even though we have also defined them as nonrational beings. What is actually in question, then, is whether there are such beings, and whether we can recognize them as such.

This is a question of fact, which cannot be answered in a system of ethics. But there is no need for us to decide it. To refute the objection advanced here it is sufficient to point out that it is directed only against the existence of duties to animals, not of those to men, and hence it defeats itself. For whether we actually come upon beings who fall under the concept of man is certainly no easier to decide than whether there are beings who have interests. Indeed, when dealing with men we have to prove not less but more than when dealing with animals: for we must produce evidence of a man's rationality, which is sometimes quite difficult.

Those who insist on questioning whether a given being is a person, i.e., a carrier of interests, can in no event answer this question on the basis of direct empirical data, except in relation to themselves. If we assume that another being has interests, and ask whether this imposes duties upon us, we must resort to reasoning by analogy. We infer certain inner processes from physical manifestations, which we know to be associated with such processes in ourselves. Such reasoning by analogy may involve greater or lesser difficulties, according to the nature of the given case, but this much is certain: either we cannot apply it at all or we must always apply it. Those who advance the argument in question must, then, in order to be consistent, assert that men have no more rights than animals—neither would have any rights at all.

To avoid this conclusion, it is argued that when dealing with men we do not depend on uncertain reasoning by analogy, because we can avail ourselves of language. In other words, it is argued that men can inform us about their interests by means of speech.

This argument is even more sophistical than the preceding one, for two reasons. First, it is flagrantly circular. If we take language to be a means of communication which serves to provide us with information about the interests of our fellow men, we presuppose that inner processes correspond to linguistic signs, and that such signs express an inner life. This assumption can be justified only on the basis of just such reasoning by analogy, which, we are told, can be dispensed with in the case of man.

Second, it is not true at all that language provides us with certain knowledge about the interests of our fellow men under all circumstances. Language consists in a conventional use of signs, and hence can serve to disguise facts as well as to communicate them. This is, then, the conclusion we must reach: If we were seriously to question the prohibition of maltreating animals with the argument that we know nothing about the interests of animals, we would have to assert that it is impossible to maltreat men as well as animals. For consistency is the least we can ask of a thinking man, and particularly of a philosopher.

Another attempt to refute the proposition asserting that animals have rights is based on the method of *reductio ad absurdum:* it is argued that assertion of such rights entails nonsensical consequences. It is pointed out that there is no clear line of demarcation between animals and creatures that cannot be subsumed under the concept of person, and our assertion must therefore include the rights of plants. This objection too is untenable. To be sure, since our knowledge is limited, we cannot always say with certainty whether a given being is an animal or a plant. But if we are honest, we must also admit that we do not always know with certainty whether a given being is a man or an animal; and yet no one would conclude on that account that we owe animals the same duties as we owe men. Thus, here again, those who advance the argument in question must, if they are consistent, deny that there are duties owed to men; for no clear line of demarcation can be drawn between men and animals either. Indeed, to draw such a line between men and animals is, for the reason given before, an undertaking much more hazardous and difficult than between animals and plants, for in the latter case only interests are involved, while in the former both interests and rationality are in question.

The self-deception which finds expression in this argument can be illustrated by the following example from geometry. Let us assume that we have proved that all angles inscribed in the same segment of a circle are equal, and that someone discovered figures of which it cannot be said with certainty whether they are circles or ellipses. According to the argument in question, we would have to conclude, on the basis that there is no clear demarcation line between circles and ellipses, that if our proposition were true it would also include ellipses; and that since it is not true of ellipses, it is not true of circles either.

All we can infer on the basis of that argument is that in some cases we must reckon with the possibility that a given being is a carrier of interests, and that we may have duties in relation to that being. But the range of such possible duties cannot extend further than our uncertainty as to whether we are dealing with an animal or not; it ends where this uncertainty no longer obtains.

It might be objected that this is not enough: for how do we know whether a plant has no interests, indeed, whether a stone that we trample under our feet has no interests? This objection is designed to show that by asserting that animals have interests we prove too much. It can be dealt with quite easily. True, we cannot prove with certainty that a stone has no interests; but to infer, from our ignorance of one thing, that we should know another, of which we are actually just as ignorant, seems more than questionable. For all we know, the stone may have an interest in being trampled by us, or a cabbage in being eaten. From the fact that we do not know *whether* we are confronted with interests, we cannot infer *what* interests we have to take into consideration.

This does not exhaust the list of pseudo arguments against animals' rights. For instance, in some cases the concept of interest is surreptitiously replaced by another concept, preferably the vague concept of life. But the criterion I have formulated is based on the concept of the person, not on that of the living being. The fact that there are more living beings than there are persons has no bearing on the question as to the scope of duties. For instance, if someone should infer, from the fact that animals have rights, mimosas too must have rights because they too respond to stimuli, we would grant the truth of the premise but not of the conclusion; for if such an inference were correct, we would have to say that an electric bell has rights because it obviously responds to stimuli. We do not say that a being has rights on the ground that it responds to stimuli, but on the ground that it has interests. From the fact that an electric bell responds to stimuli, no one will infer that it has rights.

If we apply the criterion of duty, the question of whether animals have rights can be readily answered: we have merely to ask whether, in considering an action affecting an animal, we could assent to such an action after abstracting from numerical determination. In other words, we have to ask whether we would consent to be used as mere means by another being far superior to us in strength and intelligence. This question answers itself. The fact that man has other beings in his power, and that he is in a position to use them as means to his own ends, is purely fortuitous.

67. Animals' Interest in Living

The foregoing considerations hold true no matter what animal interest is in question. On the basis of them we can decide, for instance, whether it is permissible to kill animals painlessly. We merely have to ask whether we ourselves, if we were to be killed painlessly, would consent to be killed *for that reason*. We would not, because our interest in living would be injured if we were killed, by whatever method, painless or cruel.

Interest in living, which, as we have seen, is usually valued so highly in connection with so-called duties to oneself—for instance, when the prohibition of suicide is justified by such an interest—is completely ignored when duties owed to animals are in question. Those who do not shrink from deducing a duty to themselves from their interest in their own life, should at least be consistent enough to justify a prohibition of killing animals on the ground that animals have an interest in living. As for those who have so little regard for animal life that they prefer animal to vegetable food on the sole ground that the former is tastier, they should ask themselves why they refuse to eat human flesh. A man who persists in eating animal flesh on purely hygienic grounds, yet holds these grounds to be invalid when he is offered a taste of human flesh, certainly does not rise above the moral level of the cannibal whom he despises, but who at least does not deceive himself as to his motives.

Our analysis must not be misinterpreted as an attempt to champion altruism in relation to animals. It merely reaffirms the principle of justice. That is why there can be no general philosophical injunction that we subordinate our interests to those of animals under any circumstances. Each time we are confronted with a conflict between our own and an animal's interest, we must decide, after making fair allowance for each, which of the two interests deserves to be given preference. Thus it may well be permitted to injure an animal's interest in order to avoid injuring a preponderant interest of our own; but at the same time a limit is set to the extent of the injury, which is permitted only under condition that an actual conflict is involved—this must be proved separately in each case. After such proof has been supplied, we must ask further on which side lies the preponderant interest. In no event is it permissible to regard the animal's interest as inferior without good reason, and to proceed to injure it.

This rule holds also when our interest in our own life or in the preservation of our own mental or physical powers can be safeguarded only by the destruction of an animal. Here too we must appraise the conflicting interests. For why should one sacrifice an animal's rather than a man's life? To sanction such a sacrifice as a general thing, one would have to know beforehand that a man's interest in life deserves *always* to be given preference over an animal's interest. Whether this is so, is a question that first has to be investigated. If the answer should be in the affirmative, we should be able to trace it back to a circumstance rooted in the very fact that the one being is a man, and the other an animal. This circumstance can be found only in the quality that distinguishes man from animals, namely, rationality. Consequently, we may formulate our question as follows: Can rationality be the foundation of the claim that in case of conflict, a man's life ought always to be given preference to an animal's life?

We shall test this assumption too by analyzing its consequences. If we regard fully developed reason as man's distinctive characteristic, we shall obviously have to equate children and the feeble-minded with animals, and sacrifice their lives and interests to the lives of other men. Under our assumption, we cannot object that we would thus injure the future interests of children: for death is characterized precisely by the fact that it prevents future interests from developing.

Our argumentation falls, however, if we assume that children's lives must be valued more highly than animals' on account of children's true interest. For this interest lies in the development of a still undeveloped disposition to rationality. We know that man has a claim to have his true interests taken into consideration. But we must still ask what is the extent of the rights based upon this claim. These rights certainly do not cover cases in which only sensory interests, common to man and animal, are in question. Here we are forced to a directly opposite conclusion: for once men have awakened to the awareness of their true interest, sensory interests are less important in relation to their life as a whole than they are for animals. The greater a man's rational interests, the less he strives for mere sensory enjoyment. This fact also affects his evaluation of his own direct interest in life: for this interest is merely sensory, and common to men and animals. A man can sacrifice his life for the sake of his higher interests. Animals are unable to make such a sacrifice, and in the case under consideration this must here be held in their favor.

The foregoing analysis also provides an answer to the objection that man, as a more highly organized being, has stronger interests, that his sensory interest in life is therefore stronger than that of an animal, and hence that his interest always deserves preference in the event of a conflict of interests. The assumption on which this argument is based—that sensory interests gain in strength as the organism grows more highly developed—is by no means self-evident in the light of what we have just said, indeed, is not even confirmed by the facts. Sensory interests often recede as a being reaches a higher level of development, because attention is diverted from them to other interests. Consequently, each time we are confronted with a conflict between a man's and an animal's interest in life, we must weigh the interests involved before deciding which of them deserves to be given preference.

Needless to say, a man's interest in life does not rest upon sensory interests alone. To be able to lead a rational life, it is necessary, of course, for man to live. But whoever cites this to justify his right always to give preference to his own life over the conflicting interest of an animal, without weighing the particular interests in each given case, should consider the full implications of such a view. It requires him to be consistent in subordinating sensory to rational interest even when his own interests alone are in question, and consequently denies him the right to injure his true interest in favor of his sensory interest. He thus forfeits any claim to have those interests of his respected, which are not subordinated to the interest in a rational life. How many men are prepared to accept such a conclusion without deceiving themselves?

Finally, by virtue of its rationality a being is not only invested with rights, but also assumes duties. A man who shirks his duties is certainly not superior to an animal, which is not even capable of committing a wrong. Whoever takes this fact honestly into account, will hesitate before justifying an injury to an animal's interests on the sole ground that his own life is rational.

Chapter 8. Duties to Men

68. Concept of Reason

As WE HAVE JUST SEEN, rational and nonrational beings have equally a claim to respect of their interests; but it does not follow that duties in relation to both are identical. Such an inference would be incompatible with the formal character of the moral law. The duties that arise in a given case depend on the nature of the given interests; hence it is quite possible that there is a difference between the duties we owe to rational and nonrational beings.

A discussion of what actually distinguishes men from animals as they are empirically known to us, is beyond the scope of a philosophical theory of duties. But we may ask here whether the mere circumstance that a given being is rational does not entail that we owe special duties to him. In other words, we may ask in what way our duties to men are affected by the circumstance that men are rational beings. All other qualities of human beings, qualities known only empirically, are here ignored.

Reason is the faculty of knowing what is the law; as an attribute of a being capable of action, it is the faculty of acting in accordance with that knowledge. Laws are either natural or moral laws. Our knowledge of natural laws enables us to foresee the consequences of our conduct; on the basis of our insight into the conditions under which we can realize the interests we pursue, we are thus able to choose those means by which we secure our interests in the greatest possible measure. Such a conduct is called "purposeful." A purpose is nothing but the result of an action, in so far as the idea of this result motivates the action. Consequently, a rational being has the capacity to act purposefully. In making decisions, he can emancipate himself from the influence of instinctual impulses; he can modify his decision according to his idea of the result which one or another mode of action may produce, by appraising the foreseeable effects of his conduct, and by choosing that mode of action which leads to the maximum realization of his interests.

By means of purposeful action in nature rational beings are thus able to secure the greatest possible realization of their interests. In so far as such beings have interests at all, they also have an interest in realizing their interests to the greatest possible extent, and hence an indirect interest in the possibility of purposeful action.

To deduce this interest in the possibility of purposeful action, which must be the starting point of the analyses that follow, we do not have to make any assumption concerning the content of rational beings' interests. All we need for this purpose is to assume that the beings whose interests we consider here are rational.

Now, it is clear that we can act purposefully only if we can anticipate the possibility of success. Only if we can predetermine the results of our actions, is purposeful conduct possible at all.

The situation with which we are concerned here occurs whenever we interact with others. Whenever the result of our action is exposed to other men's discretion, such discretion makes the result of our action indeterminate. Purposeful action, then, is possible only in so far as indeterminacy of the result—uncertainty due to other men's freedom to act—is ruled out.

Such indeterminacy has practical and theoretical implications. We shall first examine the practical aspect.

69. Obligation of Compatibility

The result of an action is practically indeterminate whenever the moral law does not unequivocally prescribe what ought to take place, but leaves scope for discretion with respect to actions by which men affect one another. Such practical uncertainty actually occurs because the moral law, as we know, does not always prescribe a specific course of action, even in cases of conflict, for it merely requires that the conflict be reconciled in such a way that neither party give preference to his own interest unless it is the preponderant interest. The moral law forbids the agent only to give preference to his own non-preponderant interest, but otherwise leaves him free to act as he chooses.

Every man has an interest in renouncing those interests whose realization would impair the satisfaction of his interests as a whole. The moral law does not forbid us to grant others the right to injure an interest of our own which is in itself justifiable; under certain circumstances we have an interest in granting such a right, namely, when by doing so we gain the advantage of realizing another, greater interest, which we could not otherwise realize.

Consequently we can and may freely and mutually delimit our spheres of rights, provided that in so doing we do not profit from a practical error of the person affected by our action. We are not only warranted to do so by the moral law, we also have an interest in so doing in order to realize our interests to the greatest possible extent. We are duty-bound to respect this interest. Consequently, when this interest does not run counter to some interest of greater weight, we are required by the moral law to make allowance for such an interest of the person affected, and to assent to a mutual and free delimitation of spheres of rights.

When such a delimitation of respective spheres of rights takes place on the basis of a free decision, we designate it as an agreement; when it is the result of an explicit understanding between the parties, we designate it as a compact. I shall refer to our duty to be willing to enter into agreements as the obligation of compatibility.

This obligation is different from what I call the duty to be peaceable. Peaceableness is willingness to refrain from violence in settling conflicts of interests, and hence deference to justified interests of others. The duty to be peaceable follows directly from the proposition asserting that our duties are determined by rights; it is independent of the principle of justice, i.e., the content of the moral law.

The obligation of compatibility involves a great deal more than that. It expresses the content of the moral law in relation to a specific situation: Men engaged in relations with each other ought to be willing to conclude agreements freely delimiting their respective spheres of rights. It is quite possible to conceive of a moral law which would not admit of an obligation of compatibility. This would be the case with any moral law which would unequivocally prescribe what ought to be done in each specific instance, or at least, in all cases of the type under consideration, i.e., involving interaction between rational beings. Such a law would leave no scope for compacts, for any free modification of the rights of the parties. Rather, it would itself represent such a respective delimitation of spheres of rights, excluding free choice; from such a law we could derive neither the duty to conclude agreements, nor even the right to do so. For any such agreement would be directly forbidden as an arbitrary modification of the spheres of rights delimited by the moral law.

The duty to be compatible requires only *that* compacts be concluded; it does not say *what* the content of these agreements ought to be. The content is left to the free choice of the parties; such free choice is of the very essence in any agreement. To abolish the parties' freedom in determining the content of the agreements would amount to abolishing their right to enter into agreements. The concept of an agreement whose content is prescribed by law is self-contradictory.

It must be pointed out, however, that since we have derived the obligation of compatibility from the principle of justice, the scope of possible agreements is necessarily restricted by this principle. The content of an agreement is a matter of free choice, yet free choice is permitted only within the boundaries of justice. Consequently, agreements can never be the source of a right which violates justice, whether such a violation affects the rights of the parties to the agreement, or of a third party. Even the parties directly concerned are limited in their right to conclude agreements. For under the principle of justice, from which the obligation of compatibility is derived, each party is duty-bound to conclude agreements only if these do not entail a greater injury to his interest than he would suffer without concluding them.

For this reason, actual consent of the parties is not always sufficient to make a given agreement rightful. Because practical errors are possible, i.e., because the actual interest can differ from the true interest, an agreement may involve renunciation of inalienable rights, i.e., rights that may not be renounced on the basis of an agreement. Even an agreement reached by actual consent of the parties is contrary to right if by virtue of it one party injures the preponderant true interest of the other. It must be observed, however, that only the injuring party commits a wrong in such a case, not the injured party. For there is no duty not to alienate an inalienable right.

70. Obligation of Trustworthiness

The duty to be compatible arises from the *practical* indeterminacy of the results of our actions; just so another duty arises from the *theoretical* indeterminacy of such results. When we speak of theoretical indeterminacy in this connection, we refer not to what ought to take place, but to what actually takes place.

The results of an action can be theoretically indeterminate whenever rational beings interact. For then one party becomes dependent upon the other in respect of such results; in so far as he cannot foresee the other's free decisions, his possibilities of purposeful action are limited. Each man therefore is interested in being able to foresee the conduct of all men who may influence the results of his actions: for only then can he act purposefully.

We shall discuss, first, the case in which other men influence the results of our actions through decisions based on free choice, and second, the case in which these decisions are subject to the norms of the moral law.

In the first case, the individual is uncertain as to the results of his actions because he is dependent on others whose conduct affects his interests and whose decisions are not unequivocally prescribed by the moral law. How can this indeterminacy be obviated? Since the intentions of one rational being cannot be directly known to another, communication by means of external signs is required to make them known. In other words, rational beings can inform each other about their inner processes by means of a system of symbols, i.e., external signs corresponding to specific notions, or, briefly, by means of language. For language is precisely such a system of signs correlated with ideas. To be able to act purposefully we must know the facts relevant to our action, and some of these facts we can know only on the basis of linguistic communications by other rational beings. Consequently, we have an interest in being able to depend on such communications as completely as on a direct knowledge of the facts. Whenever this interest is not outweighed by another interest, each rational being has therefore the duty to communicate his thoughts in such a way as to enable others to depend on his communications as fully as on the facts themselves. In short, each rational being has the duty to enable others to depend on him in respect of communication of ideas. This is what I designate as the duty to be trustworthy.

In so far as a man violates this duty he prevents other men from living as rational beings, from acting purposefully. And just as we can depend on a natural law only in so far as we assume it to be universally valid, we can never again depend on a man who commits an act in violation of the duty to be trustworthy. Such an act not only injures the interests of the person directly affected by it, it also implies an injury to the interests of all members of society—an injury equivalent to the one he would inflict on them if he always deceived them from that point on. For no one can trust him. The important thing here is not whether such a man violates the trust another actually places in him. In fact he can prove untrustworthy only if trust is placed in him. But a man who cannot be trusted is not for that reason any less obliged to be trustworthy. It is his duty to act in such a way as to enable us to trust him, i.e., to be worthy of trust. For his fellow men are not free to decide whether they will or will not depend on him; in order to be able to act purposefully, they *must* be able to trust him. It is on this circumstance that the obligation of trustworthiness is based.

Now let us consider our second case, in which the decisions of men influencing each other's actions are subject to moral norms. In this case, the moral law demands more than that the parties concerned give each other trustworthy information about their intentions; in addition, these intentions themselves must conform to the requirements of the moral law. The claim to be able to trust our fellow men here implies the claim to be able to depend on their rightful disposition. The duty to be trustworthy thus becomes here the duty to act as if a natural law guaranteed the rightness of the action. This is the duty to be morally trustworthy.

71. Obligation of Truthfulness

Only by deriving the duty to be truthful from the obligation of trustworthiness, and thus tracing it back to the duty to be just, are we enabled to appraise correctly the scope of the duty to be truthful, and to avoid at the same time the flaw of admitting exceptions. When the duty to be truthful is derived in this way, there is no need to provide for such exceptions—a circumstance that confirms the importance of our method of derivation.

We are confronted here by the old question as to whether we are forbidden to lie. In dealing with this question it is first of all important to choose suitable linguistic terms. If a lie is defined as an untrue statement that is forbidden, the assertion that we are forbidden to lie is a truism. When we deal with this injunction we consequently assume that a lie denotes a false statement per se, whether forbidden or not.

A lie implies an injury to the interests of the person who is lied to; but whether such an injury constitutes a wrong can be decided only by an appraisal of the interests involved in each given case. If a general prohibition against lying were to be formulated on the ground that a lie directly injures an interest, such a prohibition would be valid only if we could establish the pre-eminence of an interest in truth, which would have to be asserted a priori. Whether such an interest exists is a question which must remain unanswered here; it can be answered only in the theory of ideals. Here where we are discussing the theory of duties, therefore leaving aside a possible ideal of love for truth, we must base our deduction of a duty to be truth-ful to others, i.e., a general prohibition of lying, on the rationality of the persons affected.

Such a deduction is in fact possible. The obligation of truth-fulness in relation to others, i.e., the prohibition against lying, follows directly from the obligation of trustworthiness.

We say that a man is trustworthy when his statements cor-respond with the facts, and when we can depend on this corre-spondence as though it were natural law. The obligation of trustworthiness implies two distinct duties—(1) the duty to make our statements correspond to reality, and (2) the duty to make reality correspond to our statements. The first is the duty to be truthful; the second, the duty to be faithful.

We are truthful when we are honest in communicating our ideas to others or when our statements are in accord with the truth as we know it.

It is clear from the foregoing that a lie, i.e., an untrue state-ment, can be a violation of the duty to be truthful only if (1) it is a conscious falsehood, and (2) if another is deliberately deceived by it, if it is intended to arouse in him an idea that is not in accord with reality. The first condition makes it clear forthwith that an unintentionally erroneous statement does not fall under the prohibition against lying. Such a statement is not a violation of the duty to be trustworthy.

The second condition shows that the prohibition against lying is not violated by an untrue statement not intended to arouse an idea which does not conform to reality. The vice manifested through lying is aptly designated as deceitfulness. To determine whether a given statement is deceitful, i.e., whether it is a vio-lation of the prohibition against lying, we must know the mean-ing of this statement. Since a statement involves the use of a sign, it can have meaning only in so far as this sign is un-equivocally correlated with a notion.

A statement may, however, have various meanings: the same expression may denote one thought or another, according to circumstances. Consequently, a statement can be regarded as a lie only when it is untruthful in relation to the specific circum-stances upon which its meaning depends.

For instance, a polite phrase which may under certain circumstances express personal esteem, lacks this meaning when used in keeping with conventional rules of propriety, say, as a form of address in a letter. Indeed, omission of such a phrase, unless there are special reasons for it, would be an act of unjustified rudeness.

Similarly, a man who makes an untrue statement in jest does not violate the prohibition against lying, provided of course that his listener has a sense of humor. Otherwise the listener would be intentionally deceived.

We have a similar case when a man is not expected to express his own opinion: thus we know that a judge, in exercising his office, should refrain from expressing his personal opinion on the guilt or innocence of the defendant. If he judged a given case according to his own moral conviction, he would be lying rather than fulfilling his obligation to be truthful: for he would deceive those who rightly expect him to judge in accordance with the law.

Furthermore, we may have a case of deliberate deception in the absence of any statement, namely, when silence is equivalent to a statement. Under certain circumstances, the mere omission of a statement may become the sign of an idea. In such a case silence must be looked upon as a statement.

Finally we must keep in mind that untrue statements made to a mentally incompetent person do not fall under the prohibition against lying. For a man in a state of incompetence must be regarded as irrational; when he is in such a state he cannot act purposefully, and hence has no interest in being enabled by others to act purposefully. Consequently we do not violate our duty to be trustworthy when we fail to tell him the truth. Rather, we must in each given case determine whether a specific interest is or is not present, on account of which we may be permitted or even duty-bound to lie.

It is also clear, however, that a lie can be forbidden only if it represents an action imputable to the man who lies. A statement made under duress cannot be forbidden on the ground that it is a lie, for no one is deliberately deceived by such a statement. But even a man responsible for his actions may find himself under duress, for instance, when psychological pressure from an importunate questioner puts him under such restraint that he would betray his thoughts if he merely refrained from answering. In so far as we have the right to keep our thoughts to ourselves, the questioner can blame only himself if we lie to him in order to defend this right; for it is his fault if the choice before us is no longer one of expressing ourselves truthfully or keeping silent.

The argument underlying this conclusion goes further. The duty to be truthful springs from the rightful claim of each rational being to be able to trust others. According to the general principles of justice, this claim, like any other, can be forfeited.

A man who wishes to learn the truth in order to use it as a means to an unrightful end forfeits this claim. There is a right of self-defense against interests contrary to right. We are justified in lying when we can foresee that the truth would be misused.

Furthermore, a holder of a rightful claim may renounce it of his own accord, provided this renunciation does not rest upon a practical error. Here it might be objected that such a case is impossible: for a man can consent to be deceived, the objection runs, only if he knows in advance that the statement in question is a lie; and if he knows this, he is no longer deceived. But it is possible to conceive of an interest which a man may place higher than the truth, indeed, an interest he is more anxious to satisfy than any other interest that may be injured by a lie. For instance, a conceited person may be eager to listen to flattery, whether it be sincere or not. Or consider the case of a patient who summons a doctor to cure him. If the doctor can do so only by lying, the patient will later welcome having been deceived, and the doctor will not have been untrustworthy. It must be noted, however, that if no such consent can be assumed or if it rests upon a practical error, lying is not permitted. For instance, should the patient in our example ask to be informed about his condition, in order to make some testamentary disposition on the basis of this information, an act more important to him than his recovery, the doctor would not be justified in lying even if his purpose is to cure the patient. Indeed, his lie would be an affront of the worst kind: for he would be treating his patient as an irrational being and depriving him of the chance to act purposefully while he could still do so.

The same example leads us to a further inference. It shows that in some cases we may not only be released from the duty to be truthful, but even have the duty to be untruthful, i.e., to lie. Needless to say, such a duty can flow only from the duty to do justice. By communicating the truth we may share responsibility for an unrightful misuse of the truth by another: for if we can foresee such a misuse, we include it in the intended result of our action. Our duty to lie in such a case is a consequence of our duty not to share responsibility for the wrong in question. If we can prevent the perpetration of a crime only by lying, we are, in most cases, not only permitted to lie, but it becomes our duty to lie. The duty to be truthful, just as any other duty, can never serve as a ground for violating the principle of justice from which this duty, and all other duties, are indirectly derived.

72. Obligation of Faithfulness

The obligation of trustworthiness, i.e., the duty to safeguard conformity between one's statements and the facts, entails in addition to the duty to be truthful, the duty to be faithful. For faithfulness denotes the duty to conform reality to our statements—the duty to keep a given promise. A promise is a statement made by the promiser about a future action of his. Consequently, the duty to be trustworthy directly implies the duty to behave in conformity with a deliberately aroused expectation. We call this duty the obligation of faithfulness.

In order to delimit correctly the scope of this duty, we must grasp the specific implications of the term "promise." A communication expressing a resolve, i.e., an intention to perform a specific action, is not a promise. Such a statement may be merely a communication, and like any other statement it is subject to the obligation of trustworthiness, that is to say, to the condition that the intention expressed actually exists. But in so far as such a communication expresses no more than the fact that a man in-

tends to perform a given action at some future time, the obligation arising from it does not extend beyond the scope of the duty
to be truthful. Consequently, we cannot infer on the basis of
such a communication that the man who makes it has the duty to
carry out his intention. To say that we have now the *intention*
to do something later on, and to say that we shall *actually* do
something at a future time, are two different things. The truth
of the first statement does not necessarily imply the truth of the
second. For a man's intention of doing something at a future time
does not depend on whether he will actually do it at that time.
A promise is a statement which refers to a future action, not to
a present intention.

To determine whether a man is under the obligation to be
faithful it is not important to ask whether he seriously intends to
perform the promised action, i.e., whether his promise is honest
or dishonest. Rather, the only thing that matters is that he
promises to perform the action in question and thus arouses the
promisee's expectation that he will perform it. For thereby the
promiser has assumed the duty to fulfill his promise and thus to
perform the promised action.

Just as irrelevant as the question of whether the promiser intends to perform the promised action is the question of whether
the promisee believes that the promise will be kept. The fact
alone that the promiser intends to create such a belief imposes
on him the duty to prove himself trustworthy.

In the light of the foregoing analysis of the concept of promise,
it is clear that the duty to be faithful is a direct consequence of
the duty to be trustworthy. A promise that is not kept is a lie;
the breach of a promise is an act of untrustworthiness.

Our duty to be faithful is thus based upon another person's
claim, which in turn is based on an act of our will. It is only by
his promise that the promiser imposes on himself the duty to be
faithful. And conversely, a man is not obliged to be faithful unless he has pledged himself to be by a special act of his will.

Now, it is clear that an act of will can be a ground for a duty
only if we presuppose the existence of duties independent
of acts of will. The content of duty is objective, hence duties
cannot be created by an act of will, whether it be our own or an-

other's act. The possibility of assuming an obligation by an act of one's own will rests upon the duty to act justly, which is independent of our will, and which demands that the act of pledging one's word be linked with another act, which is a practically necessary consequence of the promise.

Our deduction of the duty to be faithful automatically excludes all cases which would otherwise have to be admitted as exceptions. Since we have used a similar method in the case of the duty to be truthful, we shall confine ourselves here to mentioning briefly a few points which have special practical importance. Recalling our previous analysis of the term "promise," we may say at once that the duty to be faithful is not based on the explicit wording of the promise; in fact the promise need not be explicit at all. Sometimes we assume a tacit obligation, namely, when we lead other persons to expect certain actions on our part, without making formal statements about them. Under certain circumstances, we assume such a tacit obligation by our mere failure to discourage other persons explicitly from expecting us to comply with existing customs. For instance, we have a duty to observe the laws of the state faithfully, even if we have not explicitly promised to observe them.

Just as there are obligations that are assumed tacitly, so promises expressly given may be restricted by tacit reservations. It is important to keep this in mind when we ask whether we are obliged to honor a promise based on an error. We must answer this question in the negative: we are not obliged to keep a promise conditional on the presence of certain circumstances if these circumstances are absent.

Furthermore, we are not obliged to keep a promise given in jest if the promisee can understand that our statement is facetious. Nor are we obliged to keep promises given to incompetents.

We are under no obligation to keep a promise given under duress, whether the compulsion be physical or psychological. For instance, a promise extracted by fraud has no obligatory character. For a promise implies an intention to encourage a specific expectation in the promisee. Where coercion is applied, such an intention is not expressed; actually, compulsion elicits the mere semblance of a promise.

The right which is the ground of the obligation of faithfulness is forfeited, if the interest in the promised action is unrightful: we are then permitted to break our promise, just as we are permitted to lie. What would otherwise be a wrong, i.e., a betrayal, is no longer a wrong if it serves to thwart unrightful interests.

It may even be a duty to break a given promise. This may be the case when the promiser would otherwise abet the commission of a wrong. This wrong would then be among the intended, foreseeable results of the promised action.

Nor are we obliged to keep a promise that is immoral, i.e., when the action promised is a violation of duty. The formal character of the moral law, however, may render a given action immoral only with reference to the particular attendant circumstances. The fact that a promise was given may bring about a change in the circumstances, as a result of which an action otherwise immoral becomes morally permissible merely on the ground of the pledged word. In such cases it is necessary to reappraise the interests involved, and investigate whether the interest created by the promise does not outweigh any other interest which would provide a ground for forbidding the action if there were no promise.

The promiser is not obliged to keep his promise if the promisee voluntarily renounces his right to its fulfillment. Just as a man may voluntarily assume an obligation by making a promise, so the promisee may voluntarily release him from this obligation. However, the promisee's voluntary renunciation of his right must not rest upon practical error.

It may even be the promisee's duty to renounce his right. Then the promiser is released from his obligation even if the promisee does not actually renounce his right. Such a case occurs when a sufficiently weighty interest of a third party would be violated if the promise were kept. Such a case may also occur when the promiser, by keeping his promise, would inflict an unforeseeable injury to his interest, an injury so grave that the promisee would not assent to it if the injured interest were his own. Under the principle of equity, the promisee ought then to renounce his right. The promisee's duty not to insist on his right arising from the promise if the promiser should find himself in such a predicament, may be called the duty to be fair. It is obvious that no general rules determining the scope of this duty can be formulated; for in order to decide whether the promiser's predicament is serious enough to require the promisee's renunciation, we must judge each case on its merits. But that possibility cannot be ruled out a priori. For human knowledge is imperfect, and we can never foresee with sufficient accuracy what circumstances may arise after our promise is given. The only rule that can be formulated here is this, that the promisee ought to renounce his claim if he must assume that the promiser would not have given his promise if he had foreseen his predicament— provided of course that the promisee does not, by his renunciation, injure an interest of his own, which outweighs the promiser's interest.

A promise cannot be binding if it is impossible to keep. The obligation of faithfulness refers only to cases in which fulfillment of the promise depends only on the promiser's will. But to make the impossible possible does not depend on his will, and he certainly can be under no obligation to do so. The simplest case of this kind is one in which the promiser is prevented from keeping his promise by circumstances beyond his control. But the promised performance may prove impossible even without the intervention of such circumstances, i.e., it may prove impossible per se.

Here we must distinguish between two possible cases. Either the promiser did not know that he could not keep his promise; then his promise results from an error, and this case must be regarded in the same light as one of an unwittingly untrue statement. Or the promiser knew that he could not keep his promise; then he gave it knowing that he would not keep it, and consequently did not intend to keep it. In other words, his promise was intended to deceive the promisee—it was a lie. In this case we may speak of a dishonest promise.

A dishonest promise is one that is not intended to be kept, whether or not it can be kept. If it cannot be kept, the promiser's wrong consists not in his failure to keep his promise, but in his having given it.

For a promise to be honest, however, it is not sufficient that the promiser be unaware of the impossibility of keeping it; rather, he must be aware of the possibility of keeping it. His promise can be honest only if he intends to keep it; and we can intend an action only under the assumption that performance of it depends on our will. We cannot intend something without knowing whether it is within the range of our will, and hence we cannot honestly promise such a thing. Consequently, a dishonest promise is not a violation of the duty to be faithful, but of the duty to be truthful.

Rash promises must be classified as dishonest promises. For instance, it is generally rash to promise to keep a secret. For we cannot always say in advance whether the keeping of such a promise depends on our will. We may, for instance, under questioning, be compelled to break our promise if we do not wish to deceive the questioner. We may easily find ourselves facing such a dilemma because silence is occasionally equivalent to an answer, so that we are left with the choice between deceiving the questioner in order to keep our promise, or betraying the promisee in order to remain truthful.

We encounter a related but much graver difficulty with promises involving feelings or convictions. Since feelings and convictions do not depend directly on our will, a promise referring to a feeling or a conviction is dishonest. For whether such a promise can be kept is a matter of accident, not of volition. For instance, all promises to remain loyal to a given religious faith all one's life, or to remain attached to another person by a bond of eternal love, belong to this category. Whoever gives such a promise either gives it unthinkingly or knows that he is lying. Thus he violates his duty to be truthful, unless he has no choice, for instance, when his promise is extracted from him under duress. Then his action cannot be imputed to him as his guilt: for in this case it is he who is deceived, and the wrong is committed by the party who forces him to make such a promise.

In the foregoing chapters we have surveyed the scope of the duty to act justly, with a view to determining the possible objects of this duty. We have seen that there can be no so-called duties to oneself; and we have divided the duties owed to others into duties in relation to nonrational and rational beings. With this we have concluded the philosophical investigation of the scope of the duty to act justly, and we have completed the last part of the philosophical theory of duties. Our next task is to develop the theory of the ethical norms that are beyond the scope of the moral law, namely, the theory of ideals.

PART 2

Theory of Ideals

Chapter 1. Analytic Principles of Formal Theory of Ideals

LIKE THE THEORY of duties, the theory of ideals falls into two distinct parts—the formal and the material. The division here is based on the fact that in each ideal, just as in each duty, we can distinguish between form and content. The form of an ideal includes all the attributes an ideal must have to be classified as such: it would be self-contradictory to subsume an entity lacking any of these attributes under the concept of ideal. The content of an ideal is what characterizes it over and above its formal attributes, i.e., that which an ideal sets before us as a task.

73. Concept of Ideal

The foundation of the theory of ideals is the concept "ideal." The term here denotes a standard of value for the conduct of rational beings in nature—a norm valid without reference to any other goal to be attained by such conduct. In so far as the realization of an ideal has objective and, in this case, positive value, we may say that each ideal sets a goal for our action, a goal which it is our task to approximate, although we are not duty-bound to attain it. We call such a task, as distinguished from the categorical imperative of duty, a categorical optative. Whereas the theory of duties formulates a system derived from the categorical imperative, the theory of ideals formulates a system of categorical optatives.

Just as there is moral valuation, so there is valuation in the light of ideals. Ideal valuation also applies to actions: only with reference to actions can it have the meaning of an ethical judgment, and relate to the will of a rational being. But whereas moral valuation, as we have seen, is based on an imperative which is not based in turn on a higher valuation, this cannot be said about ideal valuation. For in this case we are dealing with an ethical judgment that is based directly on the concept of value itself.

An ideal action is preferable only because it is valuable, whereas a moral action is preferable not because it realizes a positive value, but is valued only because it is moral, i.e., because it is enjoined by duty.

But just as we could not derive the moral value of an action from the value of its result, so we cannot derive an ideal value from the value of what is accomplished by the action in question. No matter how great the value of the *result* of an action, one still cannot infer the value of the *action* from it. On the basis of the result of an action we can formulate only a hypothetical imperative, never an ethical obligation to perform the action: that requires a categorical imperative, or optative.

The concept of the ideal implies a principle of positive valuation; but this does not mean that the converse is true, namely, that every positive valuation is an ideal valuation. The concept of the ideal implies that of value as a goal for our *action*, as something to be realized through our own contribution. Objective, positive valuation of things is not as such ethical, but aesthetic in the broadest sense of the term. It follows that every ideal valuation is aesthetic; not every aesthetic valuation, however, is necessarily ideal.

The statement that ethics is a subjective teleology acquires new significance here: even though ideal valuation is not subjective in the sense that it is subject to our discretion, it refers only to values governing our action, not to such values as are objective in the sense of objective teleology. We are dealing here not with values that characterize things in themselves, but only with values that are to be produced by our will. In this sense the theory of ideals is part of subjective teleology, and only to this extent is it a part of ethics.

Finally, with regard to the relation between the theory of ideals and the theory of duties, it is obvious in the light of the foregoing that the norms formulated in the theory of ideals are subordinated to the norms formulated in the theory of duties, since the latter are the necessary conditions governing the actions of rational beings. Hence all the propositions formulated in the theory of ideals are valid only under the general assumption that the necessary conditions imposed by duty have been met.

74. Analytic Principles of Formal Theory of Ideals

The formal theory of ideals is in turn divided into two parts. The first, general part is confined to problematic inferences from the concept "ideal," i.e., inferences that can be drawn without assuming the practical reality of this concept. In this part the concept of the ideal is expressed in analytic principles, just as was the concept of duty in the analytic principles of the theory of duties.

The analytic part of the theory of ideals can be developed largely in analogy to the analytic part of the theory of duties; we thus arrive at a system of ethical principles which are more comprehensive than the principles formulated in the theory of duties. This system includes those among the latter principles which do not refer to specific characteristics distinguishing the concept "duty" from the concept "ideal." The fundamental concept here is that of the ethical task in the broadest sense of the term. Those analytic principles which follow from the concept of such a task, and which do not presuppose the practical necessity implied in the concept of duty, can be extended to the entire domain of ethics.

The principles of universal validity, of differentiation, of autonomy, of objectivity, of ethical attitude, and of ethical readiness can thus be maintained in a broader sense. Furthermore, on the basis of our distinction between the form and the content of ideals, we can formulate a distinction analogous to that between moral and lawful valuation. In respect of form, each ideal refers to the will of a rational being, and we can evaluate that will according to whether it is motivated by its consciousness of ideal tasks. In respect of content, ideal valuation refers to what the will ought to accomplish, i.e., it appraises in what measure a given conduct satisfies the ideal norm. Thus ideal valuation can be formal or material; this distinction corresponds to that between moral and lawful valuation.

The distinction between ideal and duty is not, however, confined to content; it inheres in the concepts themselves, in the very form of the ethical task defined by each. Consequently, it is to be expected that the analogy discussed above can be carried only up to a certain point, beyond which the theory of duties and the theory of ideals are no longer parallel. In other words, in developing the analytic part of the theory of ideals we are bound to encounter a principle divergent from the corresponding principle in the theory of duties. In the light of this divergence, the formal difference between duty and ideal can be investigated and formulated in precise terms.

The principle in question is that of rigorism. For whereas we assert a rigorism of duty, we do not assert a rigorism of the ideal: the principle of rigorism is not valid for ethics as a whole. In the theory of duties we deduced this principle from the practical necessity inherent in the concept of duty. No such necessity is inherent in the concept of the ideal.

75. Rigorism and Tolerance

There is an old controversy in ethics, which is based on imperfect discrimination between duty and ideal—the dispute between a rigorist and a tolerant interpretation of ethics. Neither of these interpretations is tenable. A rigorist theory of ideals would be just as inconsistent as a nonrigorist theory of duties. At the same time, even in the theory of ideals, the maxim of tolerance can imply no more than rejection of rigorism. In ethics we always deal with demands addressed to the will, with norms governing the conduct of rational beings. In ethics there is no room for tolerance in the sense of general acceptance of any kind of action, regardless of whether it is in conformity with those norms, no room for tolerance in the sense of a general abstention from condemning actions on ethical grounds. Anyone who formulates norms is necessarily intolerant, namely, of everything contradicting these norms. Tolerance in the broad sense is thus self-contradictory as an ethical principle: for like every other ethical norm it would have to be intolerant of its opposite, i.e., it would imply intolerance of intolerance, and thereby cancel itself. Tolerance in the sense defined above can be consistently upheld only in the form of general ethical indifference, which negates any kind of ethical evaluation.

But even as we reject tolerance in this sense, we must also reject rigorism in relation to ideals. Duty enjoins us to perform an action unconditionally: duty can be only fulfilled or violated. But an ideal denotes a goal which it is our task to approach as closely as possible, but whose complete realization is not even always within our power. Consequently, we cannot say in this case that we must either realize or fail at the task in question; there remains the possibility of approximating it in greater or lesser measure. If duty and ideal are confused in this respect, we are led to the self-contradictory assertion of duties whose fulfillment is not within our power, and hence, of commands that defy fulfillment. We thus obtain a false rigorism, which represents as duty something that is actually only an ideal. This false rigorism might be called moralism, for it actually implies the moralist doctrine that there are no morally indifferent actions, and it has done immense harm to ethics. Because, in the name of morality, injunctions were formulated which proved unrealizable on impartial examination, true rigorism has become suspected of exaggeration, and ethics of utopianism. This criticism is justly leveled at false doctrines such as those asserting a duty of general love of mankind or unconditionally prohibiting the use of violence—injunctions which are doomed to remain unfulfilled in the real world.

Chapter 2. Synthetic Propositions of Formal Theory of Ideals

76. Ideal of Character

IF WE ADD, to the problematic concept of the ideal, the synthetic presupposition that it has practical reality, we obtain the major premise of the formal theory of ideals: There are ideals.

We link this major premise with a minor premise, which is an analytic proposition inferred from the concept of nature, and which asserts that whether the ideal is or is not realized is adventitious by nature. In other words, we assert that no preponderant force is inevitably directed either to the realization or the violation of the ideal. There is no natural law under which the realization of the ideal is either necessary or impossible.

On the basis of these two premises we obtain a conclusion analogous to the imperative of character formulated in the theory of duties—the ideal of safeguarding the realization of ideal tasks against the chance influences to which it is exposed in nature. In the theory of duties we have used the term "character" in the broad sense of rational self-control; here we can say that our conclusion asserts the ideal of putting character to the service of ideals. This ideal corresponds to the imperative of character formulated in the formal theory of duties, according to which the fulfillment of duty is to be secured through the power of self-control. To distinguish the ideal deduced here from the imperative of character, we shall designate it as the ideal of character. Whereas the imperative of character demands morality of character, the ideal of character demands ideality of character, i.e., it asserts the norm of idealism.

77. Ideal Conditions of Character

Because the ideal of character is analogous to the imperative of character, we can transpose the conditions of character formulated in the formal theory of duties to the formal theory of ideals. Thus we can arrive at the formal theory of ideals through mere translation. This is another advantage secured by our abstract treatment of the formal theory of duties.

The formal conditions of character are here, just as they were there, strength and spontaneity—strength as opposed to the passing surges of impulses, and spontaneity as opposed to impulses operating by the force of habit. Strength and spontaneity of character in themselves secure only what may be designated as deliberateness or rationality of conduct. Deliberate conduct is nothing but purposeful conduct, or conduct free from accidental influences. Once a given end is chosen, its realization is thus safeguarded against chance. But the choice of these ends remains itself undetermined, and is to this extent fortuitous. And since the ideal of character demands that accidental influences be ruled out, it requires that the conduct of a rational being be independent of whether his strongest impulse happens to be directed toward what the ideal characterizes as valuable. The necessary conditions of strength and spontaneity are thus supplemented by the condition of purity of character. But here purity implies more than morality; it also implies ideality, which is conformity of the will with ideal ends, not merely with duty.

78. Idealism and Utopianism

Ideality of character, like morality of character, includes two virtues. The first refers to insight into the ideal. Knowledge of an ideal can motivate the will only if it achieves adequate clarity. Even though it is clear, by definition, *that* an ideal stands for something desirable, we have no such clarity about *what* is desirable or in conformity with the ideal norm. Adequate clarification of the content of the ideal, and by the same token, of the ideal ends, is required if the idea of these ends is to motivate our will, if our will is to subject itself to them. We may designate the capacity of the mind to attain such clarity as the virtue of clarity of mind, which denotes more than the virtue of moral clarity. The latter implies only a clear sense of duty, and does not refer to the positive ends of human life. This virtue of clarity of mind, which includes but goes beyond moral clarity, is on the one hand opposed to dullness of spirit, i.e., deficient appreciation of higher goals, and on the other hand, to what may be designated as confusion of spirit, namely, confusion in respect of those goals.

There are two sources of such confusion. We may be confused about the content of the ideal goals when we are influenced by subjective interests, affects, and passions; we may also be confused about the very form of the ideal. It is this latter source of error that concerns us here; in order to gain insight into it, it will be most helpful to recall the considerations underlying our deduction of the ideal of character.

It is possible, without entertaining false ideas about the existence of an ideal and about its true content, to be confused about the form of the ideal, namely, about the relation obtaining between the ideal and occurrences in nature. To avoid such confusion, it is important to understand correctly the implications of the fact that the realization of the ideal norm in nature is subject to chance. The difficulty inherent in this problem is the source of a deep-rooted error to which moral philosophers have often succumbed, and which for that reason must be exposed here all the more sharply.

The idealist is usually opposed to the realist. An idealist is a man who fulfills the ideal of character, i.e., who is willing to live in conformity with the ideals he professes. But what is a realist? The realist's motto is: Things and people must be taken as they are. But the interpretation of this maxim gives rise to a controversy, all the more confused because it involves an equivocation. For "we must take things and people as they are" may mean two things—(1) that we must look upon them as they actually are, or (2) that we must resign ourselves to what they actually are.

In the first case, the question concerns our theoretical, in the second our practical attitude. To take things as they are in the practical sense, to resign ourselves to their actual qualities as we find them in nature, would contradict idealism. Shall we then infer that the idealist ought not to look upon things as they are? It is quite common to take this view, and as a result ethics acquires a utopian character, which makes it impossible of application. But is the idealist really characterized by the fact that he does not look upon things as they are, that he closes his eyes to the facts so as to be able to dream about them undisturbed? I should not call such a man an idealist, but a dreamer or a visionary, and we may formulate the question which is crucial here as follows: Must a man be a dreamer in order to be called an idealist?

If we are referring here to idealism in the sense of the attitude required by the ideal of character, we obviously have in mind a practical, not a speculative concept: we are not thinking of idealism in the sense of a specific interpretation of what is actually taking place in nature. In this speculative sense, idealism would amount to the belief that the realization of the ideal in nature is secured by virtue of natural law. But this kind of idealism is in contradiction with our minor premise, which asserts the impossibility of such a natural law.

Is the idealist in the practical sense bound to be an idealist in the speculative sense? Does practical idealism depend on a speculative faith? This is so far from being the case that we may safely assert the contrary, as our theory obliges us to do. A man who believed that the good is bound to be victorious in nature without his doing anything about it, would cease to be an idealist, and become a visionary. For a man cannot be an idealist if he assumes that the ideal is realized without any effort on his part. This follows directly from the minor premise in our deduction of the ideal of character, which rules out speculative idealism of any kind. The idealizing views characteristic of the visionary do indicate that he is interested in the ideal, namely, that he wishes he would encounter it in reality; but he gratifies this wish in fantasy, and deceives himself as to the fact that for all his imaginary efforts the world remains unchanged. The visionary's sentimental interest in the ideal fails to provide a motive for the will; this is in direct contrast to the idealism of disposition, which is immediately an affair of the will. The visionary is actually opposed to the realist who forms his theoretical ideas solely on the basis of a study of facts, without regard for what is desirable. Hence there is no real conflict between the idealist and the realist; rather, only a realist can be an idealist. An idealist with a sufficiently clear mind will necessarily be a realist. Realism is a virtue inseparable from clarity of mind.

True, it may be said that the idealist needs a faith in addition to his knowledge of the facts, but this faith is a conviction that does not refer to what takes place, but to what is desirable: it must be a practical, not a speculative, conviction. It is also true that this conviction is incompatible with a belief that the ideal cannot be realized, for an ideal determines its object as something that our will is to accomplish, and hence that can be accomplished. But the possibility of realizing the ideal does not imply that it will be realized by natural necessity. Practical idealism rests precisely on the assumption of the uncertainty to which all ideal aspiration is exposed in nature. Thus it rests upon our consciousness of our own freedom—our knowledge that it depends upon us whether what ought to take place in nature does actually take place.

Consequently, idealism is just as much opposed to optimism, which expects success as though it were guaranteed by some law of nature, as it is to pessimism, which assumes that all ideal aspiration is doomed to failure by virtue of some natural law. The two deny the uncertainty of the realization of the ideal, which is presupposed by idealism. Optimism, just as pessimism, may be said to be a variety of fatalism. Both are based on the assumption that the realization of the ideal in nature does not depend on our free will. The optimist assumes that the ideal will necessarily be realized, the pessimist that it cannot be realized.

Not so the realist. He forms his conception of nature without regard for what is desirable according to the ideal. He does not assume that there is some natural law under which the ideal must be realized or cannot be realized. He says that natural occurrences depend only on the distribution of forces, and that these forces are determined by natural laws, not by the ideal, not by what is desirable. Consequently, he knows that the realization of the ideal depends solely upon the forces mobilized for this purpose.

The fatalist assumes the existence of a natural law which the realist cannot accept. The pessimist is therefore essentially just as much a visionary and just as little a realist, as is the optimist. But there is an important difference between the optimist and the pessimist. Both assume that idealism stands or falls with a belief in the necessary realization of the ideal; the former bases his optimism on this belief, while the latter bases his pessimism on the negation of this belief. But the speculative faith of the optimist suffers from the disadvantage of sealing its own doom. For belief that the task set before us by an ideal is attained independently of man's will serves only to bring about the opposite. Lacking the required action behind it, the ideal becomes unattainable, just as the pessimist predicts. Hence, an ideal need only be regarded as attainable without any effort on our part, to remain actually unrealized: for this belief promptly rules out action, which is the condition of the ideal's realization. Thus it is the optimist's fault if the ideal norm remains unfulfilled, and if the pessimist proves right. Whoever begins with the illusion that the ideal is realized by virtue of natural law must suffer disillusionment. That is why the optimist, as his experience increases, is in constant danger of becoming a pessimist.

In contrast, the pessimist's unbelief makes itself true. For if something can be realized only by action, it need only be regarded as unrealizable, in order to remain unrealized, lacking such action. Thus the pessimist always wins out over the optimist: he always has more reason to present himself as the man of experience, as the true prophet. But his wisdom requires no great acumen. It consists only in predicting something one brings about through one's own conduct. The deeper reason why the optimist proves wrong and the pessimist right lies in that the optimist's seeming faith is in reality a lack of practical faith, masked only by speculative superstition, while the pessimist at least openly professes his unbelief. For to imagine that idealism depends on speculative faith in the victory of the good in nature is actually a lack of practical faith. To make idealism dependent on such a speculative superstition is to lack faith in the ideal. The optimist would display greater consistency and greater realism if this lack of faith, which he shares with the pessimist, led him to throw his sham idealism overboard.

The true idealist is neither an optimist nor a pessimist; he bases his theoretical views on the lessons of experience, and needs no clairvoyance to be a realist. He expects everything from his own actions, and nothing from the so-called course of events. His reliance is self-reliance, not reliance in fate, nor surrender to it.

79. Opportunism and Doctrinairism

A different form of the error with which we are dealing here is found in the ever recurring dispute about the implications of being loyal to one's principles—the dispute between doctrinairism and opportunism. The difficulty confronting us here arises from the question whether it is permissible to compromise, i.e., whether it is permissible to set aside an ideal goal for the sake of another goal. From the standpoint of ethical rigorism one would have to reject all compromise on the ground that in some respect it is contrary to the ideal. But such inflexibility does not stand the test of real life. Goethe says that the man of action is always unconscionable, and that only the contemplative man has a conscience. What he obviously means is that a man of action must accept compromise, and therefore must renounce the perfect realization of his ideals. Only a man who does not act can avoid compromises, and thus preserve inner purity.

But is it really true that the man of action, because he must compromise, is necessarily without conscience? We must keep in mind that renunciation of action is an omission to act, and hence itself a kind of action, namely, an action by which one makes sure that the ideal, which can be realized only through action, remains unattainably remote. A man who cannot rise to action because he objects to indispensable compromises, assumes responsibility for the fact that whatever step forward might have been taken through compromise has not been taken.

If, however, compromise denotes surrendering partial realization of an ideal goal possible under the given circumstances in favor of another goal, then it is indeed reprehensible. But that is a truism. On the other hand, compromise is not reprehensible if it denotes a concession made to secure the most valuable result possible in the given circumstances. Then both the usefulness and ethical necessity of compromise may be asserted: for we cannot assume that the action most valuable under the given circumstances will coincide directly with the ideally desirable action. If the two diverge, the ideal itself requires compromise, and a man who condemns such compromise as a matter of principle is not an idealist, but a doctrinaire.

We can condemn compromise on two grounds: either because we want more, or because we want less than what can be achieved through compromise. Where more is attainable, the acceptance of a compromise would be reprehensible; where more is not attainable, the rejection of a compromise would amount to surrender of the ideal.

If we call the willingness to accept compromise opportunism, then it follows that opportunism is a direct consequence of reasonable conduct, since ideals can be realized only step by step. Thus we may speak of an ideal opportunism, which consists in subordinating goals that are good in themselves to goals that are the best overall under the given circumstances. In other words, unconditional rejection of opportunism is not a consequence of idealism, but a sure sign of the pseudo idealism which would rather indulge in self-deception than be active in the realization of the ideal. We may say that willingness to compromise is a test of the seriousness of a man's idealism.

80. Idealism and Enthusiasm

The virtue of clarity of mind is not a sufficient condition of ideal character. It is not sufficient that our reflection should be so developed as to give us insight into the demands of the ideal; this insight must also have the power necessary to move our will. Subjection of the will to such insight we call the virtue of readiness for the ideal. We can speak of ideal attitude only when the ideal norm motivates the will.

When we say that insight into the ideal norm motivates the will, we do not mean merely that the will is in fact directed toward an action in conformity with the ideal; for this may also be the case where the will is moved by an emotional impulse, and where the action merely happens to be identical with whatever action would be produced by an ideal motive. Nor is the difference here eliminated if the emotional impulse moving the will is in turn the consequence of an ideal impulse. An affect may be aroused in us precisely because we are influenced by an ideal impulse. Such an affect, aroused by an ideal impulse and directed toward the object of this ideal impulse, is the affect of enthusiasm. An action deriving from an affect is not necessarily in contradiction with the ideal, but such an action is not reflective. Nor does a man acting on the basis of enthusiasm always act unreflectively. But he is unreflective if he acts not merely *with* but also *from* enthusiasm, that is, if enthusiasm is for him the condition for following the ideal impulse. We call such a man an enthusiast.

The idealist must consequently be distinguished from the enthusiast as much as from the visionary. The enthusiast leaves the conformity of his actions with the ideal to chance. Whether he acts in conformity with the ideal or not depends in his case on an affect. But since enthusiasm is an affect, it is not enduring. "Enthusiasm is not like a herring," says Goethe, "you cannot keep it pickled for several years." A man who follows the ideal only from enthusiasm will become unfaithful to it as soon as his enthusiasm wanes, as it will if the resistance he meets is sufficiently strong to outlast the affect. But a man who pursues his ideal with deliberation, even though he may be enthusiastic, will not be swerved from his purpose when the power of resistance cripples his enthusiasm; for his determination does not depend on it.

What is the temper of a man who emancipates the ideality of his conduct from chance and thus remains faithful to his ideal, whether events be favorable or unfavorable? His mood is one of resignation. By renouncing the impossible in advance, and concentrating his energies on realizing the ideal within the limits of the possible, he achieves that indestructible serenity which is produced only by the consciousness of standing on unshakably firm ground. Therefore resignation ought to be man's predominant mood. It does not preclude his being elated by success, but thanks to it he is less dependent on success, and willingly accepts what does not depend on his will. Only resignation guarantees steadfastness of purpose, and frees us from the danger inherent in disillusionment, because resignation from the outset makes us rule out the factor of good luck; only through resignation can we gain the kind of ethical self-reliance that is not a gift of fortune. Luck is always capricious, no matter how long it may smile on us, for it does not depend on ourselves, and consequently we cannot rely on it. A man who makes himself hostage to the vagaries of fortune voluntarily surrenders his freedom and remains at best a slave to fortune who merely happens to be lucky.

SECTION 2. MATERIAL THEORY OF IDEALS

Introduction

81. Transition to Material Theory of Ideals

THE VIRTUE of clarity of mind is opposed, as we have seen, to dullness of mind on the one hand, and to confusion of mind on the other, a confusion striking the very form of the ideal, even before touching its content. There is another form of confusion which, while relating to the content of the ideal, nevertheless has its source in a failure to understand the form of the ideal. What is misunderstood here is the principle of ideal objectivity, which is an attribute of form. The failure to comprehend this principle results in admitting the possibility of an ideal that has no universally valid content, an ideal, that is, whose content cannot be determined scientifically, being left to the subjective approval or discretion of the individual. But to determine the content of the ideal objectively is precisely the task of the material theory of ideals. That is why this task, which we are about to undertake, seems so paradoxical, particularly in the light of the skepticism prevalent today. In order to obviate this skepticism, however, it is sufficient to establish the principle of ideal objectivity. Since this principle is analytic, the advocate of skepticism can then be compelled by the mere force of logic either to grant the objectivity of the ideal or to deny the existence of ideals altogether.

Indeed, the ideal of character or, as we may also call it, the ideal of idealism, which is deduced solely on the basis of the proposition asserting the existence of the ideal, logically presupposes the existence of another ideal different from it, and with a specific content. A man is an idealist if he subjects his will to his insight into the ideal. This is possible only if we presuppose insight into an ideal with a specific objective content, which motivates the idealist's will.

But cannot this ideal be the ideal of idealism itself? Such an objection would be sophistical, for it involves a logical absurdity. If we say that the ideal which motivates the idealist's will is none other than that of idealism itself, then we would be explaining idealism, not by an ideal, but by some such statement as this: idealism motivates the will through insight into the ideal that the will is motivated by insight into the ideal. We would not be one whit the wiser, and we would face an endless regression. The elucidation of the ideal of idealism presupposes the existence of another ideal, and this other ideal cannot be again elucidated by the ideal to be explained. It is impossible to uphold the theory of ideals as a formal theory, while denying it competence to determine what is the ideal norm. Thus mere logic compels us to pass from the formal theory of ideals to the tasks of the material theory of ideals. If we repudiate this task, we must also repudiate the formal theory of ideals.

Moreover, we know from the analytic principle of ideal autonomy, that an ideal with a specific content exists, and that we can achieve certain insight into the ideal after sufficient reflection. It is a ridiculous and foolish enterprise to praise idealism, while condemning the attempt to determine the content of the ideal as impossible or superfluous.

This problem, however, cannot be solved by means of logic alone. We must go beyond the concept of the ideal, and formulate a criterion of the ideal, which we cannot develop from the concept by any device of logic. What we need here is a synthetic proposition.

Nor can the problem of content be solved empirically any more than it can be solved logically. Experience supports the statement that actions are actually striven for or regarded as worthy of being striven for; but for an answer to the question of whether these actions are really worth striving for, we need a criterion independent of all experience, which consequently must be found in a synthetic judgment a priori.

Unlike the criterion of duty, the criterion here cannot be merely formal and restrictive in character: for whereas duty only limits our choice of goals by a negative condition, the ideal is to guide our choice and name our true goals, i.e., point out those deserving of preference. For this purpose, a positive criterion is needed.

The proposition designating this positive criterion cannot be validated here but only stated as a principle. This does not mean that it is a dogma; it is a proposition that is rigorously validated in the critique of practical reason.*

We call the ideal introduced by this proposition, the ideal of culture (*Bildung*). The term "culture" is used here in a sense different from the way we have used it before (p. 34): it denotes the content of the ideal rather than the fulfillment of its demands.

* See footnote, p. xiv.

Chapter 1. Ideals of Culture

82. Rational Self-Determination

CULTURE basically denotes the shaping of minds, according to discernible patterns. Consequently, culture is a characteristic that admits of degrees. It will be the more complete, the more minds are formed on the one hand, and the more they are formed on the other. Culture depends first on the degree of variety of that which is formed, and second on the degree of consistency of the formed whole.

However, we speak of culture in the narrower sense only where that which is formed is identical with that which forms, i.e., where we are dealing with self-formation, or autonomous formation, as we may put it. Self-formation presupposes a faculty of autonomous activity. This autonomous activity is actually what we may designate as life in the narrower sense of the term: for life is the property which enables a being to form and to preserve itself autonomously. We also speak of life in a broader sense, referring to a physical process which is perpetuated through interaction between inner and outer forces, without being determined by any inherent capacity for autonomous activity. Such a system may appear more or less self-sufficient, i.e., have a higher or lower degree of spontaneity.

The term "life" in its proper sense, however, applies only to rational beings, for only these are capable of autonomous activity. The faculty of autonomous activity is reason; the faculty of forming oneself in conformity with reason, is will.

The ideal of culture, then, has meaning only in relation to rational beings; and the first thing it requires of them is to subject the conduct of their lives to their will. But the will is for its part moved by impulses. These impulses are either aroused by accidental external impressions, or they spring from the very heart of reason. If the will is determined by an accidental external impression unrelated to reason, then it depends on something alien, and we are not confronted with autonomous ac-

183

tivity. In true autonomous activity, the will is not moved by accidental, blind, instinctual impulses; on the contrary, the will dominates such impulses and being a reflective will determines itself by intervening in the mechanism of impulses and by redeeming the motive of the will from accident.

But even reflective motivation is not sufficient to secure autonomous activity in the full sense of the term. For even an impulse aroused by external impressions, i.e., a sensual impulse, can serve as a reflective motive of the will. We still must ask whether the will is determined by a sensual interest or is self-determined. Only in the latter case, only if the will is determined by reason, can we speak of autonomous activity.

Accordingly, *the ideal of culture is nothing but rational self-determination or rule of the rationally determined will over life.*

We have thus actually formulated a criterion of ideals, which is not a mere restatement, however disguised, of the ideal of idealism. Although our definition of the ideal of culture—since the term "rational self-determination" can also denote "autonomy"—might be confused with the formal analytical principle of ideal autonomy, it actually designates an entirely different principle. For the principle of ideal autonomy leaves the content of the ideal undetermined, and requires only that we have insight into this content, while in the new principle, rationality means not merely possession of insight into the ideal, but everything implied by the faculty of true autonomous activity.

We regard rationality as the distinguishing characteristic of man. But man is not only a rational being; he is also a natural being, for he is governed by natural laws, not only by ideals. Therefore, rationality exists in man only as a potential, and according to natural law it must remain undetermined whether and to what extent he is going to cultivate, during his life, what he brings into the world as his potential; it remains to be seen whether anyone who is potentially a rational being will also show himself rational in his life. For this very reason and no other, the rationality of life can constitute an ideal, and hence become an ethical task for man. The task is one of developing and manifesting what exists by natural law in man only as a disposition. The value of human life depends on whether and to what extent this development not guaranteed by any natural law actually takes place.

Hence the ideal just formulated can also be designated as the ideal of humanity; thus we may restore an old and venerable word to its original meaning, the only meaning worthy of it.

83. Love of Truth, Love of Beauty, Love of Justice

We are now confronted with the question, What specific ideals can be inferred from the principle of the material theory of ideals as we have formulated it? The ideal requires the development of reason both as a theoretical and as a practical faculty, the cultivation of both our knowledge and our interests. Practical reason as the faculty of interests embraces moral as well as aesthetic interest. Moral interest applies to what the moral law declares to be preferable. In this general sense, therefore, it is no more than interest in justice. On the other hand, I call that interest aesthetic which applies to the positively valuable as such—i.e., that which is desirable objectively and positively—in other words, the beautiful.

Accordingly, the ideal of culture requires that we develop our knowledge, our interest in justice, and our interest in the beautiful. Thus we obtain three ideals—love of truth, love of justice, and love of beauty.

For the correct understanding of our deduction and for the correct application of the ideals thus formulated, a few additional remarks are necessary.

Culture refers to the rationality of life in all of its aspects; hence, the particular ideals deduced from the ideal of culture are not independent of each other. Only by combining them all do we realize the ideal of culture.

Moreover, we assert the validity of these ideals only in so far as the cultivation of knowledge, and of our interests in justice and in beauty, depends on our will. There is no ethical obligation to possess knowledge, or to have an interest in justice and in beauty; there is only an ethical obligation to cultivate knowledge, and to develop by our human will our interests in justice and in beauty.

Finally, a purely terminological remark, which is nevertheless important if we are to avoid misunderstandings. We can speak of love for justice or for truth only in a figurative sense; for love refers directly only to the beautiful. Love is essentially an interest in what is recognized to be objectively and positively valuable, i.e., the beautiful. Hence all love, in the proper sense of this term, springs from love of beauty. But our terminology is nevertheless indirectly justified. For the content of the ideal of culture is formulated on the basis of an aesthetic valuation of our conduct. The ideal is the standard of this valuation. Now, the beauty of one's life, which originally alone determines the content of the ideal, includes the development of one's interest in justice and in truth. Hence we may speak, in a figurative sense, of love for truth and of love for justice.

84. On the Method of Deriving the Three Ideals

In the light of our last remark, it seems that love of beauty is the general ideal, from which love of truth and love of justice are derived only as particular instances. This gives rise to a dialectical difficulty, involved in the derivation of the three ideals: for previously the ideals of love for truth and of love for justice were co-ordinated with, not subordinated to, the ideal of love for beauty.

To clear up this difficulty, we must take another look at our derivation of the ideal of love for beauty. Then we find that this ideal is not a separate, independent, fundamental ideal, but that it is, and has to be, deduced itself from another ideal. To love beauty is to ascribe value to the beautiful object. But an ideal cannot be deduced on the basis of the aesthetic value of any object, it can be deduced only on the basis of the aesthetic value of our action. Hence, we are confronted with the question, What is it that gives an action a positive, and consequently an aesthetic, value? In other words, we ask what is the criterion of the positive value of an *action*. Actions by which something beautiful is produced can themselves be beautiful, in so far as reason manifests itself in them. But the exercise of aesthetic interest is here co-ordinated with the exercise of the faculty of cognition and of the moral interest.

It remains true that we ascribe value to the development of human reason on the basis of an *aesthetic* principle of valuation. It is the beauty of one's life that is manifested through the development of reason; hence we may say that the development of reason produces something beautiful, and is thus governed by the ideal of love for beauty. A peculiar relationship prevails here, which we must interpret correctly in order to understand how we arrive at the three co-ordinated ideals. On the one hand, we derive the particular ideal of love for beauty from the ideal of the development of reason. On the other hand, the particular ideal of love for beauty includes the ideal of love for the beauty of one's life, which again refers us to the ideal of the development of reason. We thus obtain an endless series. But we do not become involved in a circle; for the series in question is progressive, not regressive, because the ideal of love for beauty includes not the ideal of the *beauty* of one's life, but the ideal of *love for the beauty* of one's life. This peculiar relation is illustrated by a diagram.

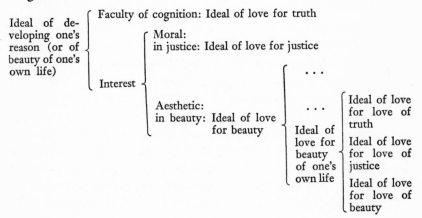

85. Love of Truth

We shall begin our discussion of the particular ideals with the ideal of love for truth, which must be distinguished from the duty to be truthful to oneself. The ideal of love for truth goes beyond this duty, since according to it true knowledge is valuable whether or not it is necessary for the fulfillment of duties. At the same time, we must keep in mind that this ideal is derived from the general ideal of culture; consequently, acquisition of knowledge can have ideal value only in so far as it contributes to culture. Moreover, the degree of man's culture does not depend directly on the wealth of his information. While his culture is the more complete, the greater his capacity to learn, information contributes to his culture only in so far as this knowledge is formed, i.e., rationally assimilated. The ideal of love for truth does not demand a random accumulation of data; rather, this ideal can be realized only by active, autonomous assimilation of knowledge; only then can we speak of an enhancement of culture. Love of truth never strives for mere data, but for the cognition of unity and integration.

The ideal of love for truth also goes beyond the duty to be truthful to others. It demands truth even where the duty to act justly does not demand it. The cultured man will not deviate from truthfulness even where duty does not forbid him to do so, but only where he is so bidden by an opposite duty.

86. Love of Justice

We have recognized that it is our duty to act justly; we may now ask to what extent we may also speak of an ideal of love for justice. For justice as enjoined by duty cannot in itself be an object of love. The law demands that we subject ourselves to the norm of justice; this law can arouse respect, but not love.

The duty to act justly demands only that we subordinate our own interest to the preponderant interest of others; but the ideal demands that justice prevail everywhere. There is an ethical interest that goes beyond the interest in one's own fulfillment of duty. For we have an interest in anything that we recognize as valuable. Now, on the basis of the moral law we obtain a valuation by which any violation of duty is directly condemned. Ethical unworth thus attaches to any situation in which the moral law is not fulfilled.

Here we have the foundation of the interest in the unconditional rule of justice in society, an interest which transcends that in fulfilling one's own duty, since it is directed toward the fulfillment of duty on the part of all other members of society. I shall designate this interest as the interest in right—an interest identical with love of justice. Because we have this interest we strive to make the rule of right in society independent of its members' sense of duty and of their willingness to do their duty, which are in themselves fortuitous, and we strive to enforce right even where good will is lacking. Here is the place for honor as an ethical value, which we had to deny it in the theory of duties. We saw there that there is no duty to uphold one's honor over and above the duty to act justly, i.e., that there is no duty to respect the dignity of one's own person; but there is, as we find now, an ideal of love of honor. For love of honor presupposes an interest in preserving one's own right, which is manifested in the readiness to react against injuries to one's right.

87. Love of Beauty

In order to understand the ideal of love for beauty, it is important to interpret the expression "love of beauty" in the light of our derivation of the ideal of beauty from the ideal of culture. Love of beauty must not be confused with the interest in the mere intercourse with the beautiful, nor with the interest in the good. Love of beauty as such is as different from mere inclination as it is from respect.

Respect expresses the interest in what is ethically good. Respect is exacted: it arises when an object is seen to be adequate to an ethical norm. But love is a free interest, i.e., not based on any compulsion; and pure love is not a sensual interest, not merely a blind interest arising from an inclination, but an interest which grants a value to the object itself, whereas inclination appreciates an object only in so far as it affects the subject.

There is an interest in the beautiful, which is purely empirical. This interest, entirely different from love of beauty, is actually directed only to the pleasure of contemplating beauty, but not directly to the beautiful as such. This purely empirical interest gives the beautiful an indirect value, in so far as it is the cause of our pleasure. The value which it grants the beautiful derives only from pleasurableness, whereas what counts most in love of beauty is the objective value of the beautiful. The empirical interest in the beautiful does not go beyond the effect of the beautiful object on the subject. Once the object has me under its sway, I enjoy it and it gives me pleasure. The existence of the beautiful object is accidental for the pleasure I have in it. The pleasure would be the same if it could be produced otherwise, i.e., independently of the existence of the object I find beautiful.

Love of beauty is on the contrary interested in the existence of the beautiful object as such, independently of any pleasure had in the contemplation of the beautiful. This love arises from the concern that the beautiful exist. Thus, the mere desire for pleasure or enjoyment differs from real love of beauty. The higher the aesthetic culture of a man, the less his need for mere pleasure, and vice versa.

88. Misunderstandings of the Ideal

THE CULTIVATION of reason is possible only if reflection is developed sufficiently to raise to clear consciousness what has lain obscurely in reason all the time. Only through reflection can reason determine the will and attain to control of life.

However, reflection or understanding * serves merely as a means to raise to consciousness the ideal goals originally set by reason.

If this be overlooked, two opposite errors will arise. On the one hand, one may uphold the requirement that decisions be determined by means of reflection, and yet a specific characterization of the content of ideal goals may be wanting, because the understanding in itself has no content. On the other hand, since these ideal goals have a source other than the understanding, one may sacrifice the requirement that decisions be reflective, and seek a content for ideal goals elsewhere. We thus obtain either reflectiveness without ideal content, or conversely, a content without reflection. In each case the criterion of the ideal is distorted.

If life is judged by logic alone, our only value will be purposefulness. Reflection can teach us only to subordinate the appropriate means to given goals having their source outside the understanding. It gives us no categorical norms to determine the content of such goals, but only hypothetical norms or rules of prudence. The relation of means to end is in itself only a theoretical relation; it expresses a natural law indicating the causes of an effect we have taken as a goal. This relation is important practically, because having set ourselves a purpose we are logically required to be purposeful. Whoever wills an end, must by the same token will the conditions for its realization: it would be contradictory to will something without willing such con-

---

* The terms "reflection" and "understanding" are used here interchangeably. See *Socratic Method and Critical Philosophy*, p. 103: "Reflection, *qua* the capacity to think, cannot enrich the content of knowledge. . . . (It) is in itself empty."

ditions. The concept of mere purposefulness, however, if correctly understood, does not lead us to any ethical norms. The false ideal of culture, according to which the purposeful shaping of a life constitutes its value, I call the ideal of utility.

On the basis of such an ideal, actions can be evaluated only from the point of view of their usefulness, and their usefulness is in turn determined by ends which remain themselves undetermined. However, the ideal of utility can be applied only when ends are given, and when the usefulness of any action can be measured by them. These ends may be set either by the agent or by other members of society; and according to whether usefulness is evaluated in terms of ends of the agent or of the others, we may speak of an ideal of personal utility or of an ideal of social utility. Clearly what would be appropriate in determining the content of an ideal would be at best social utility, since individual utility is in fact a mere precept of prudence.

But on closer scrutiny, the ideal of social utility is also revealed to be an ideal empty of content. What constitutes usefulness for society? Society as such does not pursue ends, only individual members of society do. Consequently the ideal of social utility can require only that individual members of society have ends in view. These ends may have to do with the realization of accidental or of necessary interests, i.e., they may pertain either to the welfare of the members of society or to their culture.

In the former case, the ideal of social utility would actually make the individual a mere means to be used at will by the others. The ideal would demand that he subordinate himself to the subjective interests, and hence to the good pleasure of the others.

In the latter case, our attempt to determine the content of the ideal moves in a circle. For such a principle, to be applicable, would presuppose that the content of the ideal has been determined independently of this principle, and that on the basis of this content one could decide what is required for the culture of the members of society. The content of the ideal of culture cannot be determined by what serves to realize the ideal of culture.

The error here consists in overlooking the emptiness of the understanding, and by the same token, the emptiness of the mere requirement of purposefulness.

Those who try to avoid the error involved in the ideal of social utility, but are unable to see the difference between the faculty of reason and the faculty of understanding, will be led to take for their ideal of culture a goal determined by external norms. These norms may be conceived as expressing the personal will of a human or divine being, of an individual or of a class of persons; they may be based on an exemplary pattern that is to be imitated, or they may be inherent in the demand that we observe the dead external forms of tradition or of custom. In all such cases we are dealing with an external norm, independent of our reason, and determined by some accidental fact. The ideal here can demand only blind subjection to such an external norm, but it is impossible to see on what the value of observing this norm is based. Ideals implying deference to such external norms determined by the accident of history may be called ideals of reverence.

The value of reverence is always a derivative value: it presupposes another value from which a ground for reverence can be derived. All those who advance ideals of reverence commit the error of presenting this derived value as the original one, and of overlooking the fact that a valuation independent of considerations of reverence must exist before reverence can be an ethical interest. And it is precisely this original valuation that is lacking here.

It is easy to see why those who realize that such ideals are hollow, and who nevertheless refuse to see the source of the ideal in reason, try to determine the ideal in opposition to the warped ideals of utility or reverence. But this effort leads only to another series of false ideals.

If one starts from the premise that mere utility cannot be the content of an ideal, and, lacking any other content for it, attempts to determine that content as being merely the opposite of utility, one arrives at a peculiar ideal which I call that of futility—an ideal in which mere absence of purposefulness is raised to the status of an ideal value. It is the ideal of purposelessness or inefficiency. From the correct premise that mere usefulness is not sufficient to endow an action with ideal value, the false conclusion is drawn that absence of usefulness is a condition of the ideal value. We thus arrive at the ideal of a maximum prevention of the attainment of ends originating in other interests; this leads to the extreme ideal of asceticism. For asceticism consists in striving to gratify interests as little as possible. It is true that gratification of interests as such has no ideal value; but it does not follow that ideal value attaches to violation of interests.

If the content of the ideal is defined in opposition to the pseudo ideal of reverence, mere independence of external norms is proclaimed as the ideal. Here autonomy is recognized as an ideal end, though merely as the opposite to the ideal that might otherwise be required by an external norm. We thus arrive at a false ideal of originality, which requires the individual to be as different as possible.

The true principle of autonomous activity, however, is reason; and since reason is not recognized here, this alleged autonomy is actually only a form of heteronomy. A man who seeks originality at all costs is just as much enslaved as a man who professes the ideal of reverence; indeed, the former's dependence is even greater, since he deceives himself, while the latter does not. His striving for originality makes him dependent upon the actions of others: he must wait for what they will do in order then to do the opposite. Thus his actions have no value by themselves, but only in their relation to those of others, namely, in the fact that he does something different from what they do. The ideal of originality is therefore the poorest and most wretched of all, for it is defined by mere otherness, i.e., by an empty reflective concept.

89. One-sided Ideals of Culture

In addition to such perverted ideals of culture, it is possible to formulate others which spring from one-sided interpretations of the ideal of culture, by raising one of the three particular ideals—love of truth, love of beauty, or love of justice—to the position of the sole ideal of culture. This gives rise to three one-sided ideals of culture.

The ideal of the supremacy of love for truth leads to an intellectualist conception of life, according to which the value of life is to be sought exclusively in the acquisition of knowledge, and the scientist is to be looked upon as the highest embodiment of man. This ideal is one-sided. For in the domain of nature, where human activity is required to realize the good and the beautiful, the intellectual pride of the mere theoretician does not express true humanity, but rather one of its ugliest perversions. Reason, in order to manifest itself, requires the cultivation of interest in the good and the beautiful just as much as in mere knowledge.

The aesthetic approach to life, according to which only the artist represents true humanity, is based on the supremacy of the ideal of love for beauty. Here the beauty of one's life is sacrificed to artistic beauty. But a full life includes love of truth and love of justice in addition to love of beauty. We shall therefore condemn such a conception of life as one-sided.

The ideal of the supremacy of moral interest leads to a one-sided moral conception of life. This conception cannot be applied consistently. For the moral law provides us only with a restrictive criterion of values, and cannot in itself determine any positive value of life. It prescribes a mold of life which can be realized only if it shapes life's richness. But this very richness is here sacrificed to the mere mold. Thus the one-sided moral conception of life directly defeats its own purpose.

90. Action *vs.* Contemplation

We arrive at another important opposition between two possible approaches to life, when we consider that interests may be cultivated along two different lines. For an interest can manifest itself as a mere feeling for value on the one hand, and as an impulse to act on the other. According to whether we lay emphasis on feeling or on action, we obtain a contemplative or a practical approach to life. This gives rise to a contrast between the contemplative and the practical ideal, between an approach to life that shuns action and another that rejoices in action.

This latter approach is opposed to the intellectualist conception of life, as well as to what I call, by way of contrast, the romantic or sentimental, which places exclusive emphasis on feeling.

The sentimental approach to life sets store only by man's susceptibility to external impressions, not the autonomous activity by which he shapes his life. We shall give preference to the mode of life that rejoices in action: for a life is full only if it is capped with action.

Attempts have often been made to justify the deprecation of action and the one-sided exaltation of emotional life, with the argument that ideal feelings are lofty, and that they are debased by contact with real life. But such an approach to life, in which action is replaced by enthusiasm, is based on self-deception: for all enthusiasm, if it be authentic, is enthusiasm for something that has ideal value, and that can be realized only by the will.

Those who embrace a sentimental conception of life content themselves with a merely imaginary gratification of the pure impulses; they seek the value of life in dreams of perfection, and thus shirk the task of realizing what is within the power of the will. They look upon the so-called realistic conception of life as inferior, pride themselves on their idealism, and scorn outward action. They justify their scorn for such action on the ground that it has no intrinsic ideal value. Now, it is true that we attach no value to action per se, for we judge a man by his attitude. But it is fallacious to infer from this—as one often does—that contemplation is superior to action. For we cannot speak of attitude where there is no readiness to act. Attitude denotes direction of the will. A man with an idealist attitude subjects his will to the ideal norm, and hence is ready to act in conformity with the ideal. This latter ideal cannot be again defined as an ideal of attitude: it refers to acts, it directly sets a task for the will.

The active approach to life is also sometimes deprecated by equating it with the ideal of restless busyness serving no higher purpose. In reality, there is no contradiction between the ideal of an active life and true serenity; for tranquillity that is truly inward rather than mere lifelessness can only be the consequence of a man's self-contentment. And a man cannot achieve self-contentment by being inactive, but only by living in harmony with his higher goals, only by being active on their behalf.

Contemplation is held to be superior to action on the basis of still another error, to which a noncritical ethics can easily succumb, and which we shall therefore discuss in greater detail. This error consists in setting up devoutness (which is itself a misconceived religious ideal) as an ethical ideal. Is such a religious ideal of a contemplative life superior to the ethical ideal of an active life? Before discussing this question, we may point out at once that we can speak of an ideal of devoutness only if it stands for an ethical task. Consequently, it must be either identical with the ethical ideal as such or implied by it. The very definition of the ethical ideal excludes the conception of devoutness as an independent ideal, distinct from the ethical ideal.

As for the ideal of devoutness itself, we must observe that devoutness, viewed as a practical attitude of the mind rather than mere faith in certain religious tenets, presupposes a specific religious interest; devoutness consists in the cultivation of this interest. We may indeed distinguish such a religious interest from the ethical interest, but in doing so we must guard against an ambiguity. A religious interest can be only an interest in whatever has objective value. But the term "objective value" may mean two very different things. We may take it to stand for the opposite of subjective, in the sense of arbitrary value. Or we may mean something quite different, namely, something we must be content to acknowledge, something we can do no more than contemplate, as opposed to something that becomes a goal for our action, that sets a task for our will. "Objective" in the former sense (i.e., when we use this term to designate a value not subject to our discretion) does not imply any conflict whatever between objective religious and ethical valuation; for in this sense ethical values are also objective values not subject to individual discretion. Only if we interpret the term "objective" in the second sense do we obtain a distinction between the ethical and the religious. We are here led to the previously discussed distinction between subjective and objective teleology. Subjective teleology deals with what is valuable for us, i.e., that which is to be created by our action; objective teleology deals with what is intrinsically valuable, by virtue of its very existence—that which we do not create and can only acknowledge as valuable.

Whoever fails to distinguish between the concepts of the objectively valuable and the ethically good is inevitably led to embrace a one-sided ideal of contemplation. This, then, is the error that accounts for the fanciful and lazy conception of life, whose advocates judge ideals, not by their practical implications, but by their value as objects for contemplation. The ideals are conceived not as something to be realized, but only as something to be dreamed about, and there arises the notion that they soar so high above the real world that by striving to realize them we can only drag them down, desecrate them. This produces a disposition to accept reality as it is, to make no ideal demands upon it. A man with such a disposition escapes from irksome reality into the realm of dreams and beautiful imagery, i.e., the realm of art. It must be noted, however, that only romantic art is escapist in this sense; for all genuine art expresses love of beauty, and thus springs from an interest in the reality of the beautiful and must always lead us back to this reality. True art cannot forgo representing ideals of life, and is consequently incompatible with a romantic approach to life. Romantic art renounces this claim, and hence its adequate expression is the fairy tale.

The self-deception implied by such an approach, which is a cloak for weakness and withdrawal from action, finds its most refined expression in hero worship, i.e., the veneration of a man regarded as the embodiment of an ideal. Hero worship is based on the failure to recognize man's imperfection, and imperils ideal aspiration by robbing the ideal of ethical significance. As the hero worshiper gains greater experience and by the same token greater insight, he suffers the inevitable disillusionment, and his faith in the ideal is destroyed together with his faith in human perfection. A human personality can never embody, but only symbolize an ideal. If this truth is ignored, if the symbolic relation is transformed into one of logical identity, hero worship becomes mere deification, and the worshipers end up by bowing to their hero whose authority they accept unquestioningly. This leads inevitably to a depreciation of the worshiper's own personality, to an attitude of resignation in regard to his own status and potential. He places his hero so high that he can no longer aspire to be a hero himself. Thus hero worship begets in the worshiper a sense of his own impotence, and cripples his ethical energy. All he can do is to devote himself to the worship of his hero in a passive feeling of self-contempt and mistaken humility, and to hope for redemption by the grace of a higher power. But such redemption, even if it were to fill us with bliss, could never compensate us for the loss of the value we could give ourselves through autonomous activity.

91. Inconsistency of One-sided Ideals of Culture

Correctly understood, the ideals of love for truth, beauty, and justice are interdependent. In fact, any attempt to cultivate one of the interests involved here—whether it be that in truth, in beauty, or in justice—at the expense of the others must fail, and the illusion that such attempts can be successful is created only because their inconsistency is overlooked. Indeed, closer investigation of the matter reveals the curious fact that the three ideals in question are governed by a kind of pre-established harmony.

The striving for truth, if it is carried far enough, must lead to insight into the value of developing one's moral and aesthetic interests, and by the same token, to insight into the superiority of an active life. Indeed, the value of cultivating one's moral and aesthetic interests represents a truth, and knowledge of this truth will inevitably be gained by anyone whose interest in truth is sufficiently developed. Consequently, one cannot in the long run develop the mind consistently along intellectualist lines; recognition of the truth of ethics will gradually reveal this inconsistency of intellectualism and help transcend it.

Likewise, the cultivation of love for beauty will prove inconsistent, unless it includes the beauty of one's own life, and implies, by the same token, recognition of the superior value of an active life directed not only toward beauty but also toward truth and justice. The one-sided cultivation of love for beauty flies in the face of striving for the beauty of one's own life. A man whose love of beauty is sufficiently developed will avoid such one-sidedness.

Finally, cultivation of love for justice must similarly lead to recognition of the value of love for truth and for beauty. Love of justice implies a striving for more knowledge and a practical approach to life; for without adequate knowledge and adequate insight into the value of things we could not correctly determine what justice demands in a given situation. Because the moral law is formal in character, its correct application requires an adequate knowledge of the circumstances and of the priority of the interests involved. Such priorities can be determined only on the basis of the ideal which alone provides us with a yardstick for appraising interests. This ideal cannot be wholly encompassed in the ideal of love for justice, for the interests must be correctly evaluated before we can apply the criterion of justice. Thus, sufficient cultivation of love for justice implies the development of a practical approach to life, and hence recognition of the ideals of love for truth and for beauty.

Thus we find that the three ideals of love for truth, beauty, and justice are interdependent, that if we attempt to cultivate our mind on the basis of only one of these we cannot avoid inconsistency, and that if such an attempt is carried far enough, we will automatically include the two others. Hence we may say that these ideals constitute a trinity.

Chapter 3. Vocational Ideals

92. Culture and Vocation

HAVING SHOWN the interdependence of our three ideals, we have also shown that any choice of one of them to the exclusion of the two others must be rejected. The ideal of culture requires the harmonious development of man's potentialities.

To forestall misunderstandings in this regard, we must note that a man's harmonious development, to which we attached aesthetic value, does not mean that his various potentialities are developed equally. We do not require that the notes constituting a musical harmony be struck with equal force, or that the colors of a composition be painted with equal intensity; similarly, we do not require of a cultured man that his various potentialities be equally developed. We do not produce aesthetic harmony by combining a number of uniform parts; such a harmony requires a dominant center to which the rest is subordinated, for harmony consists in such a subordination. A man with uniformly developed potentialities would be a man whose potentialities were equally lacking in development, and we would not regard such a man as cultured, but rather as a bore or a dilettante. A man has no aesthetic value unless some of his potentialities are pre-eminently developed.

We shall here disregard the fact that certain potentialities are usually developed one-sidedly because of the force of circumstance, because of the need for division of labor. It is my contention that we must require the one-sided development of certain potentialities as an ideal on purely philosophical grounds, independently of whether it is imposed by such circumstances. Such a pre-eminent cultivation of certain potentialities is what we call a man's vocation. The requirements of culture vary with vocations. Harmonious development of potentialities will have to meet different requirements, according to which potentialities are favored; in this sense we may rightly speak of ideals of culture, in the plural, and reject the opinion that there is only a single, fully determined ideal of culture.

In real life, the choice of a vocation is restricted by circumstance. To evaluate such a choice from the point of view of the ideal, we must therefore keep in mind that we are speaking here only of vocational *ideals*, and that, in accordance with the concept of the ideal, we do not demand their realization in each given case. Our task is to determine the standards to be applied when we evaluate a vocation from the point of view of the ideal, standards which ought to govern the choice of a vocation in so far as circumstances permit of a free choice. Now, an ideal vocation serves an ideal. Hence, there can be only three types of ideal vocation.

93. Ideals and Technical Vocations

Ideal vocations are opposed to technical vocations in the broadest sense of this term, i.e., vocations that do not directly serve ideal ends, but that secure for us control over external nature, wresting from it the means for the realization of our interests. But both ideal and technical vocations imply activity; the ideal of vocation rules out the idleness of a being given only to passive enjoyments.

The distinction between ideal and technical vocations does not mean that technical vocations are per se unworthy of an ideal life. When we assert the technical character of a vocation we leave open the question whether the means it produces serve ideal or non-ideal ends. But both ideal and non-ideal ends can be realized only if the means required for their realization are produced. Consequently, technical vocations are not only justified but even necessary in so far as they provide the means for realizing the ends of the ideal vocations. So long as the technical vocations are kept within their sphere, i.e., so long as they serve ideal ends and do not supplant the ideal vocations, or even serve inferior ends, there is no reason to disparage them. Technical means per se may be used to destroy as well as to further ideal values. They directly serve prudence, not wisdom. But even prudence has ethical value in so far as it serves wisdom. Those who scorn the technical vocations in the name of idealism, only reveal that their idealism is of the spurious variety. For the true idealist is interested in realizing his ideals, and he will always strive to acquire the technique required for this purpose.

Those who profess such pseudo idealism scornful of technical mediation can do so only because others are charged with the task of creating the technical prerequisites of life. The idealists who fancy themselves free actually depend on those others. Such an ideal of life is aristocratic in the worst sense of the term, for it can be realized only thanks to a class of slaves who pay the price for the aristocrats' higher spiritual values without themselves having access to them.

It is true that as cultural needs increase, more labor and an increasing specialization of functions are required. But justice demands that no one have the freedom to choose an ideal vocation at the expense of others, that each have equal access to all vocations, and that in choosing a vocation each have equal opportunity to take his own inclinations and abilities into account.

A technical vocation can be regarded as inferior to an ideal vocation only if it serves reprehensible ends, or is pursued with the claim that it directly realizes an ideal. This occurs when the converse of idleness, the mere rage for work, becomes an end in itself; when such work, which should be only a means to an end, becomes the very purpose of life, while the ideal ends are driven from their proper domain. Here we are confronted either with crude thoughtlessness as the consequence of the power of habit over the mind, or with a kind of mental derangement—namely, when mere labor as the supreme goal of life is advocated consciously and with conviction.

94. Vocations in the Service of Truth

In the light of the foregoing, we may distinguish three types of ideal vocation, namely, vocations in the service of truth, of beauty, and of justice.

We shall first consider the vocations in the service of truth. These are the vocations of the researcher. I say "researcher" rather than "scholar," because erudition is not culture, and the difference between them is precisely what distinguishes the true researcher from the mere scholar or man of learning. Erudition is merely the possession of a vast amount of knowledge. The researcher is distinguished from the scholar by independent intellectual activity, by means of which he extends the domain of knowledge. Consequently, scientific knowledge acquired by independent intellectual activity is superior to mere learning.

The ideal of love for truth gives rise to an ideal of science; for love of truth cannot be gratified by the mere accumulation of unrelated data, but requires knowledge in a higher sense, i.e., knowledge in the form of a scientific system. The ultimate goal of research, then, is science conceived of as the form of knowledge. Scientific form, however, must not be regarded as an end in itself. The content of knowledge must also be taken into account. Science is the proper goal of research only if it serves to extend our knowledge of truth.

The ideal of love for truth requires that science deal with reality. It requires that insight, which rests upon pure thought, be combined with information, which we obtain by investigating facts. The pure form of thinking is sterile where its relevance to facts is left out of account, and knowledge of facts remains sterile where understanding of the laws governing those facts is lacking.

It follows that the purely historical sciences are inferior in rank to sciences requiring independent thought, i.e., sciences which rise above the mere knowledge of facts and achieve systematic form. For there is an important difference between discovering the truth, and being acquainted with what learned men have held to be the truth. The latter is merely the content of historical statements; and such statements do not bring us a step closer to the truth. Historical sciences have a scientific interest only in so far as they pursue a higher end, namely, in so far as they investigate the conditions of progress in history; and the standard by which progress is judged is the ideal. This interest, then, presupposes an independent effort to discover the truth which cannot be satisfied by reliance on second-hand sources.

The same is true of linguistic sciences, which deal not with ideas but with the expression of ideas. Interest in language is in itself a technical interest, namely, the interest in the means of communication between rational beings; these means should be subordinated to the goal of communication, and should not be regarded as valuable for their own sake. The purpose of language is to express ideas; but the purpose of ideas is not confined to their expression in language

The pursuit of an ideal vocation goes beyond the development of theoretical knowledge. For we must keep in mind that an ideal vocation, although it implies the pre-eminent cultivation of a single potentiality, refers to the total personality of the man who pursues it, since it is a requirement of the ideal of culture. The development of theoretical knowledge is in itself a technical vocation, and if it does not permeate life, if it does not contribute to the rule of reason over life, it produces only skillful scholars. The pursuit of theoretical knowledge always threatens to degenerate into a mere skill, and to lead to divorce from life. When this comes to pass, a gulf arises between theory and practice.

Only the development of knowledge itself can enable us to overcome such a danger. For if this development is complete, it includes not only theoretical but also practical knowledge, i.e., ethics. Science can thus help us to bridge the gulf between theory and practice by intervening in life and setting goals for it.

Those who deny that science has a bearing upon real life advocate a pseudo ideal of objectivity, and assert that partisanship is incompatible with objectivity. But scientific objectivity demands only that the researcher be motivated by no interest other than the pure interest in truth. Truth is objective in so far as it is not subject to our discretion; it is partisan in so far as it rules out and opposes error. Hence it requires that those who serve the truth be partisan precisely in the name of objectivity, i.e., that they oppose error.

The ideal of objectivity, then, demands that we wage battle against every kind of prejudice, and hence against dogmatism. Dogmatism is manifested in the acceptance of judgments which are not supported by sufficient evidence. A man who opposes dogmatism rejects such judgments, but does not refrain from making judgments, i.e., he is not an unprincipled advocate of a certain kind of relativism, which condemns all opinions out of fear of succumbing to dogmatism. In reality, such a relativism does not free us from the rule of dogma. Its advocates, by denying that science is competent to settle questions in dispute on the basis of rational arguments, leave it to the fanatics of dogmatism to settle these questions on unscientific grounds, for instance, on the basis of interests which influence and corrupt the motives of the judgment.

The attempt to obviate such an influence of subjective interests on scientific pursuits leads to a further distortion of the meaning of scientific objectivity. It is thought that science is best protected from the assault of subjective interests when it surrenders all its claims on life. As a result, science surrenders even those claims which it is its highest mission to uphold. For there is not only a theoretical, but also a practical truth, and accordingly not only a theoretical but also a practical science, whose task is the scientific investigation of the value of life. In pursuing this task science comes into conflict with subjective interests, which seek to shape life to their own advantage. If science fails in its task of upholding the ideal claims on life in a spirit of rigorous objectivity, free from utopianism and sentimentalism, the ideal values are left at the mercy of brutal accident in the struggle between conflicting interests. Thus scientists who profess a false ideal of objectivity contribute to discrediting the ideal goals of life.

Science suffers an even greater loss of dignity when the researcher not only desists from defending the truth, but also puts his work at the service of designs that go against the ideal ends of life. This gives rise to a perversion of mind, which, while never questioning the validity of ethical ideals, uses them as a cover for sordid pursuits. Such a sophistical attitude seeks to obscure the truth wherever it contradicts people's desires; instead, subjective interests with the help of pseudo arguments are represented as meeting the requirements of the ideal. Ethical principles have such power over man that they are effective even when their content has been falsified. This state of affairs is exploited by those pursuing sordid designs. They artfully pervert some ideal, representing it as underlying their purpose, in order to whitewash their designs and even to set them up as ethical principles.

Authentic science is dedicated to fight against such abuse of science. No matter how cruelly ideals may be trampled underfoot in life, it is the task of true science to preserve them in its shrine, so that they may be, from this refuge, passed on to life.

Scientific freedom requires that no limitations whatsoever be placed on the sternest exploration of truth—this requirement is directly implicit in scientific objectivity as we have defined it. But would a limitation of freedom of inquiry be in order if some ideal were in conflict with the love of truth? We consider this question answered in advance by our discussion of the self-refuting character of all one-sided ideals of culture. If we consistently adhere to the ideals of love for beauty and justice we will be inevitably led to recognize the ideal of love for truth. The ideal of love for truth is therefore not only compatible with the other ideals, but is actually implied by them. In other words, there can be no ideal setting an ethical limit to the task of inquiry into truth.

It is the noblest task of the scientist to stand guard over the freedom of science. Whoever ventures to seek the truth only within limits arbitrarily set by some authority, degrades himself to the status of a skilled artisan, and yields up, together with the honor of his vocation, the prestige of science itself.

95. Vocations in the Service of Beauty

Let us now consider vocations serving the beautiful. If we class such vocations under the concept of art, we must give this term a sense which in some respects is narrower, and in others broader than is usually the case. For we shall designate as art any vocation serving the ideal of beauty.

The creative vocation, viewed as an ideal vocation, does not serve mere aesthetic pleasure. Pleasure depends on the sensations of the individual, and pleasure cannot be prescribed by any ideal of culture. The ideal task of art is to assert the objective significance of the beautiful; for love of beauty refers only to this objective significance.

The ideal of love for beauty must further be distinguished from the ideal of cultivating one's taste. The ability to form correct aesthetic judgments can in fact be cultivated in accordance with an ideal of good taste, but concern with such cultivation does not necessarily coincide with interest in the beautiful; taste may refer to merely imagined, or reproduced beauty as well as to real beauty. But the ideal of love for beauty aims at direct contact with the beautiful, and is not satisfied with representations of it, even as the ideal of love for truth demands a direct relationship with truth, for which second-hand contact is no substitute.

While thus restricting the scope of the concept of art, we must broaden it sufficiently to include all vocations serving the beautiful. Since love of beauty extends to natural beauty in the broadest sense, it embraces the beauty of life itself. Consequently, the vocations serving beauty include the vocation of giving beautiful form to life, and hence the art of creative human development. Creative vocations in the current sense of the word are but an insignificant fraction of the vocations serving beauty.

In fact, the pure interest we designate as love of beauty is essentially an interest in perfection, i.e., a religious interest in the beautiful—a circumstance that is overlooked by those who confuse love of beauty with a merely subjective interest in the contemplation of beauty, with aesthetic pleasure, or with mere judgments of taste independent of any interest in the reality of the beautiful, although referring to it objectively. This accounts for the fact that all true and great art has always served religion: for art is genuine and great only if it serves love of the beautiful, and hence religious interest in the beautiful. The vocations serving religion—if we take this word in its noblest sense, excluding superstition—must therefore be classified as vocations serving love of beauty.

96. Vocations in the Service of Justice

We deduced the ideal of love for justice from an evaluation, in terms of right, as to whether or not a given social condition meets the requirements of justice. Interest in justice goes beyond interest in fulfilling one's duty, and aims at upholding right in general. The object of this interest, in so far as it is directed toward society, is not the attitude of individual members of society, but their conduct toward one another. Only the pedagogue is directly concerned with developing man's rightful attitude. The ideal of love for justice aims at safeguarding the rule of right in society against haphazard influences, at making it independent of how individual members of society are disposed toward right. The vocations serving love of justice are therefore vocations serving the ideal of a just society, i.e., a condition in which right is upheld regardless of whether the individual members of society happen to be men of good will or ill will. Such safeguarding of right is possible only on the basis of an organization that champions right.

Such an organization is what we call the state. The ideal vocation in the service of love for justice is the vocation of the statesman.

Now, the state as it actually exists is a fortuitous product of nature; for the powers that be are compelled by no natural law to work toward a just society. Consequently, since the state is not directly under the control of the individual, men *qua* rational beings are confronted with the task of creating an institution for the purpose of bringing the state closer to the ideal of a just society. An institution aiming at conquest of political power is called a political party. Political parties become embroiled with one another, because each pursues a different end, and each strives to control the state in order to use it as a means to this end. If we pursue the ideal end of a just society, the ideal of love for justice requires us to create a political party devoted to the realization of that end. Thus, side by side with the statesman in the narrower sense we have the politician.

The politician's vocation is ideal only if it serves ends prescribed by the ideal of a just society. Consequently, the ideal politician will fight those who seek political power in order to further subjective interests and those who seek to make power subservient to a perverted social ideal. The political task so defined joins the tasks of the scientist and the pedagogue. The scientist's function is to formulate the content of the ideal and to validate it as the only worthy end, while the pedagogue's function is to steer man's will in the direction of this end.

97. Vocational Ideals and One-sided Ideals of Culture

It is important, with respect to the theory of ideals of culture, not to confuse the ideals of vocation, which demand the pre-eminent cultivation of specific potentialities, with the one-sided ideals of culture which we must condemn. These one-sided ideals are incompatible with the requirement of harmonious development, while the ideals of vocation are based on that very requirement, which we can satisfy only by cultivating specific potentialities in preference to others; for, as we have seen, there can be no harmony without a dominant focal point. We thus have to choose, from among our potentialities, one that is to be pre-eminently developed; but this does not mean that greater merit attaches to the development of the chosen skill than to others. Contrariwise, one-sided ideals of culture always seek culture by cultivating a specific potentiality while denying merit to the cultivation of others.

Since the ideal vocations which we have deduced are all based on ideals, we must consider them as equal in value. They merely represent different methods for attaining culture. This, however, does not exclude the possibility of establishing an ideal hierarchy of ideal vocations. In this sense, we may ask which vocation deserves to be called the highest, not in respect of the subjective gratification it promises the individual—for this is not an ethical question and hence not susceptible of a universally valid answer—but in respect of the objective importance and dignity of the task involved. Since we have acknowledged that an active approach to life is preferable to a contemplative life, we shall give precedence to the vocations serving justice, for the others are much more devoted to the development of knowledge and interest.

Chapter 4. Ideals of Friendship

98. Impossibility of Duty of Sociality

SINCE ANTIQUITY, the ideal of individual culture has been put side by side in ethics with the ideal of communal culture, and there has been a dispute as to the relative rank of these ideals. One of the oldest and most controversial ethical problems concerns the relation of the individual to the community. We are here confronted with two opposed views. According to the first, the individual fulfills his ethical destiny only in so far as he serves the community: direct ideal value attaches to the community, and the individual's value is measured only by his services to the community. According to the other view, the very contrary is true: only the individual has direct value, while the community is merely a means, and can be valued only in so far as it serves the individual. Here, then, the individual is the basis of valuation, and whatever value is ascribed to communal life is exclusively determined by the value ascribed to the individual.

In the light of the principles we have so far formulated, we must say at once with respect to this controversy that strictly speaking there can be no such thing as a duty of sociality. All duties are derived from the moral law which is negative in character, for it only enjoins us not to disrespect the interests of others; it does not positively enjoin us to make the interests of others our own. Consequently, there can be no duty to live in a community, let alone to found one. Even a man living isolated, apart from society, does not thereby violate the moral law.

Those who insist on deducing a duty of sociality notwithstanding, claim that only a man who lives in a community can act morally. Hence, they argue, man must live among his fellows in order to fulfill his moral destiny. Such an argument obviously proves too much: true enough, a community is an indispensable condition for moral action, but it is just as much a prerequisite for immoral action. It follows that a man who lives outside a community cannot act morally, but neither can he act immorally.

Consequently, the community taken in itself is morally neutral. There can be no direct duty to join a community, let alone to found one, even though duties arise only when one lives in a community.

99. Objective Aesthetic Value of Community

From the fact that it is impossible to speak of a duty of sociality, it does not follow that there is no ethical difference between living in a community and living in isolation. Such an inference would be justified only if every single ethical task could be derived from the moral law. There are, however, tasks that are derived from the positive, ideal value of action. Consequently, it remains an open question whether or not communal life as such has ethical value.

To be clear on this point we must guard against one false argument. The aesthetic value of a community may vary, since it results from the interaction of individuals. But such aesthetic value does not warrant inferences concerning the ethical value of communal life. An ethical task appeals only to the will of the individual. But a community has no will, and hence cannot be charged with ethical tasks. It is not a rational being capable of having ideals, and can be judged only by aesthetic, not by ethical standards. The question as to the ethical value of communal life must therefore be distinguished from the question as to its objective aesthetic value. What we ask is not whether the community has value as a result of action, but rather whether the action leading to the formation of a community has value.

100. Ethical Value of Community Derived from Ideal of Beauty

On what basis can we assert that an action leading to the formation of a community has value? Obviously, on the same basis on which we assert the positive value of any action, i.e., on the basis of the ideal of culture, as we have formulated it. Beyond the ideals of culture, there are no positive tasks for the will of the individual, hence none arising from his relation to the community. Culture is rationality of life, and we have found that we judge the ideal value of an action by what it contributes to the rationality of life. Consequently, we may formulate our question as follows: Does a man contribute to the rationality of his life by living in a community?

We have seen that a community, as a product of the action of individuals, can have aesthetic value. Now, among our ideals of culture are some actually involving rational actions which are valuable not only in themselves, in the subjective sense, but also in their results. This is the case with the ideal of love for beauty. The striving to create beauty, which is an outgrowth of our aesthetic interest, contributes to the rationality of life, and thereby itself acquires aesthetic value. And since the community, as a product of the individual's action, has aesthetic value, such value attaches to life in a community and to communal tasks. Accordingly, action by which a community is formed has value in proportion to the value of the form of community created by such action. Thus we derive an ideal of living in a community from the ideal of love for beauty.

This derivation provides us with a solution to the problem of the ethical significance of the community. We must keep in mind, on the one hand, that the community has objective aesthetic value independently of whether and to what extent it serves as a means to the realization of individual interests, and on the other hand, that the ethical value of the individual is not determined by the extent to which his actions further the objective value of the community. Rather, the furthering of the community constitutes an ethical task only in so far as it contributes to the individual's culture. But it can contribute to the individual's culture only in so far as it expresses his interest in the value of the community.

Now, the value of a community depends in turn on the extent to which it constitutes a self-determined unit, i.e., the extent to which the individuals are associated in it, not on the basis of a principle that is external and alien to them, but on the basis of their own autonomous activity. Such a principle of autonomous activity is, strictly speaking, present only in rational beings; for only these have the faculty of spontaneous autonomous activity, namely, reason. Consequently, the value of a community of rational beings is determined by the extent to which reason governs the reciprocal relations of individuals.

Reason is the faculty of gaining insight into laws and of acting in accordance with laws. Beings who follow the dictates of reason thus act in accordance with a principle that is valid for all of them; for the laws guiding them are universally valid, and hence independent of individual instances of application. Consequently, rational beings as such have something in common, in so far as reason prescribes the same directives for action for each of them. But they have this faculty of reason only potentially, and by nature it is accidental whether or not this potentiality is developed, that is, whether the unitary character of reason does emerge in a rational community. And precisely because this is a matter of accident, the rational shaping of communal life is an ethical task. This leads us to the ideal of communal life.

101. Respect and Love as Conditions of Friendship

The highest form of community is friendship. According to Kant, friendship is the union of two persons through reciprocal respect and love.

Respect is certainly a condition of friendship. For friendship is a spiritual community, and as such it requires the communication of ideas. Consequently, each member of such a community must be able to trust the other: we must be sure that our friend will not use his knowledge of our ideas in a manner opposed to our interests. Hence, confidence in the other's reliability—and by the same token respect for his moral character—are necessary conditions of friendship.

Respect is not, however, a sufficient condition. For friendship between two beings is possible only if each of them regards the other as a person valuable in the positive sense, who not only meets the requirements of duty, but who is, in addition, worthy of love because of his autonomous spiritual activity. Consequently, Kant's definition is correct: friendship is actually based on reciprocal respect and love.

102. Love and Sympathy

Love for another being, which is part of friendship, must be compared to self-love. For there is a self-love which is pure, expressing the interest in the beauty of one's life, i.e., in one's own culture. This culture consists in devotion to the ideals of truth, beauty, and justice. The concept of pure self-love will doubtless be looked upon as paradoxical: for how can devotion to something that is not ourselves, namely, to truth, justice, and beauty, be called self-love? But the paradox is only an apparent one. We love ourselves with a self-love that is pure in so far as we seek the value of life in devotion to ideals. The sacrifices our devotion to ideals imposes upon us are in reality only sacrifices of selfishness, of happiness. Such sacrifices are not sacrifices of self-love, or of the beauty of one's life, but only of enjoyment of life, or of sensual interests. It is in this sense that we must understand the profound truth of the saying that "he that loseth his life shall find it."

It is somewhat more difficult to evaluate those cases in which pure self-love is opposed not to selfishness, but to sympathy for others.

Sympathy is not the same thing as love. Sympathy rests upon a sensual interest, an inclination. It is concerned with the other's welfare, with his enjoyment of life; love, on the other hand, is concerned with the other's personal value, and by the same token, with the beauty of his life. Sympathy consists in the sharing of joys and sorrows, and thus arises in relation to the actual interests another happens to have; love is directed toward the other's objective, i.e., true interest, whether or not this true interest coincides with his fortuitous actual interest. Consequently, a conflict between pure self-love and *sympathy* for others is not the same as a conflict between pure self-love and *love* for others. Love for another person rests upon an interest in the beauty of his life, and hence it springs from love of beauty. But love of beauty is an ideal of culture, and hence there is no contradiction between the ethical ideals of love and of culture: in paying tribute to the ideal of love we enhance the beauty of our own life, and by the same token, realize the correctly understood interest of pure self-love.

103. Love as Fondness and as Benevolence *

Love for another person assumes two forms—fondness and benevolence. Fondness expresses sensitiveness to another person's value; benevolence implies a desire to enhance his value, to bring him nearer to perfection. I am speaking here only of pure love; we say that such a love is benevolent when it is directed toward the objective value of the other's life, independently of concern for his subjective well-being.

There is a love from which the element of benevolence is absent. This element must be absent where there is no scope for the desire to improve the other person. This is what happens when the love object is idealized; for then it is regarded as absolutely perfect, and the desire to enhance its value cannot even arise. But such idealization of human beings, who are necessarily imperfect, is actually something less than love, for it is blind to the true interest of its object. Pure love imposes practical tasks on our will, and cannot rest content with a mere feeling of fondness for another person.

104. Patronizing Love

The tasks implicit in the ideal of benevolence flow from the other's true interest; for pure benevolence is aimed at the realization of that interest, which is always directed toward autonomy and can be realized only through autonomous activity. Consequently, attempts to coerce or inveigle a person into pursuing his true interest reflect a basic misunderstanding of the nature of love.

Autonomous activity can spring only from rational insight; we cannot be induced to act autonomously by persuasion, only by conviction. The practical challenge of pure love can therefore be only furtherance of the other's insight, to enable him to

* *Liebe als Wohlgefallen und als Wohlwollen.*

realize his true interest by autonomous activity; pure love rules out any attempt to compel another person, by force or subterfuge, to pursue his true interest. Indeed someone so treated, by being deprived of the possibility of self-determination, actually suffers a violation of his true interest; for he is treated not as a man, i.e., a rational being, but as a nonrational animal. Patronizing love rests upon such a lack of respect.

105. Importance of Love for Truth in Communal Life

When a man is in error concerning his true interest, our benevolence toward him can be expressed only in our desire to enlighten him as to his true interest. Benevolence will thus always produce a striving for mutual enlightenment about true interests. When we fail to strive to enlighten a man about his true interest, we are indifferent toward it; in such a case we cannot speak of love, but at best only of sympathy for his actual interest.

This shows that no one can be the object of pure love unless he loves the truth; for only then is he accessible to rational arguments, and willing to be enlightened as to where his true interest lies.

106. Requirement of Reciprocity of Love

Friendship requires not merely love, but reciprocity of love, through which alone the ideal of friendship is realized. This is because love leads to the communication of thoughts. But by communicating our thoughts to another we abolish the rightful barriers between him and ourselves. For we have no duty to communicate our thoughts; we have only the duty to be truthful, i.e., when we communicate our thoughts, we are obliged to do so in a truthful manner. Thus each man has the right to keep his thoughts to himself. A man who communicates them to another renounces this right, and thereby his relation with the other man is no longer based on mere rights. But love of honor requires that the abolished relationship be superseded by a relationship based on communion, i.e., on reciprocal devotion. The renunciation of right which is manifest in devotion is commendable only when it is reciprocated. Unless one person's devotion to another is to imply the surrender of his own personality, the other must reciprocate his love. For when the first party renounces his right, he can preserve his dignity only if the other party reciprocates his love. To continue a love relationship that remains one-sided and unreciprocated is therefore contrary to love of honor.

This does not mean, however, that we have a *right* to have our devotion reciprocated; such reciprocity is only an ideal. It cannot be a duty, were it only for the fact that a response to love does not depend on one's will. Confusion between the ideal of reciprocal love and an alleged right to have one's love reciprocated gives rise to various misinterpretations. One who claims reciprocal love as his right is no more to be commended than one who, knowing he has no such claim, nevertheless pours out his devotion unrequited. Likewise, the recipient of such devotion is disrespectful when he accepts it as a right due him, in the knowledge that he is not obliged to reciprocate it.

Here we must, however, distinguish between two different ideals. There is an ideal of love which is independent of the ideal of communion. Love for the beauty of another person does not necessarily imply the wish to live in communion with that person. It is true that both the ideal of love for the beauty of another person and the ideal of communion express the ideal of love for beauty; but the beauty of the beloved person is different from the beauty of communion with that person. The first ideal refers to the beauty of the beloved person. Hence it implies fondness for this person and benevolence toward him, but not necessarily a desire for lifetime communion. Goethe's apt saying, "If I love thee, what business be it of thine?" applies only to the ideal of the beauty of the beloved person. It does not apply to the ideal of communion, which implies communication of thoughts, and by the same token, reciprocal love.

107. Love and Hate

The opposite of love is hate. There is a conception of the ideal of love, according to which love excludes hate. I contend that such a conception distorts the ideal of love, and that, rather, love and hate are correlated. For there is no ideal of love pure and simple. All ideal love is love of the beautiful. The ideal of love requires preservation and enhancement of the value of the beautiful. Hate, on the other hand, is the interest in destroying the ugly. Consequently, any aesthetic interest involves both love of the beautiful and hate of the ugly. Unless there is hate of the ugly, there can be no love of the beautiful and, more generally, no pure love.

However, two things must be kept separate here. I do not mean to say that the ideal of communion requires us to hate all persons whom we cannot love; for there is a great difference between a man who deserves to be hated, and a man who merely does not deserve to be loved. This distinction springs from that between absence of culture and what we may designate as the downright baseness of a man. Lack of culture results from deficient insight into the ideal; baseness, on the contrary, actually presupposes insight into the ideal and consists in an attitude of scorning ideal values. We similarly distinguish between amorality and immorality. We despise the immoral, but not the amoral man. Accordingly, we regard only outright depravity of attitude as deserving of hate, but not mere deficiency of insight into the beautiful. Coarseness or crudeness is merely lack of culture. But depravity is positive baseness of attitude, conscious disregard of the ideal. There is a similar difference between error and deception. Error is not hateful, but deception is because it implies a deliberate disregard for the ideal of love for truth.

The ideal of love for the beautiful demands that we wage a struggle against everything that opposes it, hence a struggle against error as well; for truth can be victorious only if error is brought to bay. That is why it is impossible to deduce a general ideal of forbearance and peaceableness from the ideal of love. True, there is no such thing as an ideal of struggle per se, just as there is no ideal of love per se. There is an ideal of love only with reference to what deserves to be loved, and an ideal of struggle only with reference to what deserves to be combated.

There is still another difference, however, between struggle and hate or between hostility and hate. Error must be combated, but deception merits our hate. The ethical ideal directly implies an ideal of struggle against error and injustice, and an ideal of hate for the mean.

No contradiction is involved in the ideal of love for one's enemy; for the ideal of struggle against error and objective injustice does not rule out esteem for the character of those whom we combat and benevolence toward them. But this implication of the ideal of love must not lead us to ignore the ideal of hate, i.e., we must not refrain from hating that which deserves not only to be combated but also hated. Therefore, the founder of the religion of love was quite consistent when he said, "I came not to send peace, but a sword."

108. Love of Mankind

The foregoing considerations enable us to decide whether ethics can formulate an ideal of love for mankind. The answer to this question depends on what we understand by the ideal of love for mankind. It might mean that we have a fondness for our fellow man, or that we are benevolently disposed toward him. Obviously we can speak of an ideal of love for men only in the second sense. Fondness for mankind would be a fantastic ideal; it would presuppose an idealization of men which is incompatible with love of truth.

Love of mankind can be shown only by striving to procure for others a chance to realize their true interests through autonomous activity: This is what a pure benevolence toward men demands, for men, as rational beings, can lead valuable lives only through autonomous activity. Love of mankind thus forbids us to compel others, openly or insidiously, to realize their true interests.

Beyond this merely negative requirement, love of mankind can be expressed only in the desire to enlighten others, i.e., to help illuminate their true interests. Love of mankind demands more here than does love of justice, which asks us only to see to it that no wrong is done to others, while love of mankind aims to aid others in attaining a life valuable in a positive sense.

109. Community of Ends as a Condition of Friendship

Although reciprocal respect and love are necessary conditions of friendship, they do not exhaust its meaning. For the ideal of friendship is the ideal of a practical communion, i.e., a community of ends. Activity directed toward common ends must be added to reciprocal respect and love in order to give friendship its full significance.

Now, it is easy to see that not every community of ends is ipso facto friendship. A gang of criminals constitutes a community of ends, but the bonds uniting them are not the bonds of friendship. This is because the ends pursued by such a community are secondary, derived ends. It is in respect of these secondary ends that the members of a criminal gang act together; the community here is accidental. What the criminals have in common is actually only the means for the attainment of their ends, the robbing of other persons; the actual end pursued here is not a common one, for each criminal strives to enrich only himself as much as possible. In helping one another to realize this end, they merely observe a precept of prudence, and each individual uses the other as a mere means to attain his private end. Analogous relations obtain between persons co-operating in many other enterprises, for instance, between the manager of a business and any of his employees: each party seeks only his own advantage, and what is common to all is only the means, in this case, the operation of the business.

Friendship, however, requires co-operation not only with respect to subordinate, derived ends, but precisely with respect to direct or ultimate ends. The ideal of friendship will therefore be the more completely realized, the more completely the ultimate ends of each friend coincide with those of the other. We thus obtain various degrees of friendship, according to the extent of coincidence between such ultimate aims.

We can speak of common ultimate ends only in so far as such ends are not merely private ends of individuals, i.e., ends determined by subjective interests. A true community of ends is possible only in relation to an objective, ideal end.

110. Culture as a Condition of Friendship

An important inference can be drawn from the foregoing statement, namely, the inference that friendship presupposes culture. For the formation of a true community of ends it is not sufficient that each of the individuals involved pursue ideal ends; they must also agree in the definition of these ends. Different individuals regard very different and often contradictory things as ideal ends; indeed, even those who relate such ends to the ideal of a rational life, will hold different views as to what a rational life requires, according to their respective degree of intellectual development. And even if the parties involved agree that a rational life implies love of truth, beauty, and justice, they may not agree as to what the particular requirements of these three ideals are. But a practical community is possible only in so far as there is agreement on the practical view of life, i.e., agreement as to the particular things that constitute the value of life. Unless a community of ends, which is the condition of friendship, is to be based on the chance that the parties involved are equally lacking in culture, agreeing in their errors and their lack of reflection, such a community is possible only if both parties are cultured (*gebildet*) and correctly judge the objective value of life.

Thus friendship, in the sense of the ideal, is possible only between sufficiently cultured persons. For only if each of them gains an objectively correct view of life, can there be certainty that their views of life will be alike. Now, this practical view of life which the friends must share for friendship to be possible, includes an element that is a condition par excellence of friendship, namely, love of truth. For without love of truth there can be no mutual enlightenment or instruction; but if both parties have it, they can always arrive at a common practical view of life, even if originally there was no agreement regarding it. A common interest in truth is therefore the most important condition of friendship; unless it is present the ideal cannot even be approximated.

It is not, however, necessary that friends pursue the same vocation; this would be more than what friendship demands. Two

persons can pursue the same ideal end, yet each of them may cultivate a different pre-eminent ideal interest. In fact, the ideal value
of friendship is enhanced precisely as the differences between
the vocations of the friends offer scope for complementing their
personalities, and as harmony between their practical views of
life prevails despite the differences between vocations.

That is why the most sublime friendships are those between
a man and a woman. For the natural difference between the sexes
is greater than any differences that may result from a different
choice of vocation, and hence it offers a greater opportunity for
each friend to complement and enrich the value of the other's
life.

111. Intensity and Range of Friendship

The degree to which friendship approaches perfection can be
judged by its intensity and by its range; so far we have discussed
only its intensity. What I call the range of friendship is the number of persons involved in this relationship. Obviously, the more
persons are involved in it, the closer it is to perfection, provided
its intensity is not decreased thereby. Only experience can teach
us to what extent this condition can be met. There is no ideal in
the light of which we can set a priori limits to the number of
persons who can be admitted to a community of friends.

The general condition governing the possibility of such extension can, however, be formulated a priori. The question confronting us here is whether affection for one person does not
restrict, in proportion to its intensity, the intensity of affection
for another person, and under what condition such restriction is
ruled out. Everything here hinges on whether our obligation not
to betray the confidence of one of our friends is compatible with
our obligation to be frank in communicating our thoughts to
another friend. Now it is clear that these obligations can be
mutually exclusive only if our two friends are not united themselves by a bond of friendship. If they are united by such a bond,
we do not violate our duty not to betray the confidence of our
first friend by frankly communicating our thoughts to the second, for then our first friend trusts our second friend just as much

as he trusts us, and we cannot tell the second anything that the first would not be willing to tell him. Consequently, we can add new members to a community of friends without thereby decreasing the intensity of the bonds uniting them if each new addition is a friend of every member of the community.

112. Aesthetic Origin of the Ideal of Friendship

The foregoing discussion makes it completely clear that perfect friendship is an ideal that can be approximated more or less, namely, to the extent to which the conditions of friendship, as we have formulated them, can be met. But the realization of these conditions does not depend directly upon our will, and hence there certainly can be no question of duty here, but only of something that is part of the beauty of life. If an individual finds such conditions realized, this is a favor of fortune, and whether or not he succeeds in his striving to realize them will also be a matter of chance. In this sense, friendship must be regarded as a gift of chance, and this fact appears in a special light when we keep in mind the aesthetic origin of the ideal of friendship. For the aesthetic value inherent in the harmony obtaining between the parts of a unitary whole cannot be inferred either from a natural law or from the moral law, and is therefore accidental in relation to laws of any kind. Indeed, in this sense we may say that the essence of beauty is its adventitious character.

I shall sum up the conditions of friendship deduced here in a formula which I regard as exhaustive: Friendship is an active union based on mutual esteem and love, and formed for the purpose of realizing common ideals.

Chapter 5. Ideals of Public Life

113. Derivation of Ideals of Public Life

WHEN WE CONSIDER the ideals of community life we must go beyond the ideal of friendship. The reason will be clear in the light of the considerations that follow.

Rationality, whether it be the quality of an individual or of a community, has two aspects—(1) a rational concern with ideas, and (2) rational activity aimed at changing the environment. These two aspects, however, are closely interrelated. A rational concern with the inner life implies readiness to act rationally, and rational activity presupposes a concern with ideas and convictions. Now, it is clear that we cannot speak of a community's inner life. Only an individual can have ideas, pursue interests, will ends; a community cannot. A community is not an individual; rather, it is composed of individuals, each of whom has his own inner life. But the isolation of the individual can in a sense be overcome. Individuals can communicate their thoughts and feelings to each other, and thus enter into more or less close relations with one another. Such social intercourse can be perfect only if it is based on mutual confidence; for only on such basis are individuals willing to open their inner lives to each other. That is why mutual confidence is a condition of friendship.

To form friendships a rational being must find other rational beings willing and able to enter into a relation of trust with him. This implies harmonious adjustment of complementary dispositions, which enhances the beauty of life in relation both to the individual and to the community. For such a harmony to occur in nature between rational beings remains a matter of chance. Consequently, it does not depend solely upon them to what extent they form friendships. Under certain circumstances friendships may even be impossible.

The value of a community, however, does not depend on mutual confidence alone. In discussing friendship we have seen that it involves a factor of range as well as a factor of intensity. While intensity depends on the degree of mutual confidence obtaining between the members of a community, range depends on the number of persons a community can include. Now, the value of a community is also measured by its range. For a friendship in conformity with the ideal is not merely a community of men based on mutual esteem and love; it is also a practical community, i.e., a community of ends. Consequently, its value is also determined by the degree to which it comes close to the ideal of uniting all rational beings in the pursuit of common ends.

When rational beings form a community of ends, they do not depend on whether their dispositions happen or not to be in harmony; all that is required is that in each of them reason be sufficiently clear to show him the ends common to all as rational beings. Consequently, we can set aside the factor of intensity, i.e., the perfect mutual confidence that should obtain in a communion. We can thus formulate the ideal of a practical community which, instead of being based on friendship with its dependence on the mutual confidence of its members, rests on the fact that its members pursue common rational ends. The ideal of such a community has a good claim to embrace all rational beings.

Such an extension, however, presupposes in turn that the community has adopted specific external forms serving the common ends in order to secure its independence of the personal relations obtaining between its members.

To the degree that any activity serving the individual's inner life, i.e., his ends, is outwardly observable, that activity is public. For this reason, I shall designate the ideals of a practical community which is secured by external means and is thus independent of the factor of mutual confidence, as ideals of public life.

114. Virtue of Community Spirit

Ideals of public life apply to a community of rational beings, and demand of it subordination to rational ends. This does not mean, however, that these ideals set tasks for the community rather than for the individual. A community as such neither pursues ends nor fulfills tasks, but it can be made to serve ideal ends by its individual members, when the outward form of the community is in conformity with such ends. It is only in this figurative sense that ideals of public life may be said to set tasks for a community. If the concept of a task is taken in this broader sense, we find that there is an exact analogy between ideals of public life and ideals of culture. For ideals of public life determine the rational ends of the community, just as ideals of culture determine the rational ends of the individual.

This analogy between the ideals of public life and of culture enables us to give the theory of public life a structure similar to that of the theory of ideals as a whole. This once more confirms the fruitfulness of the method we have adopted.

In analogy to what we did in the formal theory of ideals, we can, even before discussing the content of the ends of public life, draw an important inference on the basis of the mere assertion that there are ends which public life ought to be made to serve. For we can say that public life is actually made to serve these ends only if its very form has been adapted to them.

The virtue to which the ideal of public life thus gives rise can be designated as the virtue of community-mindedness (*Tugend des Gemeingeistes*); I define it as the readiness of individuals to form a community serving public ends.

115. Strength and Spontaneity of Community Spirit

Community spirit, just as the mind of an individual, can be said to have character. We do not thereby assume the existence of a mystical entity different from the minds of the individual members of the community; the term "character" in this context merely denotes the form of the community. The virtue of community-mindedness, just as the individual's virtuousness of character, is characterized by strength, spontaneity, and purity.

Community spirit manifests its strength by asserting itself against conflicting private interests of individuals. But community spirit should be not only strong, but also spontaneous, it should not freeze in the mold it creates for itself, nor be stifled by convention; it should use external forms only as instruments for the attainment of higher ends. These forms should not be regarded as ends in themselves and artificially preserved as such; they should remain capable of constant development. Consequently, the vitality of community spirit is reflected in the fluidity of social forms, in their capacity for adaptation to changing circumstances and to the particular ends which these determine. Thus we must demand an open, planned guidance of public life, and we call such guidance public prudence.

116. Purity of Community Spirit

Prudence as an element in community-mindedness safeguards the shaping of public life against accidental influences, and makes it serve specific ends. But what these ends are still remains to be determined. Strength and spontaneity are not sufficient conditions of community-mindedness; for on the basis of prudence alone, the community can be made to serve reprehensible as well as commendable ends.

A correct choice of ends presupposes purity of community spirit. Community spirit can be strong and vital without being pure; it can express itself in violence, visionary dreams, superstition, lust for power and riches, or crude pageantry. Purity of community spirit is expressed in adherence to the ideals governing the beauty of public life. The dominance of such ideals in public life constitutes that which we call a society's culture, as analogous to an individual's culture, which is also determined by ideals.

Only a community life governed by ideals can be called public life in the full sense. For public life, by definition, does not serve private ends, whether these be pursued by some, many, or even all members of a given society. What matters here is not the fact that individuals have agreed on the choice of ends to be pursued by them, but the specific character of such ends. They cannot be arbitrarily selected ones. True public life can be secured only if the ends determining the community are adopted as his own by every sufficiently cultured individual. Purity of community spirit and the public aspects of life require that the community serve such ends.

Just as purity of character presupposes the virtue of clarity of mind, so purity of community spirit presupposes clarity of community spirit. An individual can adhere to an ideal only if he recognizes it as such. Similarly, a given community can serve ideal ends only when, by its very form, it acknowledges them as public ends.

Clarity of community spirit therefore requires above all that specific public ends be publicly recognized as such. A merely formal ideal of idealism is just as insufficient here as it is in the life of the individual. A practical community is possible only if all of its members acknowledge the same ends as ideal. For if there is a difference of opinion as to the content of the ideal ends, a practical community is impossible. Such a community can exist only on the basis of agreement as to the choice of means for the attainment of its ends; and how can there be agreement as to means if there is no agreement as to the ends? Consequently, the union of minds which is sometimes proclaimed as the ideal of the community, can be achieved only when those minds have grouped themselves according to the conflicting ends set for the community by various factions. Mere idealism is futile as a rallying cry in the founding of a community, just as it is in the life of the individual. Clarity of community spirit thus requires first of all that specific ideals be formulated as public ends.

Mere agreement on ends, however, does not realize the ideal of community even where the ideal itself is the common object of subjective aspiration. It is not enough for public life to be governed by a common but possibly false opinion about its ends. No, public life must be instinct with the very ideals of community life itself. The ends to which community spirit is devoted must consequently be determined in such a way that they are safeguarded against accident both in the subjective and in the objective sense.

117. Culture as the End of Public Life

We shall now turn to the task of determining the content of the ideals of public life. The first question that arises here is whether ends of public life are possible at all. We have seen that such ends cannot differ from those pursued by the individual.

Now, the individual's ends are determined either by his subjective interests, i.e., his inclinations, or by his objective interest in culture. Accordingly, he pursues either what we call enjoyment of life, happiness, and individual welfare, or what makes for the value of life.

Subjective interests determine only private ends, namely, the ends of selfishness. But objective interest provides us with public ends in the true sense, i.e., universal and necessary ends of every sufficiently cultured individual. The realization of these ends is a public task, and it provides us with a standard by which we judge the culture of a given society.

There is no such thing as a social ideal of welfare. Subjective interests determine only private ends: each individual pursues his own subjective interest, and in realizing this interest he can only incidentally choose the same means as other individuals. This may give rise to a problem of social expediency: we may ask to what extent society can be effective in procuring the means for gratifying the subjective needs of individuals. If we designate by the term "economy" the whole complex of processes by which the subjective needs of individuals are gratified, then economic life may actually become a social concern. But whether and to what extent society ought to concern itself with economic life is a question of prudence rather than ethics. The organization of economic life is essentially a technological problem, which cannot be solved on the basis of an ideal of welfare. Consequently, the ideal of public life can be determined only by the ideal of culture.

118. Technology and Culture

What is the relation obtaining between the requirements of this ideal and the tasks of technology? Technology is the art of marshaling external means for the attainment of given ends, and hence for realizing the physical conditions of public life. Does an age which is primarily concerned with such tasks deserve to be called an age of technological culture? The answer to this question will depend on the nature of the ends which technology serves. The mere procurement of means is certainly not an objective of culture; nor is it opposed to culture. Rather, each culture must also be a technological culture; for it would be absurd to strive for the realization of cultural ideals while neglecting the task of procuring the means without which a cultured life would be impossible. But an age in which technology is subservient to selfish interests is even further removed from the ideal of culture than an age looking down on technology as such; and the more its selfish technology is developed, the less will it deserve to be called an age of culture. An age which subjects a highly developed technology to selfish ends can only be called diabolical. For in such an age the organization of public life is left to the mercy of subjective, private interest, and more than that, the rule of these private interests is firmly secured by the most elaborate technological means.

119. Welfare and Ideals of Culture

Before determining the content of cultural requirements, it is necessary to relate these requirements properly to the ends of welfare. For even though welfare, as we have seen, does not determine the ideal of public life, it has a direct bearing on this ideal.

While there is no ideal of social welfare, there is an ideal of just distribution of welfare in society, which is implicit in the ideal of love for justice. Justice does not require that each member of society be guaranteed a specific measure of welfare, but it does require equality in gratification of needs, so that no member of society is wronged as regards his share of the means serving the gratification of needs. The distribution of these means ought to be governed by the principle of equity as well as of retribution.

Moreover, since no one can attain culture unless his needs are in some measure gratified, the ideal of culture indirectly requires that all members of society have access to the means indispensable for the attainment of culture.

120. Value of Enlightenment

Among the cultural requirements that have a direct bearing on the life of a community, there is one that must be met before any further cultural aspirations are possible at all. The ideal of culture, as we know, implies rational self-determination; but rational self-determination presupposes adequate enlightenment. For enlightenment, as Kant puts it, is the emergence of man from a state of dependence for which he is himself responsible. A man is in a state of dependence if he is incapable of using his understanding without being guided by another. A man is responsible for being in such a state when he is prevented from using his own understanding and will, not by some external misfortune, but by his own lack of courage. Thus the ideal of enlightenment is a direct consequence of the ideal of rational self-determination, to which all cultural requirements can ultimately be reduced, and is therefore independent of any alleged ideal of welfare, which enlightenment might further or impede.

There is an old controversy as to the desirability or peril of enlightenment. This question is actually of no concern to ethics. Even if we decided that enlightenment is dangerous, we would still have to assert its ethical value, for this value is firmly rooted in a direct ethical ideal, hence is superior to any subjectively determined value that enlightenment might threaten. Consequently, we shall surmount any possible dangers involved in enlightenment not by restricting its scope, but on the contrary by extending it, in the expectation that whatever damage a little enlightenment might cause, more enlightenment will repair. We must put up with such hazards, for in order to avoid them we would have to sacrifice that which gives value to life.

121. Possibility of Enlightenment

Ethics is no more concerned with the possibility of enlightenment than with its usefulness or harmfulness. It might be objected at this point that it is impossible to guide all members of society toward culture, and that consequently enlightenment is a privilege to be reserved for the few susceptible to it.

It is obvious that this objection refers to an empirical problem: for how could we decide a priori how many or how few men can attain a specific degree of enlightenment? But we can safely leave this problem unsolved. No matter how many are assumed to be incapable of enlightenment, one can never infer, from such an assumption, that we have the right to characterize anyone as incapable of enlightenment unless he has been given an opportunity to develop his understanding. For how else could we decide whether or not he qualifies as one of the chosen few?

Consequently, every individual has an equal right to the external means indispensable for the attainment of enlightenment. To what extent he makes use of those means, is a matter that each individual must decide for himself.

122. Enlightenment and Romanticism

Those who deny that man can achieve a significant life through his own efforts, may take recourse to the notion that he can do so only by virtue of an act of grace, and that his only task is to qualify for such an act of grace. But those who resort to this expedient fail to grasp that man can achieve a valuable life only through autonomous activity. There is no substitute for self-determination.

Anyone who strives for grace notwithstanding must be motivated solely by considerations of prudence, for instance, the expectation of a life of bliss in the hereafter. To what extent an individual engaged in such efforts contributes to his earthly or heavenly welfare, is thus a question of mere prudence, which has nothing to do with ethics. All he can gain is a means for increasing his enjoyment of life, rather than an enhancement of the value of his life. Whether or not enlightenment be possible, and whether or not an individual striving for it become forever entangled in error, we must maintain that it is more consistent with human dignity to live in error at one's own risk than to become dependent upon a superior power for the sake of one's welfare.

It is clear from the foregoing that enlightenment does not merely happen to be a tendency associated with a transient historical period, but that it is a necessary requirement valid in every age. An historical period, to be distinguished from all others as deserving to be called an age of enlightenment, would have to be animated by an unshakable faith in man's ability to shape his life by his own efforts, and to repudiate as a degrading form of tutelage all promises of redemption by grace.

Needless to say, it is a long way from the mere acceptance of the task set for us by the ideal of enlightenment to its actual realization. To subject life to reason takes an arduous effort of the mind, and understanding is always exposed to the possibility of error. By subjecting life to the verdict of his understanding, man plunges into multiple dangers of error, to which those who entrust their lives to the guidance of instinct are far less exposed. It is thus the very nature of enlightenment that whoever attempts to realize this idea seemingly strays from the path leading to a secure and harmonious life.

Those who judge the value of any aspiration by its immediate results, will therefore despair of the possibility of a culture of enlightenment. They will interpret any attempt to realize it as springing from ill-considered subjectivism and anarchic tendencies. Such misinterpretations give rise to efforts to arrest the process of enlightenment, and to seek culture in the negation of autonomous activity. An age that negates the possibility of enlightenment on the ground that previous attempts to realize it have failed may be called an age of romanticism.

So-called romantic culture epitomizes reason that has come to despair of its own power. It is a culture of men who despair of themselves. Instead of asserting human self-determination, it glorifies historical tradition, and instead of seeking to reshape the world in conformity with human ideals through man's autonomous activity, it seeks to restore faith in tradition and authority. Insight, whether lucid or imperfect, is thus replaced with the twilight of confused emotions; the autonomy of human reason is identified with subjective whim, and repudiated on this ground; free thought is fettered by traditional religious forms, and free action is supplanted by the dead hand of custom.

It is clear, however, that once reflection has been awakened, doubts about the validity of tradition and the infallibility of authority can be silenced only by means of self-deception; for such doubts can be honestly resolved only by rational arguments. But the romanticist makes no effort to discover rational arguments, for he does not believe that such an effort can be successful. Yet the insecurity engendered by reflection cannot be overcome by restricting reflection and criticism of its results, but only by furthering and consummating reflection.

Enlightenment is sometimes condemned on the ground that it surrenders life to the cold and prosaic rule of the understanding. But the warmth we are supposed to win by renouncing reflection is a false warmth, and the beauty of life we are supposed to attain by disavowing enlightenment is a false beauty. Doubt and analysis mark man's first steps toward autonomous activity, and hence toward culture. To turn back on this path means to end up with a pseudo culture, which is essentially a negation of all culture; for respect for truth is the very foundation of culture.

123. Ideals of Equality and Freedom

If we inquire into the content of the cultural ideals which enlightenment is to serve, we must first of all consider the ideal of love for mankind in conjunction with the ideal of love for justice. The relation between these two ideals is similar to that obtaining between the ideal of love for justice and the objective of welfare. Justice in itself does not require that we foster the individual's enjoyment of life or welfare; nor does it require that we further his culture. On the basis of justice alone we can formulate only the negative requirement that no individual be unjustly prevented from gratifying his interests, whether these be interests arising from inclination or interests in culture. This requirement, in so far as it is applied to public life or the organization of society, may be designated as the ideal of equality. It refers to the distribution of the means serving to realize subjective interests, as well as to each individual's opportunities for attaining culture. It demands equality in respect of both.

There is, however, with regard to this ideal, an important difference between the possibility of realizing subjective interests, namely those in welfare, and the possibility of gratifying objective interests, namely those in culture. We shall clearly recognize this difference if we consider that we can gratify another man's interest in the enjoyment of life, but not his interest in culture. For he needs no autonomous activity to enjoy life, provided he has been supplied with the necessary means; but his interest in culture can be realized only by his own autonomous activity. Hence the question arises, How can the ideal of equality be applied here at all? For according to the ideal of self-determination, all one man can do for another in this respect is to remove obstacles preventing him from gratifying his interest in culture and to provide him with an opportunity for gratifying it. But in so far as such obstacles exist, the ideal of equality implies the task of removing them, so that no individual will be at a disadvantage as against others, as well as the task of providing every individual with an equal opportunity for attaining culture.

Activity in behalf of men's culture is directly required in even greater measure by the ideal of love for mankind. This love aims at bringing men closer to perfection, and hence it strives to eliminate everything that restricts autonomous activity. With regard to public life, love of mankind thus leads to the ideal of freedom.

The ideal of freedom requires that each man be vouchsafed the opportunity to attain culture through autonomous activity, in so far as this can be done by the removal of external obstacles in the way of such activity, whether they be natural or artificial. It is the ideal of a society in which each individual has the material opportunity for attaining culture.

Even though an individual can attain culture only through autonomous activity, in order to live autonomously he must survive in the first place. Consequently, the physical prerequisites of his existence must be assured; otherwise he could not live, whether as a cultured or an uncultured man. But this is not enough. For if he is compelled to spend all of his energy to secure the necessary means of subsistence, or if others prevent him from making use of his external freedom, he has no access to culture. Both material want and spiritual tutelage can prevent an individual from attaining culture through autonomous activity; the ideal of freedom imposes upon us the task of removing such obstacles.

124. Economic and Cultural Requirements of Social Justice

With respect to the task of clearing away obstacles deliberately put in the way of the individual's autonomous activity, the requirements of love for justice coincide with those of love for mankind. Both demand that we act positively in behalf of those members of society who are unfairly underprivileged. We have seen in the theory of duties that the inherently negative requirement of justice not to disregard the interests of others yields to a positive requirement where persons affected by our action are unable to defend their own interests. Where an individual is prevented from achieving a valuable life through autonomous activity because of unfavorable circumstances or because others separate him from culture by artificial barriers, love of justice demands that we clear away these obstacles in so far as they keep him in an inferior position, and that we provide him with an opportunity for autonomous activity equal to that of other members of society, whether he will later make use of this freedom or not. He certainly cannot make use of it when he is denied it.

125. Right to Culture

We have introduced the ideal of freedom side by side with the ideal of equality. Nothing could, however, justify the assumption that some sort of pre-established harmony governs the realization of these two ideals. Rather, we must ask which of them should be given preference in the event that they conflict. This brings us to the controversial question of which has precedence, the ideal of culture or the ideal of right.

The challenge of culture is, properly speaking, by no means

beyond the sway of right; indeed, the ideal of justice is a necessary element of the ideal of culture. For if the ideals of culture embrace all public ends, one of these ideals is certainly the ideal of right, which love of justice strives to realize.

But with this consideration we have not yet faced the question of what to do if one ideal of culture, namely, that of right, enters into conflict with other ideals of culture.

Here it seems plausible to argue for the priority of the ideal of right, since justice, the content of the moral law, directly represents a duty; thus it would appear that in accordance with the rigorism of duty, every other end would have to be subordinated to the realization of right. But such an argument leaves out of account the fact that we are dealing here with ideals, and hence that we are concerned with right only in so far as it too represents not a duty but an ideal, namely, the ideal of the realization of a just society.

For this reason, our task here is to choose not between an ideal and a duty, but between two ideals. In order to decide which of them has to be given preference, we must recall that the ideals of public life, or the communal ideals, are based on the objective aesthetic value of the community.

What, then, is the value conferred upon a society by the ideal of justice as compared with other communal ideals? A just society is, by definition, a society that meets the requirements of the moral law. It alone confers no positive value upon a community but is merely the necessary negative condition of the value of any community. Only the ideals of culture determine the positive value of a community. But a community that violates justice utterly forfeits any positive value, which otherwise might attach to it; consequently, in the event of a conflict between ideals, the ideal of justice must be given precedence. A violation of justice cannot be condoned in the name of any communal value, no matter how high. If a community is to be a cultural community, it must regard right as inviolable, as sacred; or, as Kant puts it: "If justice perish, what profits it a man to dwell on earth?"

This proposition, when applied, seems to lead to difficulties: for the law of right is not a material but a formal principle, and it cannot be applied without taking into consideration the requirements of culture. For in appraising interests, as we must do to arrive at a just decision, we are concerned not only with the respective strength of each interest involved, but also with its objective preferential value, which is determined by the positive ideal of culture. Thus it would seem that in this case we have shown a cultural requirement to be the more valuable. But all that we can infer from this is that a lover of justice must possess sure judgment on the positive value of culture. This does not mean that in each case the rightful decision must inevitably fall to the side of higher culture. The maximum of culture is not per se the criterion of right in public life. We cannot say a priori that a powerful sensual interest may not be found to outweigh a positive requirement of culture. But even if in a given case a cultural ideal may tip the scales, we still decide on the basis of the ideal of right and not of this positive cultural ideal which of the ideals is to be given preference in a conflict of interests.

126. Organization of Public Life

The ideals of public life offer certain challenges to a community of rational beings in nature. But under natural law it remains a matter of accident whether the public ends determined by these ideals assert themselves against opposing interests. Whoever strives to realize public ends is therefore faced with the question of the means that will enlist the preponderant strength in nature on his side.

We must concern ourselves with this question here in so far as it is susceptible of a philosophical answer. First of all, even before going into the content of the ideals of public life, we can draw one important inference on the basis of the very concept of public life. For whatever ends reason may prescribe to public life, the very concept of such ends implies the requirement that social life be shaped in such a way as to make their realization possible, indeed, necessary, at least in so far as this realization depends on the form of the community. Public life arises wherever a community of rational beings is formed. But whatever ends may be regarded as rational, the necessary condition for their realization is the general possibility of purposeful conduct. The possibility of acting purposefully rests in turn on the predictability of the results of action. Thus purposeful action can be secured only if the uncertainty of its result is excluded. Consequently, public life above all requires forms of social intercourse, which safeguard from accident the results of men's actions arising from their interrelations. Rational intercourse must pre-eminently be peaceful intercourse. This requirement springs not from the ideal of right, but independently of it, from the very concept of an ideal of public life. For where brute force regulates interrelations between rational beings, it becomes a matter of accident whether intercourse between them is in conformity with the ideal of community, however the content of this ideal may have been determined. Thus peaceful intercourse must take the place of relations based on brute force. But the forms of peaceful intercourse are secure only by virtue of social organization.

We say that a society is organized when the realization of its ends is safeguarded against accident. Consequently, social organization rests upon external institutions which make the determination and realization of the social ends independent of the insight and whim of individuals. Social organization thus implies first of all the creation of forms of intercourse consistent with the ends of the community, and second, the enforcement of these forms so that their observance be not subject to the discretion of individuals. Hence public life requires (1) laws regulating social intercourse, and (2) a power superior to the individuals in order to enforce the forms of social intercourse.

Social organization serves a threefold purpose. This is why: A man who has relations with another may be dependent on him, i.e., be subject to his discretion, in three possible ways. To begin with, such a dependence may result simply from physical coercion. Then, one man may depend upon another for the realization of his interests. He may be able to satisfy his needs only to the degree that the other, controlling the means for their realization, permits. Here again we must consider two cases separately—subjective and objective interests, i.e., the gratification of interests referring to enjoyment of life, and of interests referring to the value of life.

Accordingly, social organization performs these functions. (1) It regulates the physical dependence of one individual upon another: this is the political organization of society. (2) It regulates the dependence of one individual upon another in respect to the means for gratifying needs: this is the economic organization of society. (3) It regulates the spiritual dependence of one individual upon another: this is the cultural organization of society. The first function of social organization is concerned directly with external physical relationships, the second with what may be called the exchange of goods in the narrower sense, and the third with the communication of ideas.

127. Despotic Organization

We may further ask what ends a given organization of society serves. Now, it may serve private or public ends. A social organization serving private ends, we call despotic. Accordingly, despotism can assume three forms—political, economic, and cultural. We shall consider each of these in turn.

Despotism characterizes a society that is governed not by the ideal of public life, but by the arbitrary rule of one, several, or many individuals. Arbitrary rule is always determined by the mere strength of a private interest. Three kinds of despotism are possible according to the three facets of the organization of society.

Arbitrary rule may, first, be based directly on brute force when society is subjected to the power of a despot. This I call political despotism. Whether brute force is actually applied or used only as a threat is immaterial here. It makes no difference if the individuals voluntarily submit to the despot thus making it unnecessary for him to resort to brute force: for a threat is effective only if it is backed by brute force. Despotism is thus possible even in a society whose organization is formally peaceful, namely, a society in which the despot lays down his will in the form of laws whose observance he enforces by the mere

threat of violence. The power serving the organization of society is called the police power, and in so far as it is used not only
internally but externally, military power. Thus political despotism governs by means of military power, and this form of despotism may be called military despotism or militarism.

Arbitrary rule, secondly, may prevail in economic life. Economic despotism consists in the rule of some individuals over
others on the basis of monopoly. Monopolism arises when certain members of society have exclusive disposition of specific
kinds of goods, so that they can at will prevent other members
who need such goods from enjoying or consuming them. These
others thus become subject to the will of the monopolists, who
can dictate to them the conditions under which alone they will
be allowed to enjoy or consume the goods in question, i.e., to
gratify their needs. This form of despotism may be called mo-
nopolistic despotism or monopolism. The particular form of
monopolism which consists in the exclusive ownership of the
means of production may be designated as capitalism; for capitalism is a form of society in which a specific class owns the
means of production, i.e., the means of procuring the goods
required for the gratification of needs. Where goods serving
to gratify needs are not directly available but can be obtained
only by means of labor, men depend on the use of means of
production, and in this way they become dependent on cap-
italists who dictate to them the conditions under which they
can earn a living. The exploitation of a situation of distress deliberately produced or maintained for the purpose of gaining
private advantage is called extortion. Economic despotism therefore rules by means of extortion, just as political despotism rules
by means of brute force.

Finally, arbitrary rule in the organized communication of
ideas characterizes spiritual despotism. For there is not only a
monopoly of material goods, by means of which some individuals keep others in economic dependence, but also a monopoly of spiritual goods. Some individuals exclusively control the
real or imaginary means of salvation, and use this control to
keep others in a state of spiritual dependence. Those others
submit to the dictates of the spiritual monopolists, because they

cannot or think they cannot attain salvation on their own. Spiritual monopoly thus consists in the exclusive possession of the keys to salvation, or in the art of persuading others that one has them. And spiritual despotism organizes the communication of ideas in such a way that some people depend on others for knowledge of the means for achieving salvation. By controlling, or at least claiming to control the instruments of salvation, the privileged, acting as guardians, subject others to their arbitrary rule. An organization regulating the dependence of some men on others in respect to knowledge of the means of salvation is called a church, and the despotism based on it is known as clericalism. Like capitalism, clericalism rests upon a form of extortion, since it exploits the spiritual distress of some people for the purpose of securing rule over their conscience.

It is clear from our definition of despotism that a despot must strive for exclusive personal power. For as long as he has rivals, his own rule will be constantly imperiled in step with their power; he can make his rule secure only by eliminating any competing source of power.

As a result, any division of power among the three types of despots can rest only on a temporary truce, which none of them can in the long run consider satisfactory as a realization of his goal. Rather, the nature of despotism is such that any concession to it will inevitably produce a state of affairs in which the various forms of social organization will be combined under a single despotic power. Until then, each despot is exposed to the danger that his designs will be frustrated by his fellow despots.

The motives that impel a despot to tolerate no despot of different kind within his domain, also impel him to strive continually to enlarge this domain by external conquests. For so long as other despotically governed communities exist outside his sphere of power, he is not secure against the danger of foreign intervention. Hence each despotically ruled community tends to absorb the communities outside it. This striving for world domination is known as imperialism. Thus, each despotism is by its very nature imperialistic; and since the goal of imperialism can be realized only by world domination, the condition of human society, so long as despotic organizations exist at all, must remain unstable, unless there is a single despotic organization embracing all mankind.

128. Mistaken Social Ideals

Despotism is antithetical to an organization of society aimed at the realization of public ends. But the elimination of despotism is only a negative requirement of the ideal of public life; and we must ask now what positive public ends ought to take the place of the despot's private ends.

The answer to this question is implicit in the theory of ideals of culture. The ideal of personal self-determination implies that culture is possible only through the individual's free and autonomous activity. But culture requires certain specific external forms of communal life if the individual's freedom—without which there can be no autonomous activity—is to be secured. Consequently, the possibility of public life depends on the invention and the development of (1) the art of public education aimed at fostering the individual's participation in culture, i.e., his free autonomous activity, and (2) the art of government, which determines and secures the external forms serving the ideal of public life.

Failure to understand that these are the ideal ends of public life leads to various misunderstandings about social ideals. Where such mistaken social ideals prevail, the ends of public life will not be realized, even if those who control the organization of society are without selfish intentions.

All mistaken social ideals are rooted in the failure to grasp the nature of reason as the faculty enabling men to set themselves the true ends governing their lives—an error fallen into all the more easily because pure rational cognition is originally obscure.

Whoever, as a result of this error, rejects the rational principle of self-determination is compelled either to replace true public ends with subjective private ends, or, if he refuses to subject society to merely private interests, to represent the public ends as set by a being superior to individuals, whose will is then law for the individual.

Let us consider the first alternative. Only the subjective ends of welfare are recognized here as public ends; this leads to the formulation of the so-called ideal of public welfare, a false ideal of human happiness. Such a conception of public welfare, which holds the realization of subjective human interests to be a public end, implies a direct contradiction. For welfare, as the realization of subjective interests, and hence of private ends, cannot be a public end. The theory based on this confusion between subjective and public ends may be called the empirical theory of public life.

The pitfalls of this theory can be avoided only by the establishment of objective ends, i.e., ends not determined by merely private interests. But if we fail to recognize practical reason as a faculty determining the objective value of human life, and nevertheless seek to establish objective public ends independent of the individual's arbitrariness, we can do so only by asserting the fiction of objective ends that are determined not by the interests of individuals at all, but, independently of these, by the purpose of a higher being. This theory which is based on the fiction of objective ends so defined may be called the mystical theory of public life.

Social mysticism can appear in two guises, according to whether the higher being whose goals determine the ends of public life is assumed to be society itself or the creator of the world.

The first brand of mysticism—one might call it sociological—regards society itself as a supra-individual entity, as an organism in the full sense of this term, i.e., a being with a life of its own, whose ends designate those according to which society is to be organized. This gives rise to an ideal of self-assertion and expanding power of society. Here the state—the organized social power—becomes an end in itself.

The second, or theological brand of mysticism, defines the objective ends as those of the world's creator. This leads either to the idea of the divine education of mankind, or to that of God's self-revelation in history. The logic of this theory requires that the public ends be set not by the state but by the church; for the divine will can be communicated to society and rule over it only through the intermediary of a spiritual social organization, namely, a church. The carrying out of this idea requires a special caste of priests proclaiming and translating into practice the ends of a ruler of the universe. The social ideal formulated on such a basis is that of clericalism, i.e., an ideal of a society ruled despotically under a mandate of the divine will.

It is clear, however, that neither of these two forms of mysticism marks any specific content for the ends of public life. For to be able to shape society in conformity with the ends of the social organism or with those of God, we would first have to know what these ends are, and to determine their content mysticism must borrow from some other principle. But even assuming that we could actually discover what are the ends of the social organism or of God, we would be unable to determine the ideal of public life on such a basis. For we would still have to explain why the ends of any being, no matter how powerful, whether it be the social organism or the deity, should be decisive for the shaping of society by men, and by what right the ends of such higher beings can claim to be human ends. Private ends, even those of an all-powerful being, cannot by definition be the ends of public life. And yet mysticism can provide us with no ground for considering such ends except the power of the being that sets them for itself. Suppose we assume that the particular capacity of a being for setting us goals by its own purposes is recognized solely by the objectively superior value of those purposes. In that case, we would be caught in a vicious circle, for we would have to presuppose some other criterion for the objectively valuable. So we are left with only the absolute superior power of the being in question as the ground for regarding its ends as superior. Such a theory, according to which the will of a higher power, and hence an authority, determines the content of the ideal of public life, can be carried out consistently only in the form of theological mysticism. For if power is the attribute that binds us to any given end, then all ideals of public life can ultimately be derived only from the ends of the most powerful of all beings, that is, God.

129. Anarchism of Public Life

Both the empirical and the mystical theory of public life base their ideal upon a heteronomous principle, i.e., a principle placed above human reason, to which, it is claimed, human reason must bow. Blanket repudiation of heteronomy in determining the ideal of public life leads us to the principle of autonomy. But if autonomy is understood to imply no more than the repudiation of heteronomously determined ideals, we are led to the ideal of anarchy, according to which there is no such thing as a public end determining the shaping of society, to which the private ends of individuals would have to be subordinated. The life of society would thus be shaped by the unrestrained sway of private interests. As an ideal of public life, however, the principle of anarchy is just as self-contradictory as are the heteronomous principles. For even if the private interests of the members of society were to coincide, we still could not, on such a basis, formulate a public end determining the shaping of society. For the concept of a public end implies that it shall be independent of any fortuitous coincidence among the actual interests of individual members of society.

Since the anarchist theory of public life stems from opposition to the despotic excrescences of social organization, it can assume three forms, according to which of the three possible aspects of despotism is the main target of its attacks.

Political anarchism combats all political organization of society. Consequently, it condemns the institution of the state as such. For a state is possible only through a government, i.e., a power superior to that of the individual members of society, to which the private interests of individuals must bow. Now, it is true that every government must be controlled by individuals; hence, if these individuals use the governmental power to serve their private interests, the government will necessarily be despotic. But governmental power does not necessarily have to serve the private interests of the rulers; it can also be used by these rulers to serve public ends. In nature, the superior force necessarily prevails over the weaker. This natural law cannot be circumvented in any social order; it will also assert itself in an anarchist society. But if it is impossible to eliminate the rule of superior force, we are left only with the choice between letting lawless chance prevail and attempting to make superior force serve the public law of right. Hence, if we wish to secure in nature not the rule of whatever power happens to be the stronger, but the rule of right, we can succeed only through the instrumentality of the state. Political despotism can never be eliminated by anarchy, but only by just government.

Economic anarchism consists in rejection of any organization of economic life. It implies the principle of unrestricted freedom of trade, resting upon the dogma of a pre-established harmony of interests. But if economic forces are allowed completely free play, the economically weak are at the mercy of exploitation on the part of the strong. Thus, here too, our only choice is between lawless accident and an organization of society fighting against exploitation. Economic despotism can never be eliminated by economic anarchy, but only by socialism.

Ecclesiastical anarchism condemns any state intervention in religious life. It adheres to the principle of unconditional tolerance, and rests upon the dogma that once the struggle between religious groups has been confined to the use of spiritual weapons, the spiritual enslavement of men becomes impossible, and the individual's freedom of self-determination will be secured. But spiritual rule can be established without recourse to violent measures; man's awakening to spiritual autonomy can be far more effectively foiled by gentle blandishments. The principle of unconditional tolerance thus opens wide the door to spiritual terrorism, and in effect surrenders the freedom of conscience to the priests' lust for power. Spiritual despotism cannot be eliminated by the anarchist principle of so-called freedom of thought, but only by the organization of reason.

130. Possibility of Nondespotic Organization

The various forms of anarchism are based on the belief common to all of them that all forms of social organization must be rejected in order to prevent the surrender of the individual's will to alien arbitrary rule. Thus everything here hinges on the question of whether a social organization that will not end in despotism is possible, and if so, how. For in every social organization the individual's will must bow to a higher purpose, and the submission of the individual's will to a purpose not his own is despotism. How then is a nondespotic social organization possible?

This problem will seem insoluble, i.e., the concept of a nondespotic social organization will be regarded as self-contradictory, so long as no ends are recognized other than those determined by the actual interests of the individual.

This error will in turn be inevitable so long as reason is ignored because of its original obscurity or confused with the understanding which is merely the empty faculty of random reflection. Those who commit this error either limit themselves to private ends of individuals, or else are driven to postulate mystical ends which are objective in the sense that they are determined by the will of a superior being, rather than by interests of individuals. Now, since practical reason is originally obscure, it is true that the ideal ends which alone can determine the ends of public life are not necessarily expressed in the actual interests of the individual members of society. For the extent to which the individual is conscious of his own true ends depends on the degree to which he has developed his reflection. By disclosing such ends—which become objects of the individual's actual interests only if he develops his reflection—we begin to see how the problem of nondespotic social organization can be solved. For when society is organized to serve true public ends, the individual will of each member of society must indeed bow to a higher purpose, but this is by no means a purpose that is not his own; on the contrary, he cannot fail to recognize it as his own if his reflection is sufficiently developed. Consequently, an organization of society in which the determination and realization of ends are not subject to individual discretion will not be despotic if these ends are not private but common to all sufficiently cultured members (*Gebildete*) of society.

We call by the title of regent anyone who wields power in order to direct the organization of society toward its proper goal. Now, whether or not a society has a despotic form does not depend on who the regent is, but on what ends the government serves. But if it is intrinsically a matter of indifference who rules in a given society, all the less should it be left to accident whether the regent, whoever he be, subordinates his private interest to the public's. This condition is unfulfilled only when the government is controlled by men sufficiently cultured to recognize public ends as such, and to pursue these without regard for their private interests. To this extent it may be granted that everything depends on who rules: government should be in the hands of the adequately cultured.

Here it will be asked: Who is cultured? And who shall decide on whether a man is sufficiently cultured to be a ruler? The first question is answered by our theory of ideals of culture; hence I need not answer it here once again. It will be sufficient to recall that the cultured are certainly not the "erudite." But regarding the second question, namely, who is to judge whether a man is sufficiently cultured to rule, and hence, who is competent to choose the regent, the only rational answer here is: Those who are themselves sufficiently cultured to answer the first question, and who are willing to be guided by this answer —consequently, the cultured members of society. To instruct others to do so would be as foolish as it would be pointless, because they would neither understand nor follow such instructions: they would have to be cultured themselves to be able to do so.

The problem of how a nondespotic organization of society is possible must, however, be considered again in reference to the content of the public ends. For so far we have solved this problem only formally, i.e., only in so far as it involves the concept of a nondespotic organization; we know that such an organization is possible in so far as it serves public ends. Now the content of these ends is determined by the ideals of freedom and equality. The ideal of freedom stands here for the rational self-determination of the individual members of society. But how can a social organization serve the realization of an ideal which can be realized only by the free autonomous activity of individuals? Thus our problem is here posed again. For personal self-determination and organization, i.e., subjection of the individual will, seem to contradict each other. Thus the question requires an answer that goes deeper. Subjection of the will of individuals to public ends, in so far as the content of these is determined by the ideal of freedom, cannot be enforced: free self-determination and external compulsion are indeed mutually exclusive.

The resolution of this difficulty comes about from the consideration that men, as rational beings, are capable of developing their reason, and can thus be led to self-determination. The development of human reason for the purpose of leading man to self-determination is education. It is, then, by means of education that the public interest must be made the actual interest of all individual members of society. Consequently, *the organization of public life can be only the organization of education*. Every other kind of organization is in fact bound to strangle rather than to develop the free mind, and thus must degenerate into despotism. Duress as a means of organization without despotism is justifiable only for beings incapable of education and hence of reason in the proper sense of the word, or for beings capable of education but maliciously opposed to the public interest notwithstanding the enlightenment they have received. It is true that no one can be compelled to be free, but injustice can be prevented by compulsion. Law can be enforced; use of compulsion for the securing of justice serves public, not private ends.

The reason why the possibility of an organization of free men represents a problem lies essentially in the circumstance that the true interests of men are originally obscure. Consequently, public ends are not self-evident; their very existence often remains unknown. This encourages the opinion that the subjection of individual waywardness to organization is possible only in the service of the private interests of others, and thus must end in despotism. From this the seemingly inevitable inference is drawn that despotism can be eliminated only by the rejection of any form of social organization. And true enough, if one ignores the public ends determined by reason, all one can do is either to give way to despotism in order to avoid anarchy, or inversely, avoid despotism by repudiating all forms of social organization. In other words, from the correct principle of autonomy one falsely infers here the principle of anarchy, and from the correct rejection of anarchy, or from insight into the necessity of social organization to realize the ideal of public life, one falsely infers the inevitability of despotism. The error is identical in both cases: it involves the confusion between the concept of social organization with the subjection of the individual members of society to arbitrary rule. As a result, the principle of autonomy, i.e., of independence from the arbitrary rule of others, is confused with anarchy, i.e., the independence of the individual from any higher ends whatsoever. We can avoid this error, and combine without contradiction the two correct assumptions that each serve as a premise for a false conclusion by disclosing the originally obscure true interest of the individual as the principle of public ends, thus discovering the possibility of organized freedom.

The resolution of the error can be illustrated by a diagram.

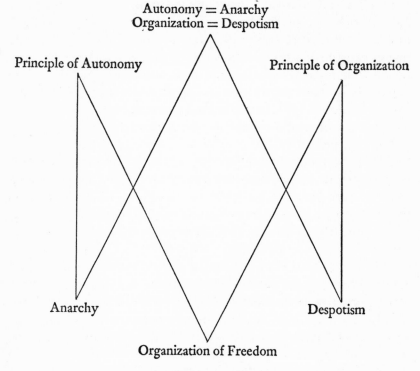

Autonomy = Anarchy
Organization = Despotism

Principle of Autonomy

Principle of Organization

Anarchy

Despotism

Organization of Freedom

131. Party of Right

Public life has two enemies—lack of clarity regarding public ends, based on error, and lack of willingness to serve these ends, based on selfishness. For public life to be developed, both enemies must be defeated. Eradication of the error that leads to nonrecognition of the true public ends can be expected only from an enlightened philosophy. I have just indicated the only possible method by which this can be accomplished. Once the truly public ends are recognized as such, only the preliminary condition for their realization is created, for there is still the other enemy to be vanquished, selfishness, the root of despotism. While the first task is gradually carried out by the progressive development of science, the carrying out of the second requires the conquest of power, which may then be made to serve true public ends.

Thus we are led here to an ideal of struggle, which implies the superiority of an active view of life to a merely contemplative one. The former asserts the value of fighting ardently in the service of public ends: a man who has attained clarity about the ideals of public life is directly faced by the challenge of taking up the cudgels for them. The ideal of public life sets a task for men's will. Society as such has no will, and cannot act or pursue ends; the ideals of social life can be realized only by the action of individuals. They can accomplish this task only by combating all efforts to harness society to the service of merely private ends. The false ideal of general tolerance amounts only to a false ideal of general indifference. Only a man who does not care for truth and justice can remain tolerant in the face of error and injustice. An interest in preserving and propagating the truth, and in asserting right necessarily implies an interest in suppressing and destroying error and in eliminating injustice.

We must guard here against an error resulting from a misinterpretation of the ideal of community.

The ideal community cannot be realized merely by the union of all men, or of a group of men who happen to be associated by the contingencies of nature; the ideal community is a community of like-minded men, i.e., it is based on spiritual affinity, not on fortuitous kinship. A community of minds implies a community of ideal ends. Only such a grouping deserves the name of a cultural community; otherwise we have a mere physical aggregation carrying no ethical value.

The ideal of true community presents us with a challenge. It can be realized only by those who unite in its service, and wage war against its foes. Such a militant community aiming at the transformation of a mere physical aggregation into a cultural community, can at first be only a party within a given society. Thus we arrive here at the ideal of a party which sets itself the goal of bending the power ruling the physical community to the ideals of public life. The physical community can become a cultural community only through the victory of such a party. For in nature, culture can manifest itself only by fighting against unculture, and right only by fighting against wrong. Which trends in a given society will be victorious must depend on the prevailing relations of strength. It is the distribution of power in a given society that determines the ends on behalf of which it will be administered. Under natural law, it is the strongest party in society that gains the upper hand. Public ends can become dominant in a society only if they are represented by sufficiently strong interests, i.e., when a sufficiently powerful party stands up for them. The ideal of public life can therefore be realized only indirectly, by the concerted action of those who strive for the dominance of public ends, i.e., those members of society who are sufficiently cultured.

Consequently, the only possible immediate application to be drawn from the theory of ideals of public life, yields a challenge to the cultured members of the community to join hands in a party powerful enough to harness public power to public ends.

Idealism can manifest itself in public life only as a striving to influence the real distribution of power in society, and to shift it in such a way that preponderant strength serves the public ends. This is also the only correct way of applying the precept of realism to public life. Although conquest of power in itself can under no circumstances be regarded as an ideal, the will to power is an indispensable condition of all ideal aspiration in public life. In nature, superior power is ineluctably victorious, and the only question is whether one wishes this power to be despotically misused, i.e., exploited for selfish ends, or made to serve public ends. Whoever wishes to exclude the first alternative, must work for the second, and thus strive to conquer the greatest possible power in society in order to wrest it from the hands of those abusing it for selfish ends.

The advocates of the opposite view, who uphold an ideal of tolerance, are not, generally speaking, motivated by ethical considerations, but by a prudent awareness of their weakness. A man too weak to expect to be victorious in a conflict certainly reveals his circumspection when he preaches tolerance; if there is no battle he himself will at least escape defeat. Such tolerance is never an ethical ideal, but merely a maxim of prudence for the weak. To give such weakness the name of virtue would truly amount to making a virtue out of necessity. It is a pseudo virtue by means of which the weak cloak their frailty, giving it the appearance of an ethical quality.

The false ideal of tolerance must not be confused with the correctly understood ideal of peaceableness, nor must the ideal of struggle be confused with a false ideal of bellicosity. We must distinguish between tolerance and peaceableness, just as we must distinguish between struggle and war. If these differences are ignored, a false ideal of belligerence, contradicting the correct ideal of peaceableness, will be derived from the ideal of a militant view of life; and the correct ideal of peaceableness will by the same token be distorted into a false ideal of general tolerance or nonpartisanship. Only by distinguishing between struggle and war, between peaceableness and nonpartisanship, can we bring the ideal of peaceableness into accord with a militant view of life. More than that, peace which rules out violence in settling conflicts between physical communities, is the very first prerequisite for a struggle in behalf of the ideals of public life. Such a struggle can indeed be undertaken only if there is no state of war, which requires the union of all the forces in a given physical community for the sake of effective external action, and hence rules out internal party conflicts which would weaken the defense of the community as a whole. The breaking of the domestic truce marks the opening step in the cultural struggle by which alone a true public life can be realized. Therefore, the first struggle we are required to wage in the name of the ideal of a militant view of life, is the struggle for peace; until this struggle has been won, public life remains a utopia.

The task of leading the struggle in behalf of a true public life becomes a duty for the cultured man. There are several reasons for this.

First of all, only a man who by virtue of his clear insight understands the conditions of a just communal life and of true public ends, can have the mission of realizing these. As a man's insight deepens, his duties necessarily increase. Beyond his immediate obligations, he will recognize it as his duty to stand up as best he can for those who are unable to defend their rights because others prevent them from doing so. These others may be motivated by ill will, ignorance, or deficient insight into the right arising from the true interest of men. In all these respects, it is a matter of accident whether justice reigns in nature; for its observance depends on the extent of the knowledge, insight, and good will of the individuals involved. Thus, the task of safeguarding the reign of justice in society against accident devolves upon the educated man.

This obligation arises for the cultured man for still another reason. We may ask to what extent the advantage the cultured man enjoys over other members of society is a consequence of merely accidental external circumstances. If his advantage stems solely from a favorable state of affairs which enabled him to enjoy an extensive education while others were excluded by misfortune or malicious intent, the privileged are duty-bound to make up for their good fortune: for even another man's wrongdoing can create an obligation for us if his victims need our help.

The advantage of the cultured man consists firstly in his economic position, in so far as it enables him to give his life a positive value beyond mere subsistence, and secondly in the opportunities afforded him for participating in culture.

Under certain circumstances, for instance, in times of low social mobility, the majority of the members of society meet with insurmountable obstacles when they try to rise by their own efforts to a life of human dignity. Under such circumstances it may be unworthy of an educated man to take up a scientific or artistic vocation—ideal vocations otherwise—because what is ordinarily only a challenge to his love for justice becomes under such circumstances a duty, an unconditional obligation to set all other interests aside, no matter how strong or worthy. Under such circumstances it is contemptibly selfish to benefit from fortuitous privilege and dodge one's duties to society—all the more so when such evasion is embellished by stressing the idealism of one's vocation. Such men may be called parasites of public life.

The more goods a man possesses, whether they be material or spiritual, the greater is his obligation to see to it that goods are equally distributed, and if he shirks this obligation, the greater his robbery of others. From the point of view of justice, it matters little whether such an abundance of goods has been acquired by the deliberate spoliation of others, or whether a man merely clings to accidentally acquired goods, denying them to those who have a claim upon them.

The underprivileged can fight for justice only if the interest they have a right to realize is alive within them. Only an *actual* interest can be effective in the social mechanism, and set in motion the forces that will compel its gratification; and only an actual interest can motivate the oppressed to unite in battle for their rights. In so far as such a group of people striving for the improvement of the conditions of their existence is engaged in a struggle for justice, it is not guided by selfish purposes. For justice is never a private end in society, but the necessary end of every cultured man. Therefore all cultured men are on the side of those who are fighting for their rights. In such a fight waged by the oppressed classes cultured men must not stand aloof, but must recognize their own goal in the goal of the oppressed.

The champions of justice can come from only two camps. First, there are summoned to this battle those who themselves must fight for their own rights to the degree that they have been deprived of them (for the less a man has, the less can he lose along with his life); and second, those who are willing to make the greatest sacrifices—the oppressed on the one hand, and the cultured on the other. As Karl Marx said, "We need, in order

to regenerate society, an alliance of the suffering and the thinking, of the proletariat and science."

But however important this task may be, it is not the noblest
social task of the cultured man.

Men's sensual and by the same token actual needs clamor
spontaneously to be gratified, and the further removed from
gratification, the more they tend to awaken sympathy, and thus
to set in motion the powerful lever of social justice. But where
the right of men to realize their *true* interest is in question, the
situation is quite different: for here right is not directly represented by an actual interest.

In this case, the extent of an individual's insight into his true
interest and, more generally, the extent to which the need for
things that give value to his life awakens in him, depends on the
development of his reflection. Such an individual's true needs
are no longer the greatest when they are actually felt as needs.
For he rises to the consciousness of his human destiny and thus
reaches the first level of life worthy of men, and as his need
for true values awakens he finds sympathy and, by the same
token, at least possible outside help. On the other hand, those
who most need help can least expect it from mere sympathy;
here sympathy becomes an obstacle rather than a help, for sympathy aims at keeping men from being conscious of their
distress. Thus sympathy becomes here a welcome excuse for
cold-hearted men, which enables them to cloak their basic indifference. There is no greater fraud than the assertion that love
of mankind directly enjoins us never to make anyone unhappy.

Here the cultured members of society are the *only* ones who
face the duty to wage a fight for justice, and for this reason this
obligation is all the more sacred for them. Indeed, not only are
they the only ones called to wage this fight; they must even expect that those for whose rights they fight may turn against
them, as may those who sympathize with the oppressed, who,
concerned to keep their fellow men contented, whether from
sympathy for the unawakened or from plain selfishness, are re-
luctant to see them emerge from their spiritual tutelage. In this
fight, then, the cultured members of society must go it alone,
and oppose all the rest of society. The prospect of victory in

this fight seems all the poorer the higher its purpose, and hence the worthier it is. For what is at stake here is not the mere enjoyment, but the true value of life.

Yet this situation does hold one comfort for those who persist in defending a seemingly lost position. For the community that is here formed to fight for justice is not based on a coincidence of actual interests, but is the necessary community of all those of adequate culture. It is the true church invisible that has no dogmas or ritual, and that is administered solely by the priests of truth and justice. In a community based only on the actual coincidence of subjective interests each individual ultimately seeks only his private advantage, and thus the community is not truly a community of ends but merely of means for the more effective realization of individual interests; but in this other community, it is the true goal itself which binds different individuals by virtue of its universal validity. With the growth of culture in society, this community must therefore gain in strength and in numbers. In the physical community, the closer one comes to the goal, the greater the danger that the community will disintegrate—for the goal here is only the division of the spoils; but here, with each step that brings one closer to the goal, the bonds of the community grow stronger, for the goal is the same for all.

It is by no means a matter of arbitrary choice on the part of the cultured man whether he joins such a community: it is his bounden duty to join it.

So long as the overwhelming majority of his fellow creatures are utterly disfranchised; so long as individuals, by means of their economic or political privileges, can sacrifice whole classes and whole peoples to selfish aims; so long as there exist powerful institutions which, by lying propaganda, nip in the bud the free spiritual development of man, and in the name of the religion of love trample underfoot the most sacred rights of man; indeed so long as the last trace of such institutions has not vanished from the earth—just so long *ought* the educated man to feel that he owes a debt to his dispossessed fellow creatures, and just so long can he have no higher interest and no higher calling than fulfillment of the duty accruing to him from this situation; indeed, he ought to measure the value of his own life by the extent to which he fulfills this duty.

Whoever evades this task, forfeits his claim to be called a cultured man. For he is either deficient in love of truth and in willingness to acknowledge his duty, or he shows a lack of active love for mankind and for justice—more than that, he becomes directly guilty of a breach of his duty, and thus does not even meet the condition that would entitle him to be called a *moral* man.

Appendix

Introduction to *Socratic Method and Critical Philosophy* *

BY JULIUS KRAFT

THIS first American publication of selected philosophical essays by Leonard Nelson (1882–1927) marks the beginning of a comprehensive effort to bring to the attention of the English-speaking world the work of a creative German philosopher which, up to now, has been generally unknown, and the significance of which is almost entirely unrecognized. This lack of international attention is all the more noteworthy since Nelson's philosophical work is characterized by a rare clarity and timeliness, and his life, which was devoted to thinking and teaching and to the educational and political renewal of human civilization, was the life of a citizen of the world.

The breadth and quality of Nelson's writing can be measured by the fact that it embraces almost all branches of philosophy, and that in both its critical and its constructive aspects it is concerned with problems of the first order. Nelson did not hesitate to challenge the entire structure of such epochal doctrines as Cohen's and Natorp's neo-Kantianism, Mach's empiricism, and Spengler's historical mysticism; he developed a fully documented and penetratingly executed reinterpretation of the history of metaphysics since Hume; and he accomplished the imposing task of erecting a complete system of ethics together with its epistemological foundation. In like manner Nelson's practical work was concerned with the root difficulties of social, political, and educational conditions, never with their surface problems. As a philosophical teacher Nelson demanded of his students the keenest clarity of understanding, and himself adhered to unique standards of lucidity in instruction, making him a modern Socratean [1] in deed and not merely in word. It was characteristic of him not only inside, but outside the university as well, that he translated his teachings into action. Not satisfied merely with contemplation and writing, with lecturing and discussing in the old and distinguished University of Göttingen, he founded

---

* This introduction is reprinted here because of its useful and concise outline of Nelson's philosophical lifework.

1. Nelson's lecture, "The Socratic Method" (see *Socratic Method and Critical Philosophy*, p. 1), gives a vivid account of the method of philosophical exercises practiced by him at the University of Göttingen for eighteen years (1909–27).

his own Philosophical-Political Academy (at Melsungen near Cassel) for the education of responsible political leaders.[2]

Whatever may be the lasting value of Nelson's theoretical and practical work, its scope and level entitled it to serious consideration. How is it that his work, and especially his philosophical writings, failed to attract more general attention? The answer is very simple: Nelson was a philosophical heretic of the twentieth century, and his heresies were of such an outspoken and universal character that they earned him the sworn enmity of the dominant philosophical schools in Germany and brought him into conflict with her whole cultural atmosphere. Public indifference to Nelson in Germany, however, was bound to have the most adverse consequences for the international recognition of his work, and so it had.

Nelson's fundamental heresy was his conviction that there is one, and only one, philosophical truth, and that it is attainable by thinking.[3] This conviction, inspiring his whole life, was squarely opposed to the spirit of his time, which, for the first one or two decades of the century, was characterized by skepticism, and then turned more and more in the direction of mysticism, developments that were climaxed by the imposition on the German people of National Socialism as the obligatory world-view—just five years after Nelson's premature death. This unexampled cultural breakdown may be viewed as a dramatic historical commentary on the practical import of warnings Nelson had uttered time and again. He had always contended that the rejection of rational philosophical truth by his contemporaries could result only in subjection to an invented irrational "truth." The intense awareness of this danger gives to Nelson's critical and constructive writings a uniquely passionate tone. He is never indifferent; he always takes a determined stand. But it is the stand of a thoroughly prepared case. Even the severest critic will not find in Nelson's writings that "dim magnificence" which, as Macaulay says, "if it is admitted into a demonstration . . . is very much worse than absolute nonsense."

Nelson's philosophical work—the most mature parts of which are the *Lectures on the Foundations of Ethics* [4] and the yet unpublished "Lec-

2. A future political history of Germany will have to record how, out of this Academy and the youth groups connected with it, came a number of heroic men and women who fought against the National Socialist regime and who, since the fall of that regime, have borne with equal courage their share in the struggle for a new and better order in Germany.

3. A nontechnical account of this guiding conviction may be found in the essay, "The Art of Philosophizing" (see *Socratic Method*, p. 83).

4. *Vorlesungen über die Grundlagen der Ethik*, Vol. I, *Kritik der praktischen Vernunft* (*Critique of Practical Reason*) (1917); Vol. II, *System der philoso-*

tures on the History of Metaphysics" [5]—is the achievement of a superior power of abstraction and of an iron will, both of them formed and purified by theoretical and practical influences of great significance. The most momentous of them is a philosophical rediscovery that Nelson made when only a high-school student. Just as Felix Mendelssohn-Bartholdy (to whom Nelson was related through his mother's family) rediscovered Bach's forgotten masterpiece, "The Passion According to St. Matthew," so Nelson rediscovered the forgotten writing of a forgotten philosopher, J. F. Fries (1773–1843), whose work had fallen into oblivion by a coincidence of adverse cultural and political circumstances, namely, the crushing effect of post-Kantian philosophical mysticism—as cultivated by Fichte, Hegel, Schelling—and the police state of Metternich.

The rediscovery of Fries's *New or Anthropological Critique of Reason* (2d ed., 1828; reprinted in 1935), his *System of Metaphysics* (1824), *The History of Philosophy Set Forth in Accordance with the Progress of Its Scientific Development* (1837–40),[6] and of numerous other books and essays by him and his pupils (particularly E. F. Apelt) was the spark that kindled the flame of devotion to a rebirth of critical philosophy, which burned all through Nelson's life. Nelson's study of Fries convinced him that the Fichte-Hegel-Schelling school was mistaken in arrogating to itself the role of carrying on the work of Kant, and that, therefore, the failure of its speculations did not imply the failure of critical philosophy. The study of Fries convinced him further that the cultivation of critical philosophy excludes the blind acceptance of the Kantian letter. Continuing and extending the penetrating critical analysis applied by Maimon (1754–1800) to Kant's transcendental proofs (which Maimon demonstrated to be circular), Fries subjected Kant's whole system to rigorous criticism. The result was to eliminate metaphysical agnosticism and epistemological subjectivism from the structure of critical philosophy.[7]

---

phischen Ethik und Pädagogik (System of Philosophical Ethics and Pedagogics) (1932, posthumously); Vol. III, System der philosophischen Rechtslehre und Politik (System of the Philosophy of Law and Politics) (1924).

5. "Vorlesungen über die Geschichte der Metaphysik," Pt. I, "Fortschritte der Metaphysik, insbesondere bei Hume und Kant" ("Advances in Metaphysics Particularly in Hume and Kant"); Pt. II, "Rückschritte der Metaphysik seit Kant" ("Regress in Metaphysics since Kant"); Pt. III, "Fortschritte der Metaphysik seit Kant" ("Advances in Metaphysics since Kant").

6. Neue oder anthropologische Kritik der Vernunft; System der Metaphysik; Die Geschichte der Philosophie dargestellt nach den Fortschritten ihrer wissenschaftlichen Entwicklung.

7. Fries's central technical procedure is a reconsideration of the relation between metaphysics, epistemology, and psychology of knowledge, a highly im-

This structure is determined by the requirement that philosophy be established within the limitations of human knowledge. Trivial though it may seem, this requirement is nevertheless a most fruitful principle, the disregard of which has largely characterized the history of philosophy. Though it obliges us neither to assert that space, time, causality, the moral law, or even God is inherent in a "universal consciousness," nor to advocate a demolition of metaphysics, it does demand of us that we give an account of the elements of knowledge out of which it is possible for the human mind to construct metaphysics. Fries undertook to show how the method of the critique of reason had to be modified if it was to apply to the foundation of the theoretical sciences, and to ethics, art, and religion. Without falling into epistemological subjectivism or metaphysical agnosticism, he demonstrated how this revised critique supported the fundamental finding of Kant about Leibniz' logicism and Hume's empiricism, namely, that both collapse under the impact of the theory of the synthetic a priori propositions. He went on to show that Kant was also right as against Aristotle, whose realism breaks down before the distinction between the phenomenal and the noumenal aspects of the universe.

His lifelong association with critical philosophy, although the most significant, was not the only formative theoretical influence on Nelson's intellectual development. There were at least two others, mathematics and social science. His mathematical studies under Hessenberg, and under Hilbert whose friendship and high intellectual esteem he enjoyed, gave him a thorough acquaintance with mathematical methods and sharpened his logical tools. His friendship with Franz Oppenheimer [8] introduced him to the sociology of the state and to economic theory, and exposed him to an honest criticism of Marxism. As a consequence, all

---

portant methodological subject taken up again in one of Nelson's first essays, "The Critical Method and the Relation of Psychology to Philosophy" (see *Socratic Method*, p. 105). This essay is the best introduction to the delineation of Kant's transcendental and Fries's psychological method of the critique of reason and of the related distinction between the analysis ("exposition") and the validation ("deduction") of philosophical principles.

8. The names of both Hessenberg and Oppenheimer appear as co-editors of the *Abhandlungen der Fries'schen Schule. Neue Folge*, established by Nelson in 1904. The first *Abhandlungen der Fries'schen Schule* was established in 1847 by Apelt (author of a comprehensive textbook on critical philosophy in its Friesian version, *Metaphysik* [1857], re-edited by R. Otto [1910]), Schleiden (the biologist), Schlömilch (the mathematician), and H. Schmid (a Fries pupil who made important contributions to the philosophy and psychology of religion and published very stimulating *Lectures on the Nature of Philosophy* [*Vorlesungen über das Wesen der Philosophie* (1836)], re-edited by R. Otto [1911, 1948]).

his life he was opposed to the dogmatism of historical materialism, and when, after the First World War, he made a trip to Russia, he did not hesitate to speak out against what he considered to be the errors of this doctrine. Nelson's ethical system, however, with its insistence on a realistic approach to human society, bears witness to the fruitfulness of his acquaintance with social science.

Even more important proved to be his contacts with social reality, which largely determined the direction of his philosophical work, that is, its gravitation toward ethics. Nelson was reared in a highly cultured Berlin family, his father a distinguished lawyer of idealistic outlook, his mother a woman with considerable talent for drawing, which her son inherited. Young Nelson did not find high school or university very congenial; he looked back with horror to his later high-school years. His concern with philosophical scrutiny, which developed very early, suffered under the dogmatism that pervaded the teaching methods of even one of the best high schools in Berlin, and his keen sense of personal dignity and independence made him hate the traditional methods of school discipline. Nelson's university studies at Berlin, Heidelberg, and Göttingen gave him a solid grasp of mathematics and the natural sciences, including psychology, and of their methods. Yet in none of these universities did he find satisfaction for his philosophical longings. His technical philosophical education, therefore, was acquired almost entirely through self-study guided by his rediscovery of Fries.[9]

The field to which the tools thus acquired were to be mainly applied was largely determined by the historical events of the time: the First World War, the social and cultural tensions of the Weimar Republic, and the international political crisis stemming from the Russian Revolution. Nelson lived through these events not as a passive philosophic bystander but as a man who increasingly felt the responsibility to contribute his gifts of clear thought and unswerving purpose to the struggle to free mankind from the recurrent torment of political "destinies." Nelson's zeal for a higher form of social existence than can be found in a world torn by wars, class conflicts, and cultural disintegration made it imperative for him to devote his thought to a study and appraisal of all serious movements in the furtherance of peace, social justice, and cultural progress. Practical considerations, then, and not theoretical

9. Nelson's philosophical dissertation, "Jakob Friedrich Fries und seine jüngsten Kritiker" ("Jacob Friedrich Fries and His Most Recent Critics"), *Abhandlungen der Fries'schen Schule. Neue Folge* I (1904), analyzes, reformulates, and defends Fries's transformation of Kant's transcendental critique into a psychological one against Kuno Fischer, Hermann Cohen, Windelband, Scheler, and others.

preferences, determined Nelson's preoccupation with ethics, and the logical rigor of his ethical system is the expression not of an intellectualistic motivation but of an intellectually refined conscience.

Nelson was a person of fearless directness who never equivocated, his work even showing evidence of a certain intellectual and practical obstinacy. He pursued the ideal of the acting philosopher in the Platonic sense of the word, yet in certain phases of his educational and political activity there is a tendency to fanatical activism, and his philosophizing was not entirely free of overemphasis on the finality of results and on the exclusiveness of specific approaches to complex problems. Correspondingly, there were traces of harshness in his personality. But his self-sacrificing devotion to truth and justice was such a powerful force in his life and in his work that his limitations may be said to be merely what Goethe called the *"Erdenrest zu tragen peinlich."*

Notwithstanding Nelson's preoccupation with ethics, he made great contributions to theoretical philosophy, witness his papers on general epistemology and the methodology of science, and his unpublished history of metaphysics, a historical systematic introduction to the entire field of critical metaphysics. Nelson's most exhaustive work in general epistemology, his *On the So-called "Problem of Knowledge"* (1908),[10] has to be viewed in the light of the fact that the prevailing trend in Continental philosophy during at least the first decade of the century was almost exclusively toward preoccupation with *Erkenntnistheorie.* This *Erkenntnistheorie* is, of course, an echo of Kant's critique of reason, though only a very remote one, indeed. The neo-Kantians, the empiricists, and the phenomenologists had substituted for the basic problem of an analysis of knowledge the problem of finding a criterion for the validity of knowledge in general. This problem admits only of circular "solutions" and is therefore fictitious. The elimination of this problem, however, was by no means intended to discredit epistemology and metaphysics. On the contrary, the critical review of the post-Kantian epistemology in *On the So-called "Problem of Knowledge"* shows how powerful were the tools supplied by Fries's epistemological methods for the foundation of rational metaphysics.

Whereas this essay departs in important points from Kant's procedures (though not from his systematic intentions), Nelson's contributions to the methodology of mathematics and the empirical sciences are chiefly concerned with the reformulation and defense of some of the basic theories of the *Critique of Pure Reason.* Kant asserts that both

10. *Über das sogenannte Erkenntnis-Problem.*

mathematics and empirical science stand or fall on the assumption of synthetic propositions a priori. Nelson very early recognized the crucial character of this assumption, and never lost sight of it. This is evident in the "Remarks on Non-Euclidean Geometry and the Basis of Mathematical Certainty" (1905–6), in "Is a Natural Science Free of Metaphysics Possible?" (1908), and in his lecture on "Critical Philosophy and Mathematical Axiomatics," [11] which he delivered in 1927 shortly before his death. All these essays have the character of preparatory studies testing the Kantian assertion regarding synthetic propositions a priori on scientific developments, such as non-Euclidean geometry and mathematical axiomatics, unknown to Kant, and on modern methodological theories, such as mathematical conventionalism and Mach's empiricism. The result is a strong vindication of Kant's fundamental discovery.

This outcome is, in a sense, less remote from the present state of methodological discussion than may appear at first glance. The nominalistic dissolution of science into man-made symbol systems—this newest phase in the evolution of empiricist methodology—entails the consequence that consistent empiricism is incompatible with the assumption that there is scientific knowledge. Contrariwise, adherence to this assumption compels the abandonment of an empiricist methodology. That such an abandonment cannot be carried out in the form of a new logicism is sufficiently established by the failure of logicistic undertakings from Leibniz to Russell.[12] The hour has come, therefore, to reconsider seriously the feasibility of a methodology of science that employs as one of its basic constructive tools the concept of the synthetic proposition a priori.[13] In the process it will become apparent that such irreconcilable

11. "Bemerkungen über die Nicht-Euklidische Geometrie und den Ursprung der mathematischen Gewissheit"; "Ist metaphysikfreie Naturwissenschaft möglich?"; "Kritische Philosophie und mathematische Axiomatik." "Critical Philosophy and Mathematical Axiomatics" appears in *Socratic Method*, p. 158.

12. Nelson did not overlook the epistemological importance of logic proper. His "Remarks on the Paradoxes of Russell and Burali-Forti" ("Bemerkungen zu den Paradoxien von Russell und Burali-Forti [zusammen mit Kurt Grelling]"), written with Grelling, formulated for the first time the now familiar paradox of words being either autological or heterological. It should be noted further that two outstanding symbolic logicians, Bernays and Ackermann, owe their philosophical education to Nelson.

13. Another pupil of Nelson, Grete Hermann, subjected modern physics and its current positivistic interpretations to the scrutiny of a philosophical analysis guided by Nelson's methodological approach to science. Her carefully reasoned results corroborate the necessity and specify the formulation of synthetic propositions a priori for physics. See Hermann-May-Vogel, *Die Bedeutung der modernen Physik für die Theorie der Erkenntnis* (1937) (*The Importance of Modern Physics for Epistemology*); G. Hermann, "Die naturphilosophischen Grundlagen der Quanten-

doctrines as mathematical conventionalism and mathematical intuitionism, physicalistic positivism and the mystical philosophy of physics of Eddington and others, all contain valid elements, which find their place in a philosophy of science whose cornerstone is the Kantian conception of the synthetic proposition a priori.

To the solidity of this cornerstone Nelson's *Lectures on the Foundations of Ethics* [14] testifies constructively. This may seem paradoxical in view of the formalistic character of Kant's own ethics, but here again the Kantian letter and the Kantian spirit are not alike. The systematic structure of critical philosophy by no means entails a categorical imperative without content. This Kantian doctrine, being a logicistic remnant in his system, is not required by critical ethics. Nelson demonstrated this thesis in a historical-logical analysis, *The Critical Ethics of Kant, Schiller, and Fries. A Revision of Their Principles* (1914),[15] in which he also systematically traced the development of nonformalistic critical ethics in the writings of these men.

Ethics, then, holds up as its fundamental concept the category of a task, without being forced into a formalistic doctrine of duties. Armed with this insight, Nelson undertook a further step in preparation of his practical philosophy: a devastating attack against the positivistic philosophy of law which, confusing the world of changing legal arrangements with the unchangeable norm of justice, ends up in political relativism and thus destroys a main condition of political progress, namely, the possibility of well-founded political ideas. The exposure of the positivistic theory of constitutional and international law and of legal relativism made in Nelson's *Jurisprudence without Justice* (1917) [16] is distinguished not only by its logical forcefulness and brilliance but also by its moral courage. Published in the war year 1917, it contains at its conclusion a consideration of "Jurisprudence and the War" that minces no words in castigating the abuse of legal science engaged in a "dance around the Golden Calf of sovereignty." [17] Prior to this Nelson had asserted the necessity for the limitation of sovereignty when, at the

mechanik" ("The Philosophical Foundation of Quantum Mechanics"), *Abhandlungen der Fries'schen Schule. Neue Folge* VI (1935), No. 2; Hermann, "Über die Grundlagen physikalischer Aussagen in den älteren und den modernen Theorien" ("On the Foundations of Physical Statements in Old and Modern Theories"), *ibid.*, VI (1937), Nos. 3–4.

14. See note 4.
15. *Die kritische Ethik bei Kant, Schiller und Fries, Eine Revision ihrer Prinzipien.*
16. *Die Rechtswissenschaft ohne Recht.*
17. The combination of irresistible logical criticism and prophetic scorn characteristic of *Die Rechtswissenschaft ohne Recht* is again evident in a philosophical

outbreak of the war and in the face of militaristic hysteria, he had publicly defended at the University of Göttingen the ideal of international peace.

The year 1917 also saw the publication of another work of Nelson's, which is likely to be regarded as his greatest: the *Critique of Practical Reason*.[18] Nelson knew what he was about when he selected this Kantian title and dedicated his work to Hilbert. He took up again certain fundamental unsolved epistemological problems of ethics and approached the task of their solution with tools forged by Kant and Fries and refined by mathematical axiomatics. These are the tools employed in solving both the *quaestio facti* and the *quaestio juris* of ethics, that is, the *formulation* of the principles of ethics and their *validation*. If Nelson's *Critique of Practical Reason* contained no more than the formulation ("exposition") of the principles of ethics, it would still be a notable philosophical achievement. Its analysis of such concepts as "duty," "right," "justice," "equality," "retribution" is unparalleled for clarity and simplicity. One has only to compare these Nelsonian abstractions with the contemporaneous efforts of Scheler and N. Hartmann to "intuit" phenomenologically the essence of ethical values to realize the difference between philosophical discrimination and philosophical confusion. A particularly original outcome of Nelson's research in ethics is his exposition of "ideals" or "categorical optatives," whereby the Kantian restriction of ethics to a theory of duties is removed and the way is opened to an ethics which not merely forbids but also formulates positive goals worthy of human effort.

The validation of ethical principles is carried out through their psychological "deduction," i.e., by proof of the fact that our ethical feelings, namely, our conscience and our ideal evaluations of human life, are of a qualitatively unique character. They cannot be broken down into sensual elements like fear or libido, yet they are capable of reduction to nonsensual elements that are not directly contained in our consciousness. These nonconscious elements of ethical feelings belong to what Fries called "immediate knowledge," and they are the nonintuitive but rational basis of ethics. It has often been asserted (from Kuno Fischer to Cassirer) that Fries's psychological "deduction" is a form of "psychol-

---

pamphlet entitled *Spuk. Einweihung in das Geheimnis der Wahrsagerkunst Oswald Spenglers* (*Spook. Initiation into the Secrets of the Prophetic Art of Oswald Spengler*), published not long after the end of the First World War. This time the immediate object of exposure was one book by one man, but indirectly he aimed at the spirit of a whole generation. The book is Spengler's *Decline of the West*, representative of a generation that had lost confidence in itself and was therefore only too willing to lend its ear to a prophet of impending doom.

18. See note 4.

ogism" and therefore of empiricism. There is no better refutation of this statement than Nelson's psychological deduction of the principles of ethics, which he in no way derives logically from psychological principles, but the bases of which he ascertains psychologically in the qualitative characteristics of "practical reason." The "deduction" of ethical principles is, then, at the same time a vindication of the rational nature of man.

"Exposition" and "deduction" do not exhaust the content of the *Critique of Practical Reason*. It also contains a lucid methodology of ethics, an analysis of the idea of the free will, and finally an axiomatics of all possible ethical theories.

This is really, as Nelson felt it to be, an attempt to conquer a vast new territory for philosophy. Its fruits are apparent in the *System of Philosophical Ethics and Pedagogics* and in the *System of the Philosophy of Law and Politics*.[19] The term "system" in combination with ethics has long had a somewhat stuffy sound. Too many "systems" of ethics have broken down for us to regard new ones with anything but skepticism. Yet granted that philosophy has to deal with the problems of ethics, their exact treatment requires a systematic form. The recurring breakdown of ethical systems does not prove the fictitiousness of ethical systematization, but rather the necessity to improve radically the rigor of ethics. This is accomplished in Nelson's systematic treatment, which, guided by the postulate of mathematical axiomatics, seeks to derive the theorems of a system with a minimum of assumptions. Only a concentrated study of this ethics can give an adequate idea of the striking way in which the application of this postulate insures a richness of content entirely beyond the reach of system haters.

The present writer was privileged to attend several of Nelson's courses in ethics, where he underwent the stirring experience of coming into possession of new tools for solving old problems, an experience intensified by Nelson's superior art of philosophical teaching. What was presented in those courses orally the reader will find in Nelson's *Systems*. He will discover how problems generally considered to be undecidable suddenly become decidable when they and the means available for their solution are rigorously formulated. It would serve no purpose to list at length those ethical problems of personal conduct, education, politics, and to report Nelson's answers to them. The innermost spirit of his *Ethics* forbids such a survey procedure. This spirit is a reassertion of an autonomous ethics, that is, of an ethical certainty that is subject to argument.

19. See note 4.

Nelson's system is a monumental protest against authoritarian certainties and nonauthoritarian uncertainties in ethics. It re-establishes the principle of a morality without dogma, of a social order without arbitrary privilege, and of a culture without empty pretension.[20] This re-establishment is carried out for ethics proper by insisting on the exclusiveness and primacy of the duty of justice to be practiced toward man and animal and by an amplification of the realm of duties by the realm of ideals. The classical ideals of truth, goodness, and beauty are unified into what may be called "the ideal of rational self-determination" (*vernünftige Selbstbestimmung*), and education and politics are shown to receive their ethical goals from that ideal. Consequently, the philosophy of education formulates ethical principles of an education for freedom from fear and freedom from intellectual bondage, and the philosophy of politics formulates ethical principles of a social order in which, under qualified leadership, peace, social justice, and cultural freedom are institutionally guaranteed.

The critical mirror Nelson places before mankind reflects the abyss that separates ideal and reality. To shrink from this abyss or to seek consolation in forces beyond the human realm is a clear sign of ethical self-deception. Ethical integrity demands that we look into the mirror, evaluate what it reflects, and then arrive at a clarified ethical judgment. It may be confidently asserted that if we face Nelson's *Ethics* squarely, we shall come away with a new approach to the theoretically central and practically vital problem as to whether rational ethics—and that means also the rational foundation of educational and political theory— can be realized or is no more than a dream. If only part of Nelson's constructions should prove to be valid, they would substantially confirm the conviction of the greatest philosophers since Plato that rational ethics is within the reach of man.

20. As those pretensions typically confuse empirical, ethical, and religious ideas, a sharp distinction among them is all the more important for the health of cultural life. Nelson's "The Scientific and Esthetic Conception of Nature" and his "The World-View of Ethics and Religion" (see *Socratic Method*, pp. 44, 62) provide important and impressively formulated clarifications of such a distinction.

Nelson's approach to religion, which he never developed systematically, is guided by the Kantian attitude of distinguishing between the phenomenal and the noumenal aspects of the universe, which implies an awareness of human apartness from the eternal. This attitude is incompatible with mystical certainties about the "numinous objects" into which one of Nelson's early collaborators, Rudolf Otto, transformed Fries's antimystical philosophy of religion in his well-known and stimulating books, e.g., *The Idea of the Holy*. Through Otto's theory of religion, elements of Fries's philosophy swelled the broad stream of religious mysticism which had found its philosophical formulation in James's "religious experience" and later in Scheler's "religious intuitions." In addition to Otto, the psychiatrist Kronfeld and the distinguished physiologist Meyerhof belonged to Nelson's philosophical circle.

Nelson's epistemology and his system of ethics have remained up to now a part of what may be termed the unofficial European philosophy of the beginning of the century. It awaits a rediscovery like Nelson's rediscovery of Fries's work. Official European philosophy, at first relativistic, then more and more mystical, had no use for Nelson's antirelativistic and antimystical ethics of practical reason. It therefore either ignored Nelson's work or ridiculed it as a "belated rebirth of eighteenth century rationalism"—disclosing thereby that it preferred high-sounding historical superficialities to the effort of systematic penetration. Having dismissed Nelson condescendingly, official European philosophy indulged all the more in prophecies of destiny, abandoning the clarification of human tasks as an outdated prejudice. Instead, it brooded over the essence of human existence, which Heidegger painted in the grey of despair and to which Jaspers gave a no less illogical, if somewhat less monotonous, interpretation.[21] The price for this dismissal of rational ethics is the creation of an anthropological scholasticism that plays with Kierkegaardian paradoxes and Hegelian dialectics, a result to be seriously pondered by any philosophy that does not want to run afoul of logic.

Thanks to the efforts of Russell and Whitehead, Hilbert and many others, logic experienced a revival in the twentieth century. So far, however, it has had scant constructive results for philosophy as a whole. In fact, "the new logic" has been misused to bring about a renewal of logicistic and even nominalistic claims, which debase philosophy to a system of tautologies, if not of meaningless symbols; a further impressive demonstration of the fact that new scientific devices, such as the invention of logical calculi, cease to be a blessing if they are subjected to arbitrary philosophical interpretations, in this case the interpretation that modern logic is incompatible with metaphysics, that is, speaking epistemologically, with systems based on synthetic propositions a priori.

Precisely the same incompatibility is being asserted concerning other fundamental sciences. Mathematics is claimed as a branch of logic; physics is considered a combination of observational and conventional elements. Behavioristic psychology has, of course, only contempt for "metaphysical fictions" like the concept of a mental reality. Finally, the social sciences and the humanities are objects of a fierce competitive struggle between those who want to compress them into more or less consistently developed physicalistic schemes and those who consider them fertile ground for the seeds of their particular political and

21. See the present writer's *Von Husserl zu Heidegger. Kritik der phänomeno-logischen Philosophie (From Husserl to Heidegger. Critique of Phenomenological Philosophy)* (1932), and "The Philosophy of Existence. Its Structure and Significance," *Philosophy and Phenomenological Research*, Vol. I, No. 3 (1941).

religious preferences, thus transforming them from fields of knowledge into means of indoctrination.[22] Art and religion, too, share a similar fate in being treated alternatively by preconceived psychological and sociological schemes or by serving as pretexts for unchaining the unholy, age-old hatred of reason.

But all this—the denunciation of rational metaphysics in the name of science, art, and religion—is only a claim, and not a claim of modern science, art, and religion themselves but of the interpretation given to them by an antirational philosophy. Viewed in this light, this denunciation is nothing but a usurpation that ought to be overthrown by a rational reinterpretation of the widened intellectual horizon of the nineteenth and twentieth centuries. Such an intellectual endeavor will bring about fruitful interaction between old ideas and new achievements. The old ideas will be progressively freed from the dross of their historical shortcomings, and the new achievements will be understood as those of a human, that is, of a rational, mind with insurmountable limitations. Thereby it will become apparent that the radical wings of twentieth-century philosophy, empiricism as well as existentialism, have aims that find much more satisfactory realization in a rational philosophy. These aims are, on the one hand, the rejection of obscurantism and, on the other, the search for a meaning of human existence. Rational philosophy pursues them by a nonempiricist philosophy of science and by its ethics and its philosophy of religion.

Nelson has set a great example by vastly enriching these disciplines in the spirit of Kant and Fries and by demonstrating thereby once again that it is not the eulogizing of and blind submission to great men but the meeting of unfettered minds that brings about deepening of philosophical judgment. It is almost superfluous to add that the attainment of this end is also a practical requirement of the hour. A famous historian of our day describes our predicament as "civilization on trial." In that trial history holds out no hope of a favorable judgment for a generation that indulges in intellectual self-mutilation. The rediscovery of reason—in science, in ethics, and in religion—thus becomes a prerequisite for recapturing the meaning of life. In this rediscovery and in this recapture Nelson's philosophical work can be a powerful ally.

22. A typical expression of these fundamental uncertainties concerning the methodological interpretation of the social sciences and the humanities is the theory of *Geisteswissenschaft* established by Dilthey and radicalized by existentialist methodology of history. A systematic analysis and appraisal of the doctrine of *Geisteswissenschaft* will be found in the present writer's *Die Unmöglichkeit der Geisteswissenschaft* (*The Impossibility of "Geisteswissenschaft"*) (1934).

Index
(Excluding Appendix)